To Sheffield,
and John, -
you understand -
for there both grandfathers!
with best wishes

# The Old U(VA) and I

## 1961-1965

by

Frank Briggs

DORRANCE
PUBLISHING CO
EST. 1920
PITTSBURGH, PENNSYLVANIA 15238

Dorrance Publishing Co
585 Alpha Drive
Pittsburgh, PA 15238
Visit our website at *www.dorrancebookstore.com*

ISBN: 978-1-6491-3372-4
eISBN: 978-1-6491-3600-8

In Honor and Memory of

B. F. D. (Benjamin Franklin Dewees) Runk

Grand Marshal and Dean of the University

# Acknowledgments

In writing this book I learned that the whole process is harder than I thought it would be. It's a lot of work that requires ample help.

First, Carline Chamberlain spent hours in the UVA Special Collections archives finding pertinent documents. Liza Yates created the dust cover design that embraces the book with lovely simplicity.

Several classmates reviewed the chapters as I wrote them. Beta pledge brother, Ted Hogshire, was especially helpful in keeping me, as best he could, on course. Joe/Jose Brown provided embellishments and names that I had overlooked. John Casteen critiqued my book and made some suggestions. He also pointed out a basic flaw in the closing chapter, which I have rewritten.

University of Virginia professor and historian Emeritus, Sandy Gilliam, is a Beta ten years my senior. His encyclopedic knowledge of University lore spanning a seventy-year period is incredible. Joel Gardner who started at the University the year I left, also provided valuable insights. Reading his book showed me that I was writing about the end of an era that had existed for generations.

Chuck Johnston, my prayer partner and friend of over thirty-five years, an English teacher, and headmaster, provided a different view. As a non-UVA (Vanderbilt) graduate, he made sure I was writing to the non-Virginia reader as well.

The whole team at Dorrance Publishing was wonderful in their instruction and patience. They took a raw manuscript and turned it into this finished product.

However, my greatest thanks go to Ed Curtis, the copy editor. From me he received a conglomerate of disorganized thoughts and run-on sentences. Like a great chef, he took these ingredients and turned them into something worthwhile.

My beloved wife of fifty-five years, and counting, provided her usual candid, non-sugarcoated input. It was she who told me how much Ed had needed to do to make it readable. To find out her name you will have to read right until end of the book!

# Contents

# Preface

My original intent of these recollections was to make a few notes to re-call and coordinate my days at the University of Virginia, my experi-ences and reflections, to leave to my descendants. Then a pledge brother, Ted Hogshire, suggested I check out an excellent book by Joel Gardner, *From Rebel Yell to Revolution: My Four Years at UVA, 1966– 1970*, which chronicled the period immediately after mine (1961–65). It dawned on me that I was writing about what Gardner called "The Old U." But what he referred to as the end of an era, I believe was a massive expansion beyond the old boundaries that brought about some needed changes.

Of particular importance are the significant achievements the Uni-versity has made toward racial conciliation and justice. In terms of gender equality, the facts speak for themselves. The incoming class is 54.9 percent female, and current students outperform their male coun-terparts by .06 in terms of GPA. Teresa A. Sullivan in 2010 became the first female president of the University. In the Greek community, once a bastion of exclusivity, the sixty-one fraternities and sororities are now woven into the fabric of student life. Moreover, according to the Uni-versity website, these organizations contributed over thirty-eight thou-sand hours of community service and raised over $223,000 for charitable and philanthropic causes. The fraternity/sorority GPA was 3.350.

In my own fraternity, Beta Theta Pi, there have been vast positive changes. While the fraternity core value "to build lasting bonds of friendship and brotherhood" is as strong as ever, the days of excessive drinking and hazing pledges are now regarded as repugnant. The 2019 GPA of the UVA Omicron chapter is 3.51, and the fraternity is a leader in intramural results. Additionally, the house has devoted countless hours in concert with the sisters of Alpha Chi Omega sorority to put on an outstandingly successful philanthropic program.

One of Thomas Jefferson's greatest legacies is his mantra of "following the truth wherever it may lead." I hope great care will be exercised to continue permitting full expression of different individual beliefs. For over two hundred years this concept has guided the University to the reputation for excellence it enjoys today.

For the most part these recollections are organized chronologically, though, in a number of instances, I have expanded earlier events by adding information gleaned from the prism of knowledge gained in later years.

When citing a "something I heard" or a "they said" as a supposed fact or statistic, I will try to specify the hearsay element. There are also events and people who are out of place chronologically or are placed in the wrong fraternity or story. Please accept that these are the memories of an unknown first-year man's improbable journey to the student council presidency in an era that no longer exists. This is not a documentary or a history, and I have not verified them through additional research.

# Chapter 1

# The Beginning

My Virginia saga began when my parents—Frank and Barbara—drove me from our home in Pittsburgh, along with all my worldly possessions, southward toward Virginia. It wasn't until we were about an hour from Charlottesville that it began to hit me that I was going to a new and different world.

I've since learned many times over that most people put a great deal of thought into where they go to college. They agonize over many things: large school or small, location, curriculum, academic fit, room-mates, cost, and myriad other considerations.

I had done none of these and given almost no thought to the matter. I knew college was the next step in the process, and I was given a number of schools to consider by my family history and Blair college counselor.

My mother and I made a wonderful trip together to visit Washington and Lee, the University of Virginia, and William and Mary. In years past I'd been to Cornell, where my father had been a star in the hotel school, and Princeton, which was both near to Blair and to my parents' points of origin.

Each of these five institutions received an application from me, and responses from Cornell and Princeton quickly reduced my options to three. My final decision was Virginia because they were the first to accept me and my mother thought the grass had not been properly groomed at W&L.

That chore being done, I went back to living on a day-to-day basis. For me at that time, and for some years later, the long view was a week, while the response to any situation was doing whatever expediently and pragmatically resulted in peer acceptance.

I will now provide some background on my family's history of relocations that might reveal the source of this attitude. While each location will be a chapter of its own, since this memoir concerns my years at Virginia, I will omit many details unless they seem necessary.

I was enrolled in kindergarten at a French-Canadian school in Montreal, Canada. At the age of five, I entered first grade at a splendid English private school, Lower Canada College (LCC), at a time when those of British descent still had a significant presence in Quebec. After the school year ended, we left the Great White North, and our Canadian home vanished in the rearview mirror. After a stay with family, the next three grades of my education were spent at Ashwood Elementary School in Hot Springs, Virginia, a small mountain community that was home to the famous Homestead hotel, where my dad was the general manager.

After the school year ended three years later, I went to a summer camp. When my parents picked me up after camp, we did not return to Hot Springs. Those relationships vanished with no goodbyes, and we moved in with my maternal grandparents—Charles and Grace Smith—whom I loved dearly. I started fifth grade at Wanamassa Elementary School in Wanamassa, New Jersey. Suffice it to say I experienced my first dramatic shift in culture.

At the end of my first semester there, we packed up again and moved to Houston, Texas, where I attended Oran M. Roberts Elementary School. My sixth and seventh grade years were spent at the Kincaid

School. At this time, I began developing some real relationships and roots, both with peers, city, state, and region. I was reacquainted with the vast differences between the North and the South.

Then one day in late spring, my sister Kingsley ("Lee") and I came home from school and told Mom, "The kids at school say we're moving to Pittsburgh, Pennsylvania."

Mom said, "We had hoped to be able to tell you before it was in the newspapers."

So once again the moving trucks arrived.

One day as we traveled north, we spent the night at a small motel in the Appalachians, and I looked down on a newly flooded TVA lake and thought, *When I grow up, I'm going to come back and live here in the South*. Years later, after matriculating at the University of Virginia, I knew I was back home!

Meanwhile, we spent the summer at the beach with my grandparents, and then moved into a house in Pittsburgh. That fall I started eighth grade at Andrew W. Mellon Junior High School in Mount Lebanon.

While Pittsburgh is a wonderful place, my first three years there were a disaster socially, academically, athletically, and especially behaviorally. After two years of steady decline, I was sent to Blair Academy in Blairstown, New Jersey, for another totally unsatisfactory year. But things then began to change. That summer I lost thirty-five pounds, took swimming seriously, and found two well-grounded friends. Upon my return to Blair, two incredibly propitious things happened. First, most students start boarding school in the tenth grade, so the incoming class didn't know the old me, and second, I repeated a year that made it the first time I was with people my own age. For me, Blair became a tremendous source of real support.

I was college bound in 1961. As we approached Charlottesville, my thoughts began to focus on how uncool Dad's clothes were, especially the plaid shirt he was wearing that day. At that time, and for the next thirty-five to forty years, one of my primary objectives in life was an adaptive, chameleon approach to come across as a part of any group I was close to.

My father, a practical man who had no concerns about fitting in, wore what he thought was appropriate for moving his son into a dormitory room and not for looking preppy or collegiate. But I was so preoccupied with this shallow thought that I failed to take in the larger picture.

After spending a night on the road, we arrived at Emmet House midmorning and entered the housing office. I was assigned to room 206. After hauling my stuff up to the room, we were directed to the Barracks Road Shopping Center to get some things Mom felt I needed for the room. After spending years at boarding school and summers at camp, not to mention at home, I never thought about providing anything myself since the school, camp, or my mom always took care of it. When I later moved to Atlanta, my roommate's mother took over. After I married in 1966, my wife handled such things.

It's been said that males in my generation are remarkably spoiled in contrast to subsequent generations regarding shared marital responsibilities in both revenue creation and domestic duties. Such was my experience.

After I was settled into my room at Emmet, I spent the afternoon with my parents, just the three of us, and it was a wonderfully rewarding experience. Very seldom had my dad and I done anything together, so this became a special occasion. Afterward we had dinner together, and then they deposited me at the dorm for my first night as a college student.

Back at the dorm, the bedlam that had reigned all day—with parents, first-year men, and assorted others swarming the halls like worker bees—was gone. Everyone had disappeared, and I realized that for the first time in many years I had no one to turn to, call up, or visit. I was alone amid thousands. Suddenly the enormity of the situation consumed me. For the second time in my life I was homesick. I felt like a six-year-old. So, I left the dorm, walked several miles north on Route

29 to the Jefferson Motel (which is long gone now) and knocked on my parents' door.

The surprised pleasure on their faces showed how welcome was my desire to seek their companionship. It was a special end to the first day of my new life—almost.

I wish I could say that I returned to my dorm room for a good night's sleep, but I didn't. On the way back to Emmet House, I passed an intriguing place called The Cavalier and stopped in for a quick look. Several hours later, after I had exhausted all of my money, I stumbled back to my new residence. It was the first of innumerable days that ended that way over the next four years.

The next morning, I had breakfast with my parents, after which, dressed in a seersucker suit, white shirt, rep tie, and cordovans, we attended St. Paul's Episcopal Church on University Avenue, directly across from the Grounds. At that time and for years to come, Virginia gentlemen did not appear in public, except at very casual events, without a coat and tie. Since I had worn a coat and tie since age fourteen, and continue to do it to this day, albeit less universally, it seems more natural and dependable than what is currently called business casual.

After church we met the minister, and Mother chatted with him. He became a friend to me over the next four years. I remember Mom saying, in what I considered a very loud voice, "Oh, look! Here's the guest book to sign." It was a difficult moment for someone who was trying as hard as I was to avoid looking like a guest.

I must explain something at this point. I considered myself a very strong Episcopalian and knew a great deal about the rituals, theology, and history of the English Church. In fact, I was an acolyte at St. Paul's and later became junior warden of the student vestry. At that time Episcopalians were the largest denomination among UVA students, and the second largest were Southern Baptists. However, as you will see in this writing, the thought that Christianity had anything to do with lifestyle never crossed my mind.

After church and lunch, my parents departed for Pittsburgh, leaving me to navigate the next leg of my life's journey. Left to my own devices, I decided to explore the McCormick Road Dormitories where I was to live.

The ten Georgian-style houses had been completed in 1950 and formed a rectangle. All were brick on the outside and cinder block with tile floors inside. Each had three residence floors, with common areas, services, offices, and maintenance facilities in the basement. Eight were arranged in a quadrangle, and each pair were joined together in an L-shape, with Hancock and Bonnycastle freestanding at the bottom. The residence floors were divided into two sections of eleven double rooms each, with a common bathroom and shower area separating the two. At the end of each hall was a phone. None of us expected air-conditioning, because there wasn't any, and the windows remained open almost all the time in the muggy central Virginia heat. With more than six hundred men living in close quarters, a ghetto, albeit upscale, was created in which music and conversations drifted through the limited and trampled grassy areas between the buildings. The concrete-block-and-tile construction magnified the sound so that if someone dropped something or rolled barbell weights to create a ringing sound, it amplified to the floor below. After a while, residents on the lower floors responded by going upstairs and either cajoling or threatening bodily harm.

The Alderman Road Dormitories were built during my time in Charlottesville, and they were designed with a more modern, suite-like approach, with many more amenities. Still, the Old Dorms, as the McCormick Road Dormitories were called, have remained the most popular because of tradition and their proximity to the central Grounds.

Echols House residents were called Echols Scholars and seemed to be less sophomoric than the rest of the incoming first-year men. The level of activity was probably highest at Hancock House and even more so at Bonnycastle House. This was probably because both houses were freestanding and somewhat removed from the other eight, with Bonnycastle Field behind them creating, at least theoretically, a calmer atmosphere. However, seemingly most advantageous, they were the houses for first-year men who had applied earlier than the rest of us, invariably by legacy children and younger siblings who knew the score. It was also known by that group that they should send in their housing application before or at the same time as their application for admission. While the housing office began assigning rooms only after the admission process had been completed, it was on a first come, first serve basis.

As a result, Hancock and Bonnycastle were populated by the students most apt to know how to party and did. Sometime in the late 1980s the anarchy became so prevalent that the basement floors were regularly flooded by fire hose battles on the floors above. The University eventually revamped the process and eliminated this privileged opportunity.

Bonnycastle was the home of one of my favorite and often frequented eateries, The Castle. It served a splendid variety of deep-fat-fried, grilled, and other high-caloric entrées, as well as a variety of pastries, ice cream, soft drinks, and iced tea. Many a morning I breakfasted there after a late night.

One night I came upon an open door and saw a skinny kid in a white T-shirt mournfully strumming a guitar. The music accompanied a Christian praise song, although I'm not sure it was being performed as such.

Many years later, I was in my den and watching the news and suddenly shouted to my wife to come see something.

I pointed at the distinguished newscaster in his forties and said in amazement, "That's Brit Hume from Danville who's now supposed to tell me how I should view world events!"

I've since learned Brit was from Washington, DC, and he has become my most trusted pundit. He is one of so many people who went on to great achievements from the bunch of immature kids who made up the class of 1961.

At our fiftieth reunion, Brit was on a panel on world affairs with fellow classmate Fred Barnes, a noted editor and commentator. The moderator was Ambassador Charlie Glazer. The president of the University at that time, John Casteen (1990–2010), was also a member of our class.

On my first solo evening, I explored the Grounds and, between Alderman Road and the dorms, found a lovely cemetery nestled in a large grove of trees, mostly tall evergreens, which provided a sanctuary-like feeling. The graveyard proved to be a pleasant retreat to which I returned many times that year, and in the years to come. The headstones, several dated in the 1860s, served as a reminder to me of the many largely forgotten Virginians who had contributed to the University I was now a part of. On my second night, however, having reconnoitered my new surroundings, I returned to the hustle and bustle of the second floor at Emmet and wondered what would be coming next.

# Chapter 2

# The Early Days

The denizens of second-floor Emmet were a microcosm of the University demographic at the time. By future standards this was quite narrow since it was almost entirely white males. Mary Washington, a women's school in Fredericksburg, was the Female Division of the University of Virginia. And while the University was theoretically integrated, African American representation was infinitesimal. There were, and still are, some large in-state schools and some of the better schools outside the Commonwealth that have traditionally sent students to the University. Long before their arrival, those kids know what fraternities or sororities they are going to rush, their living and eating arrangements, and who their friends are and aren't. Thus, they weren't part of the gang I spent my early days with; they simply resumed their lives at a new location.

The first person I met was the floor counselor (resident advisor), Charles "Chuck" Hudgens Spence. His careful grooming and patient, efficiently methodical manner and appearance were who he really was. When he introduced himself to my parents and me, he offered any assistance and generally served as a guide in those early days. As I was coming from four years at a boarding school, I wasn't quite sure what his capacity was and decided it was somewhere between camp counselor and a floor master (teacher). In my experience, a camp counselor was a kind of big brother, while a floor master was an enforcer of discipline. During my early weeks, I came to realize that floor counselors were there in case a need arose, otherwise they were pursuing their lives as the rest of us did. Since Chuck plays an important role throughout this recounting of my life, I'll not say more about him at this point.

Concerning the rules of the house, there were very few. They essentially boiled down to no girls and no destruction of University property. Smoking and drinking in the dorm were acceptable. At boarding school, students had to be sixteen to smoke, and then only in a few designated areas. Thus, I was quite startled the first time someone across the hall lit up. At the time well over half the people I knew, male and female, were smokers, including teachers and students in class. For the most part, people did not drink in class or on weekdays. On weekends and party nights, however, there may have been people who didn't drink at all, but I never knew any of them unless they were athletes in season.

My roommate, John Catron, and I got along well since, while we enjoyed each other's company, we had absolutely no shared experiences or interests. John was from Gate City, which is close to Bristol, and he was the first person from his high school ever to attend the University of Virginia at Charlottesville and one of a very few to go to college at all. He was very slightly built, with moderate features and coloring, and he moved with a quick efficiency through the day.

The Lord put us together as a continual reminder of all the gifts I took for granted. John was the son of a supervisor at Eastman Kodak, and his food allowance was $1.67 a day. In hindsight, it appalls me that I lived for nine months in the same room with another human being and knew almost nothing else about him. Did he have a mother and siblings, religious beliefs, a prior life? From his point of view, did I?

Curiosity piqued, I tracked John down and reestablished our relationship after fifty-seven years. After he took a BA in economics, John had an expanding career in information technology. After consulting to and heading major governmental IT entities, he retired in 2020. While we were exploring each other's past, we encountered a shared interest in nocturnal activities at the Rotunda. During his second year, John and his roommates discovered an access to the building's parapet. Thereafter they enjoyed views from that height with their dates. But that ended abruptly after they placed a jack-o-lantern on the rooftop. Suddenly they encountered U cops and visited with Dean Runk shortly thereafter. That august personage suggested this was their last parapet visit if they intended to complete their studies at the University. John and his friends respectfully agreed. Later in this recounting, readers will see why this tale struck a particular chord with me.

We talked in these early weeks, but did we really say anything? Moreover, a lot of time and money had been spent on my being prepared for college, while John had none of that. Had we studied together, even a little, we each had a gift to give the other.

Directly across the hall from us were Carrington Harrison III and Calder Loth, a fascinating duo who came from the same class at the Virginia Episcopal School in Lynchburg. Carrington was bulky, with cropped, astonishingly blond hair and a disconcerting way of staring at you through slightly squinting blue eyes, as if at a laboratory specimen. He came from a well-placed family in Winchester. Later that fall, he invited me on a weekend with several friends that I remember to this day as a very special experience I'll describe later in this narrative.

After we took our degrees, I didn't talk to him again for fifty years, when I called him about the class reunion. By then he had retired as an orthopedic surgeon in Staunton, and we have since renewed our relationship.

Calder, slight and fastidious in dress, had a droll, seemingly disinterested but well-practiced manner of speaking. Although much of his family originated in the Richmond area, he grew up in the small city of Waynesboro, which is midway between Charlottesville and Staunton. Both inadvertently and by choice, he schooled me in historical information, a mixture of fact and myth, about the Commonwealth, many First Families of Virginia (FFV), practices and thoughts, and historical sites and architecture, which were subjects that fascinated him and became his life's calling. The last time I'd encountered these mannerisms was in a cabin mate from Richmond and St. Christopher's School at Camp Shaw-Mi-Del-Eca during the summer between fourth and fifth grade.

(My elementary school years in Hot Springs were several hundred miles from FFV territory, and for that matter, Waynesboro lay well beyond it as well.)

One thing I learned from Calder, for example, is that North Carolina is the valley of humility between two mountains of conceit!

I recently communicated with Calder, who is consulting with the University on Grounds restoration after forty-one years as a noted architectural historian with the Virginia Department of Historical Resources. Google recounts his honors and published works.

Directly next door to our room was Kelly Wood. Although Kelly later became a fraternity pledge brother, he was an impressively quiet person who, unlike me, only spoke or responded when he had something to say, which, whenever it occurred, made him gregarious. I only experienced this after we became Beta pledge brothers. For many years he was the Norfolk Navy Yards top engineer until, after a valiant, courageous battle, he succumbed to cancer a few years ago.

Rounding out the boys in this listing is Ray Sutherland, an engineering student (like Kelly Wood and Chuck Spence). He was an affable, talkative native of the southwest city of Wytheville, Virginia, with dark hair and strong facial characteristics. After we took our degrees, Ray married and went with IBM in Atlanta, where we reestablished our relationship. As of our 2015 fiftieth reunion he lives in Connecticut.

In the rooms on the other side of the bathroom was a person I got to know who became a lifelong friend, Richard Cheatham. At our first meeting, he was a quiet fellow from Pulaski, Tennessee, but he emerged from the Harvard Law School as a self-assured lawyer with a commanding presence and an intricate knowledge of banking law. Members of his firm, the larger legal community, and clients relied on him because of his significant abilities until a fatal illness took him in his midseventies.

The rest of the floor, those without the comfort of prior relationships, I will refer to as the gang. Have you ever seen a movie starring a motley group of recruits in their first days of barracks life? They are always a conglomeration of sizes, personalities, cultures, and disparate backgrounds whose only commonality is being thrown together under the same roof upon entry to a new venture, such as military life.

That depiction is what we were, and we did everything together in those first weeks. The only other name I remember is Hiram, who was a tall, gangly basketball player from Knoxville, Tennessee, with a pronounced Adam's apple, whose parents were both professors of zoology at UT. Because I had come with four years of dormitory experience and Hiram was a revenue (major) sport athlete, we were nominal leaders of the group.

Hiram, however, had a fatal flaw in that he was in love with his high school sweetheart back home, and he often traveled back to see her, thus never fully disconnecting from his former life. At some point I'm almost certain he left Charlottesville to return home for good. For my part, I marveled at the thought that a girlfriend at home could have anything to do with one's social life at college.

Then there was a fellow named Tom, who had a high-pitched, feminine voice. Ironically, he lived right next to the hall telephone and always answered the phone, which caused callers to marvel that we had a woman living on our floor. There was also a redheaded kid who didn't mean to be obnoxious but was. The rest were basically bit players in the crowd whose presence I remember but have no memories of.

In those early days, we all took our meals at Newcomb Hall (the University Union). It was then a simple, no-frills institutional cafeteria, but now it's a sophisticated food court. We also attended some of first-year orientation there.

We all frequented The Corner, which had a variety of landmark eating, clothing, bookstores, and other remarkable establishments. This row of hallowed institutions was across from Brooks Hall and just beyond the easternmost boundary of the Grounds.

Starting at the corner of Elliewood Avenue and West Main Street (now University Avenue) was Mincer's Pipe Shop (now just Mincer's), which stocked an unbelievable quantity of University-branded items, followed by The Virginian restaurant, a narrow, paneled place that was good for a brew and a mouthwatering cheesesteak sandwich. The College Inn was another restaurant with good food but somewhat less atmospheric than its neighbor. The dominant eatery, however, was the relatively large University cafeteria, where one went down the serving line to receive excellent, basic southern cuisine. Although the food was very good, I never felt comfortable there, since, when I was in grade school at Hot Springs, it was where my mom and I always had lunch whenever we came to Charlottesville for a day of allergy shots. Somehow the remembrance of those injections always lurked in my thoughts whenever I was there.

Flanking the cafeteria were two bookstores, the University and Anderson's, which have since been replaced by the University's own bookstore in Newcomb Hall. Each place was the same as the other in terms of inventory, a list of all the books necessary for every class, and sold them at monopoly-level prices for new books and 50 to 60 percent off for used. At the end of each semester, they would happily buy back the books for 15 percent if it was in the syllabus for the next semester.

Chancellor's Drug Store merits some special attention. In addition to medical and hygienic necessities, it sold a large variety of day-to-day items. So, I had an account there, and the bill was sent monthly to my father. One day I was told, "You don't have an account here anymore.

Your father closed it." Although he and I had never discussed it, he apparently decided that writing an allowance check for the basics and then writing other checks for those items was something he would rather not do. Also, since birth control prophylactics were sold only in pharmacies and kept behind the counter, Chancellor's was the only supplier, and customers had to request them from a clerk, and the available clerk was often a woman. Thus, the fraternities made it a standard practice to send pledges, accompanied by witnesses, to purchase such packages, often Trojan Ends.

One well-known and often-repeated tale regarded Scotty, who tended to stutter under duress. When an attractive clerk asked him to repeat his request, he said, "I'd like some pro..., proph..., prophyl... rubbers!"

East of Chancellor's the street drops significantly for about thirty feet and bends to the left on the way to downtown Charlottesville, a mile or so distant. Just across the street, all that existed for hundreds of yards, to the intersection with Jefferson Park Street, was the last tentacle of the hospital, a picturesque, one-story relic containing a clinic and student health (SH).

My first trip to SH produced in me a vague anxiety that I later realized was because the building had been the allergy clinic where I spent many childhood hours receiving my shots.

After the drop was a splendid art studio named Freeman-Victorius. It featured lovely prints of the University and the surrounding environs. Then, almost directly under the railroad trestle, was the infamous White Spot, home of famous delicacies such as the Gus Burger, followed by the relatively more upscale University Diner. While there were other establishments beyond these, for most of us, The Corner ended here.

We also frequented a few watering holes and had a few raucous beerfests back at our dorm. There also were several University-sponsored mixers, one at Newcomb Hall and the other a road trip by bus, though I can't remember where to. Some people may not know what a mixer is, but those of us who matriculated at boarding schools in a by-gone age, all of which were gender-specific at the time, as were most colleges and universities in Virginia, know exactly what they're like.

The gang even went as a group to visit fraternities during the first weekend of fraternity Rush, which proved to be a good way not to solicit a bid. As the weeks progressed and we all had different classes, schedules, and interests, our widespread camaraderie gave way to smaller clusters of people who happened to live in the same neighborhood or apartment building, and our group activities became fewer, infrequent, and then nonexistent. The value of my past experience cannot be overlooked, however. My frequent family moves and abrupt school changes helped me immeasurably to develop a significant ability to adapt, empathize, and grow.

As a reference point, there was almost no similarity between my experience and those of each of my three children, all of whom went to Virginia after living a lifetime in the same neighborhood where their mother grew up, as well as graduating from the same day school.

When I arrived at Virginia, there were five boys from my boarding school, Blair, and one I knew slightly from Pittsburgh, where we lived at the time. My children, however, knew or knew of dozens of people from the school they came from and children of my schoolmates or mutual friends. I met my roommate when we arrived together at school. Our eldest daughter, Margaret Carolyn ("MC") roomed with Kemper Williams of Richmond's St. Catherine's. Kemper is the daughter of my Beta brother, Jack Williams, who was in the Bonnycastle dormitory. MC and her friends picked the roommate of my other daughter, Barbara, a girl from Memphis, and made sure Barbara pledged Kappa Kappa Gamma. My son, Bo (Frank Hay Briggs III), met his future first-year roommate, Ned Parish of Richmond's St. Christopher's, at a Peach Bowl party in Atlanta when he was in seventh grade, and they decided to room together when they got to Charlottesville.

The first six weeks in Charlottesville were a learning experience for me in adapting to a school and campus the size of a small city. In those days, classes met six days a week, with Saturday being a half day. I started three of those days by dashing a huge distance across the Grounds to Brooks Hall to be at a Geology I lecture by eight o'clock in the morning. (After that year my basic scheduling approach was to enroll in no classes that started before nine or after noon.) Mr. Allison, the professor, seated his 120 students alphabetically and kept roll. If someone was not present when his name was called, he was absent for the day, even if he arrived late. Had my name started with a Z instead of B, I could have gotten up ten minutes later.

The other classes I had were all in Cabell Hall, which was new at the time and the center of everything. Since academics were not my primary concern, I will discuss them in more detail later in a place of their own, toward the end of the semester. My other courses were Calculus I, Basic English, Military Science 101, and Latin III.

After lunch I moved into the more significant part of my day. I went down to start freshman swimming. In those days, freshman teams participated separately from the varsity, which started as a second-year man (sophomore). Since I came from a secondary school with a high-performance, well-coached swimming program, this was a real letdown because Virginia was between coaches and practice was more or less on one's own, under the nominal supervision of a volunteer graduate student.

I also joined *The Cavalier Daily* newspaper staff as a reporter and features writer. Since I'd had lots of experience at Blair, along with a fair amount of talent, I was soon given key assignments and eventually became a day editor.

Evenings were another matter, since it didn't take me long to realize that studying was based totally on self-discipline, of which I had very little or none. Several weeks into this new adventure a fellow I didn't really know, Chuck, who was from Mount Lebanon, asked if I wanted to go down the road. At that time in Virginia there were men's schools and women's schools, which was the norm, so I learned that going down the road meant visiting a women's school.

I replied, "But it's Wednesday!"

Chuck said, "So?"

The fruit was introduced into the garden, accepted, and off we hitchhiked to Madison College (now James Madison University). I don't remember any of the details of the evening except that the Rubicon had been crossed.

Another eye-opener occurred on my second Saturday in Charlottesville when I attended my first football game. Virginia hosted William and Mary.

Rules governing drinking at games had not yet been introduced, so it was an enormous BYOB cocktail party. Several rows in front of me, a man opened a suitcase, which turned out to be a portable bar, well stocked with enough liquor to last several games. To my right, two guys put a small trashcan filled to the brim with iced beer between them on the seat.

Over the previous three years the Wahoos had lost twenty-eight consecutive games, so the party seemed to be the most justifiable reason for being at the stadium. But the Cavaliers actually won that day, to remain tied with another school for the longest consecutive losing streak in intercollegiate football. The following weekend our team lost an away game at Duke, something like 45-7. I listened to the radio broadcast in my room.

As the weeks passed, I got to know Virginia better and, as always, expanded my breadth of acquaintances quickly because I could do so almost effortlessly. I've never been comfortable with solitude, although I can do it. However, wherever we lived, I always managed to hang out with a small circle of friends, one or two of whom became longtime friends. In Hot Springs it was Joe Shaver. At Roberts Elementary in Houston it was Carl Faught. At Kincaid it was Robert Robbins. At Blair it was Lee Johnston. When I moved on, these relationships ceased almost immediately, but they were extremely important to me. Only with Michael Healey (a neighbor from junior high) and Lee Johnston (from Blair) have I remained in contact with anyone before Virginia.

In Pittsburgh, my two closest friends were Dave Coulter and Alan Rimer. After my second sophomore year at Blair, I had no friends because I was no longer attracted to the old ones. At Chartiers Country Club, I met Dave, as both of us were working out in the pool, and we became friends. Alan, who knew the old me, was distrustful, but as Dave's long-time buddy, he continued to be thrust into close proximity with me, and the result was the three of us became the Three Musketeers and had cards printed to seek work in yards, clean and wax cars, and even occasional heavy housework. When we turned eighteen, we were old enough to look for higher-paying jobs. The rest of the time we worked out and swam together, dated three girls who knew each other, and were generally inseparable. Since Dave and I went away to boarding school and repeated a year, Alan was one year ahead of us and went to Duke a year before I was admitted to UVA and Dave to Ohio Wesleyan.

One morning during the summer before I went to college, I came down for breakfast and Mom told me that Dave had been killed the night before in an automobile accident returning from a mission trip to Berea, Kentucky. It was absolutely devastating to Alan and me, but it caused us to bond even more closely. Thus, he was excited to drive up to see me and Laurie Holbrook, my high school girlfriend, who came over from Mary Baldwin College.

One thing caused Alan more anxiety than anything else, and I should have known it. His mother had a great deal of trouble with alcohol, and I had been there several times when she publicly embarrassed him.

Nonetheless, by the time Alan and Laurie arrived, I had been drinking beer for some time. When he saw me, Alan's big smile turned into consternation.

All he could say was "Oh, Frank!"

We had dinner together and things improved, but it was not the reunion we had hoped for. I saw Alan a few times after that, when I went to the North Carolina schools for swimming meets in the following years, and he was a groomsman at my wedding, but we both were headed in separate ways.

Only one person transcended all those years: Anne Boleyn Pole. She reentered my life in the late 1990s and became, albeit long distance, with only occasional visits in Richmond, a dear friend of my sister and me. Anne's three surviving grandparents lived across the street from us in Hot Springs, so she and her brother spent the summers there, away from their home in Richmond, and became our constant summer companions.

One day in the summer of 2018, I called her while she was working in her garden. We had a long chat, and she remarked that she felt unusually warm and weary. The next morning, I had a dropped call from her, texted back that I was on my way to church and would call afterward. The response was affirmative; however, before I had a chance to call, her wonderful companion of many years, and my classmate from Virginia, Doug Carleton, called with the shocking news that Anne had died of a heart attack that morning after being taken to a hospital the previous night. I still regret not calling back sooner.

And so, after the first month, I knew my way around, had a large number of casual acquaintances, and was active in several extracurricular activities. But I had not yet started to dig the foundation on which my Virginia experience would grow.

# Chapter 3

# Rush

Although I assumed that joining a fraternity was something I wanted to do, I had no comprehension of how to go about doing it. As I said earlier, the first weekend of Rush, I set out with the gang from second-floor Emmet to visit several fraternities much as a group of tourists sets out in a foreign land to see whatever points of interest they can find. Along the way we encountered the Swanson twins, who I knew from Blair, who were in Sigma Chi, one of the fraternities we visited. They were cordial but no invitation was forthcoming for meals from them or anywhere else during that foray.

I received an invitation to XXX fraternity as the result of my one recommendation, compliments of an elderly neighbor in Mount Lebanon who'd been a brother of that fraternity at North Carolina State, and in fact I rushed there and became quite taken with their star female rusher, Faith. From now on I will refer to them as the XXX House for fear of disparaging them later on.

But there was one house I believed was above all others: Zeta Psi. At Blair each table in the dining hall had assigned seating, although there was some rotation of students at certain tables. At the head of each table was the table master, while at the foot was the senior assigned as table foot. My head was a Yalie, Duncan Alling, who had a lovely wife, Cynthia, from Bronxville, whose brother, Scott Sykes, was a third-year man at UVA. Once I had decided to go to Virginia, I continually heard about the perfect attributes of Scott Sykes. In fact, there was a lot of truth to it, for when I entered, he was a fourth-year star and captain of the lacrosse team, cadet colonel in Army ROTC, Chairman of the Honor Committee, and an all-round BMOC.

The first or second time I went to the Zete house for a Rush party, I came straight from a two-hour swim practice. Since I was in training, I was supposed to not drink. At the house, everyone seemed to know each other and were very relaxed. In the presence of the demigod Scott Sykes and his circle, I was stiff and uptight and, predictably, dropped from the Rush list. Around the same time, without a coach and an organized program to keep me directed, I decided to stop going to swimming. I also ate a few meals at the XXX House and quickly realized that wasn't going to be my solution.

The next week I decided, after downing some brews, that I would go back to the Zete house and show them they liked me a lot more than they thought they did. Unfortunately, when I arrived there, they didn't agree. When I continued going to the house, I was grabbed by two brothers and hustled out the door, which was slammed behind me. Interpreting this as an indication I wasn't going to be a Zete, and standing by myself on Rugby Road, I decided to go to the house across the street and have a beer. At that time, kegs were an accepted staple of Rush.

After one beer I took another cup and found a seat on a sofa in the living room. A few minutes later a brother came over and engaged me in conversation. By this time, I was very relaxed and had forgotten I was rushing, so the conversation went on easily. A little later another member joined us, followed by others, and we had a great time. I noticed our threesome plus the additions was being watched by a number of rushees who passed by in the hall, but I thought nothing of it. In what seemed like no time at all, but what must have been several hours later, it was one o'clock and time to clear out the rushees.

Then the two brothers, Rush chairman Eli Brown, president-to-be Jim Brandhorst, Steve Chipman (Eli's constant companion and apartment mate), and another asked me to join them and get something to eat. So, we went on foot to the University Diner at The Corner. It was packed. We found a table, but the servers were too backed up to get to us quickly.

After a few minutes I said, "Where's the waiter? I'm so thirsty I could drink that bottle of catsup!"

The obvious response was, "Why don't you?"

"Well, hell," I said, "I think I will."

I took the bottle and chugged it down. While I didn't think anything of it and some food was eventually ordered and enjoyed, my life and status at Virginia had changed forever!

No longer was I an unknown student from a little-known prep school. The next day I was actually invited to the Beta house for lunch. News of my feat had spread universally, and Betadom was achieved— if I wanted it.

I did, recognizing the perfect chemistry that existed.

As a side note, people on the hall had begun to dislike RA Chuck Spence because he hadn't recommended one person from his floor on the Beta Rush list. In fact, he had put three people on the list, but the Rush chairman had lost it.

With the turn of my fortune, I was welcomed at the other houses that were grudgingly deemed acceptable by the Betas. But by then I had picked up a nickname—Beta Briggs—that reduced the probability of my pledging elsewhere. Since I knew I was a "pocket bid" who was going Beta, I no longer felt any Rush pressure, and so I was able to visit the other houses a lot more and see the significantly different personalities of the various chapters. I was supposed to report back to the Betas which pledge possibilities were rushing elsewhere, but that presented no obstacle for me or anyone else.

For the final weekends, my longtime friend and high school sweetheart, Laurie Holbrook, was my date, which was great fun because by then she had no illusions about me and we could concentrate on enjoying ourselves.

My first experience with the small cities and towns in the rolling farmland of southern Virginia, which blend into those of North Carolina, occurred when Carrington Harrison asked me to go with him and two of his former classmates from the Virginia Episcopal School (VES in Lynchburg)—Lee Booth and Russ Wentz—to the Episcopal High School (EHS in Alexandria) game in Lynchburg. We spent that Friday night at Lee's house in Danville, which was on the North Carolina border.

Carrington became an SAE (Sigma Alpha Epsilon), whose house was on Grady Avenue, immediately next door to KA (Kappa Alpha), which is on the corner of Rugby Road and Grady and directly across the street from AEPi (Alpha Epsilon Pi). Of the three, the Es had a spectacular reputation for memorable parties and antics, although on party weekends the activities of all three tended to blend together in their front yards and streets. The Es also had an immensely popular and personable houseboy, Ike. He was an affable personage who, always in his white jacket, looked much like a Pullman porter and provided stability amid all the bedlam surrounding him.

The KAs could appear somewhat pompous and less effervescent in contrast to their next-door neighbors. Directly across Grady were the AEPis, which was one of three Jewish fraternities at Virginia. (The other two combined under the surviving name Zeta Beta Tau [ZBT].) Although there were plenty of bona fide scholars in each house, the Pis were the most cerebral of the three.

After we left our stuff at Lee's, we went to a well-known drive-in restaurant over the state line, which was the first time I had ever been in North Carolina. The next day we headed to Lynchburg for the game between the two rival schools, but I remember little since I had no connection to either. However, this firsthand experience with a southern prep school allowed me to meet several recent alumni who attended a completely new selection of colleges and universities: UNC, Wake Forest, etc.

The person I remember best from that weekend was Claude Freeman, who was described to me many times on the trip down as a wild man from Carolina. When I finally met Claude, the experience was only for a minute or so.

After we were introduced, he said, "Hey."

I responded, "Hey."

And we moved on. Thirty-eight years later, my son, Bo, became engaged to Beverly Freeman (UNC '96), and I asked her father, Lindsey, if he was kin to Claude.

"He's my brother."

I was not surprised. Both had attended VES and UNC.

Late that afternoon we left Lynchburg, stopped for food and drink, and then headed to a mixer at Chatham Hall, a prestigious girls' prep school in Chatham, which was ruled by a martinet addressed only as Mr. Yardley. The evening got off to a bad start when I walked through the door to meet Mr. Yardley but slammed into the glass of an unopened one. Each of us instantly knew the other was an adversary.

Suddenly my breath was taken away when I saw one of the loveliest girls I had ever laid eyes on! Anne was a tall, willowy blonde with a lively disposition. As the evening progressed, we became increasingly enamored with each other. We entwined as we slow danced until the last moment.

The next morning, we left Lee's house and stopped at Chatham Hall for visitation. As is the custom at other girls' schools, there were set times when boys were allowed to visit, including a period on Sunday. Visitors were permitted to sit in the parlor or take a prescribed walk on the campus in full view of the chaperones at all times.

Even in the full light of day, Anne was as dazzling as she'd been the night before. As we walked on the upper playing field, I learned she'd been restricted to the campus for a month for "overfamiliarity" on the dance floor. Then, after we professed great affection for one another, my group departed for Charlottesville.

As we traveled north on Route 29, the discussion turned to what we should do on the way. I suggested we stop at Sweetbriar College and visit Faith, a sophomore I was enamored with after meeting her at the XXX House Rush parties.

During the early weeks of Rush, I'd gone to the XXX House, where I encountered Faith and was fascinated by her languid manner reminiscent of F. Scott Fitzgerald's characters from the Long Island North Shore. She was an attractive five-foot-five brunette, and I found her manner of speaking through her nose and clenched teeth something I had never encountered before, except in movies such as *Auntie Mame*. She even seemed more sophisticated in the way she smoked cigarettes. I think she considered me less restrained in my down-to-earth partying than she was used to and more exciting to be with. Though she spent most of her time in the more refined atmosphere of the XXX House, forays to the other fraternities on Madison Lane and Rugby Road were eye-opening for her.

When we arrived at Sweetbriar, we learned that Faith lived in a house at the end of the main road. After we parked and asked someone to tell Faith she had visitors, it struck me that she might refuse to see us or be angry that I had dropped in with no prior notice. But then I saw her glide across the room and say in her upper-strata New Yorker finest, "Why, Frank, such a surprise! *So* good to see you!"

Suddenly I saw her for the first time in the cold light of day through the eyes of my three friends in juxtaposition to the sweet radiancy of my latest heartthrob, Anne.

"Hey, Faith. We're on our way back to Charlottesville and just stopped to say hello."

And then we about-faced, exited, and got back on the road.

By now I was eating most of my meals at the Beta house. By the way, in those days, Rush started on the second Saturday of October and lasted until Bid Sunday, which was shortly before Christmas break. One was a pledge (goat) until Hell Week, which ended on Friday night, and Rush started again the next week. It was a year-round proposition, and while it made sure all the participants knew each other well enough to make studied decisions, providing over two months of meals for non-member and nonpaying rushees, plus the expense of beer and parties, it was tremendously expensive. For first-year men, however, it was a great time with free meals, free beer, and parties with thirty-one different fraternities. After we pledged and then became brothers, it all became a series of lessons in real-life economics, namely, figuring out how to pay for it all!

One night I was returning to the dorm after Rush hours, and a fellow in front of the ATO house asked me if I'd like to come in for a beer. Ken was from Roanoke, and years later, as a trial lawyer in Atlanta, he became a good friend whose children went to both Westminster and the University with mine. When I reminded him of this moment, he could not remember it. His invitation to have a beer was a violation since it was after one o'clock, but that didn't really concern me. We went to the basement bar and party room, and I enjoyed a lot of beer. Eventually I meandered back to my room and fell into deep sleep.

The next morning, I found a piece of paper in my pocket. It was a note to myself and duly signed by me: "On my honor as a gentleman I pledge that I will eat the following meals at the ATO house." There followed a list of every meal until Rush was over. The enormity of this oath dumbfounded me, and I went to Chuck Spence to report that I could no longer eat at the Beta house. To violate an Honor Pledge meant immediate departure from the University.

Chuck's response was swift, "You stupid first-year man! Go ask your Honor counselor how valid a pledge is when it's been extracted from a rushee who had too much to drink at an illegal after-hours party."

While Chuck was not *my* Honor counselor, he was *an* Honor counselor. I continued my path to being a Beta pledge. As a result of this, I became even more dedicated to the Honor System in the unadulterated form of that time in the University's history.

As Bid Sunday grew closer and Laurie visited regularly, we spent more time at other houses and enjoyed the weekly Rush parties and meeting other people. I experienced my first Openings Weekend in all its glory, with thousands of visitors and famous combos and bands: The Fabulous Tams, Hot Nuts, and many others from far and wide. With each playing Beatles' and other celebrity groups' music, each at a different fraternity, it was like a Bourbon Street or Vegas Strip experience, equaled (I later learned) only by Midwinters and surpassed by the ultimate experience, Easters. I had asked Laurie to come to Bid Sunday with me, but the brothers told her it was not a good idea.

As Rush progressed, I continued to attend classes but without quite as much fervor. One thing that helped was that the new life science building was under construction close to my dorm window. Three days a week, I bounded out into class both because Mr. Ellison kept roll *and* heavy construction noise began around 7:30 to 8:00 and made it difficult to sleep. Thus, other than in one subject, I continued to amble along with the pack.

In the afternoons I spent more time with *The Cavalier Daily*, reporting and feature writing. Rush, though, and the whole fraternity scene continued to enlarge in my life.

And then the big day arrived: Bid Sunday. By tradition, those who expect or hope to get a bid from a coveted fraternity stayed in their rooms on Sunday afternoon, and then lines of fraternity brothers entered the dorms. I heard one group and then another enter the hall, and I wondered whether the Betas had changed their minds in the final hours of decision.

Suddenly there was a knock at the door. I opened it to see the president of the XXX fraternity formally invite me to become a pledge of the YYY chapter of XXX fraternity. As protocol required, I thanked him for the honor of the invitation and shook hands with each brother as they filed by my door. Looking back, I think all of them were dressed in dark suits to mark the solemnity of the occasion. After they left, Jim Sommers, president of the Omicron chapter of Beta Theta Pi, appeared with his membership and formally invited me, and I exchanged handshakes with the brothers. Although they certainly didn't mention it, I had the distinct feeling the proud Betas could not decide whether to be amused or irritated at having to wait for the XXXers.

At around four o'clock, those of us who were pledging were to go to the house of our choice (in my case Beta) to accept our bids. When I and my pledge brothers arrived at the Beta house, it was a sea of joyous celebration. We were warmly greeted with hugs and congratulations and herded into the front hall, where there was a full-sized galvanized trash can filled to the brim with a concoction known as artillery punch. Milk bottles were handed out and we were told to fill them. Then we toasted our glorious accomplishment to chants of "Drink! Drink! Drink!" Advice I cheerfully followed!

After a while any of us who'd received a bid from another fraternity were supposed to return them to that house since they were not going to be accepted. Each would be accompanied by a brother or brothers from the fraternity he was accepting, a practice that had probably started out as a courteous, gentlemanly practice but had devolved over the years. For any bids received from fraternities considered major contenders, the entire brotherhood accompanied the hapless pledge onto the porch to return the bid proffered by the group that had thought enough of him to offer it, while the audience looked on with victorious glee.

For my bid, however, the Betas considered it an embarrassment to have a pledge who received a bid from the XXX House. So, I went to the XXX fraternity with only Carlton Abbot, a gifted and popular architectural fourth-year man, to accompany me. At that point the day began to go downhill because the drinking of several bottles of artillery punch had not left me at my best.

After we arrived and I courteously but somewhat sloppily returned the bid, Faith came over to say hello, and I decided to take her with us. She didn't seem to mind as I took her by the arm to leave, but the XXX brothers took exception and grabbed her other arm while they tried to push me out the door. It was then that I let go a punch that missed everyone but went through a glass pane in their front door. Carlton then took over, soothed the XXXers, and steered me back to the Beta house.

I said earlier the Betas had suggested to Laurie it would not be a good idea for pledges to have dates for Bid Sunday, but many brothers did, and one of their dates saw my hand and shrieked, "Oh, it's all bloody!"

I replied, "Nah, it doesn't hurt," and punched the wall to prove it, putting a hole in the plaster in the process.

After further discussion, it was decided I needed stitches and I should probably not head to the emergency room by myself. So, Lew Siler, aka Lewdog, a football team manager, was deputized to go with me because he had not been drinking.

When we arrived at the hospital, we were ushered into a treatment room, where I was put on a table to get the stitches, and Lew was permitted to stay in the room with me. While the procedure was going on, Lew became a little fidgety and started fooling with some dials, one of which made the table go from horizontal to vertical, which resulted in my sliding off and onto the floor. This seemingly innocuous action significantly distressed the medical team, and Lew was ejected from the room. As my treatment resumed, I drifted off.

I awoke the next morning with my arms and legs strapped to a gurney in a hall of the hospital. After some wiggling, I escaped this cocoon and started for the door, only to be halted in my tracks by an authoritative nurse who stridently demanded, "Just where do you think you are going?"

"Back to my room," I replied in a calm, tired voice.

"Oh, no, you're not!" she replied.

Not seeing any benefit in responding to her, I started to move toward the door.

The nurse said, "We'll see about that!" and motioned to a nearby policeman. Happily, he was University officer Jim Batten, with whom I had a pleasant relationship. He was a man of few words but great empathy.

"Hi, Jim," I said. "Can I have a ride back to Emmet House?"

"All right," he replied.

We left with the nurse muttering about law officers who aided and abetted criminals.

I was greeted at Emmet with great enthusiasm and interest, and I realized my indiscretions had greatly added to my (dubious) reputation. I later learned that a frame had been put around my hole in the wall to enshrine the moment.

The only discordant note was when the obnoxious redhead, true to form, told me, "Your parents called last night to congratulate you. I told them not only were you not here but you were in the emergency room and having stitches."

Since there was no point in responding, I just entered my room and actually began to study a little before my first lunch as a pledge. Rush ended and my pledge period began.

# Chapter 4

# The Pledge Fall

After Bid Sunday, my home base shifted from the second floor of Emmet to Rugby Road and the Beta house. Students in class, at The Corner, the gym, church, and elsewhere became who their pledge pin said they were: Betas (Beta Theta Pi), Phi Kaps (Phi Kappa Sigma), Hallies (St. Anthony Hall; Delta Psi), KAs (Kappa Alpha Order), Elmos (St. Elmo Hall, Delta Phi), Zetes (Zeta Psi), E's (Sigma Alpha Epsilon), and twenty-five others, some of which were understood to be more equal than others. Then there was everybody else; they were called independents. Most were nice people and some were friends, but they lacked a tribe to support them in student politics, intramural athletics, extracurricular activities, housing, and most of the other facets of University life. I felt then as I do now, namely, that everyone who really wanted to be in a fraternity could be and that the fraternity-sorority system was a representation of how society is and always has been structured. Nonetheless, a healthy mix is one in which there is an effort to integrate disparate elements into the broad tapestry, without restricting one's right to choose companions. And that's easier said than done.

The time between Bid Sunday (December 12) and Christmas break was a honeymoon period for pledges and brothers who were getting used to each other and learning the nuances of daily routines, personalities, tribal idioms and taboos, and all other matters of family life.

The Beta house had four floors. The lowest was below grade in front and at grade in the rear and contained the furnace room, kitchen, dining room, and the tube (television) room. (I'll talk more about the furnace room during Hell Week next year and the kitchen in two years, when I was kitchen manager.) The dining room was a cheery, paneled room with caricatures of brothers on the walls as decoration and two rows of trestle tables. The tube room was similarly paneled but unadorned, except for a television in front of which sat a leather armchair flanked by two leather couches. Top priority for the couches went to the members of the Tube Team (TT) while the armchair was the exclusive domain of the Lord High Antenna (LHA). Membership was confirmed according to who watched the most TV. At the time most televisions were only black and white, stations were few, and the broadcast day ended at a certain time and resumed at a certain time, with only a test pattern broadcast between midnight and six. There were occasions when an LHA quietly watched the test pattern.

On the main floor of the house was a broad hallway with a fair-sized room on one side, euphemistically called the library, and a larger room with a fireplace on the other, which served as the living room. At the end of the hallway was an open telephone closet and a door leading to the bathroom and four rooms for residents, three doubles and one single. The living and dining rooms were the two gathering places during the week, while the library accommodated any spillover. On party weekends the living and/or tube rooms were cleared of furniture for dancing and combos. While UVA fraternities did not have house mothers, they were required to have one on party weekends. The objective was always to have either an elderly woman (somewhere between fifty and ninety years old) who had grown up around Virginia parties or one so aged and deaf as to be impervious to what was going on. The house mother was stationed in the farthest corner of the library and surrounded at all times by several flattering brothers while mayhem ensued everywhere else.

The third floor was residential, and the fourth had the attic on one side and a large chapter meeting room on the other. In the latter, benches lined the four walls in an unbroken rectangle for brothers; pledges sat on benches in the center of the room and faced the three primary officers at one end.

The glossary of the house included the following terms:

    horn: phone
    flash: regurgitate
    grunt: eat
    growl: defecate
    growler or whizzer: bathroom
    goat: pledge
    root: submarine sandwich or anatomical organ
    root man: Sigma Nu who ran the hoagie concession
    sweet pea or good honey: attractive female
    pooda: knowledge
    secret pooda: fraternity secret lore
    down the road or road trip: trip to a women's school
    ball grabbers: jockey shorts
    geek: nerd
    big-boy clothes: suit

As pledges, much of our interaction had been with second- and third-year guys, who are typically the most active in Rush. But now we were also in the presence of our elders, fourth-year men who had seen and done it all.

Tom Adams was a kindly person and well liked throughout the U. He was always ready to lend an ear and offer good advice.

A number of times I ate with Rod Regan, who introduced us to the new, inexpensive steakhouse just past The Corner, where we ordered extremely rare steaks served with french fries. After the fries were eaten, we apologized profusely to the waiter and explained that the meat was a little more rare than we had anticipated. The entrée was sent back on the grill, and when it was returned, it came with a new pile of fries. Rod also perfected the art of sarcasm, which once led the College Inn owner to ask us to leave.

Andrew Jackson "Jack" Bowen IV's name alone was enough to inspire respect.

Don Greenhalgh was a sincerely practicing Roman Catholic. He planned to be a priest, but he knew how to be a Beta without compromising either commitment.

The brothers recounted memorable events of past years, some that might have actually happened, some with only slight embellishments. For example, a Beta visited a girl and took a pledge brother along. While the two conversed on the front porch, the pledge developed a tremendous necessity to relieve himself. He stepped behind some bushes and did so at length in the deepening darkness of the early evening. Unbeknown to him, a few feet away, on the other side of the shrubbery, sat the parents, grandparents, and younger siblings of the daughter who'd been excused from the table to answer the door.

We also heard the story of a brother who'd been picked up in front of the house by an attractive older woman and taken to her home in Farmington. Her inattentive husband was out of town, and the brother later recounted hours of Turkish delights. As with many tales of sexual exploits, whether they actually occurred or were fantasies didn't particularly matter, because they were entertainment.

Other tales were based on truths involving the brotherhood, such as cutting down the fifteen-foot Christmas tree on property owned by a Beta family. When the felled tree was being loaded, we were accosted by an extremely agitated landowner, who pointed out that it was his property and not ours. Since I was a pledge, it wasn't my problem, so I never learned the solution except that we had a lovely tree.

One Midwinter party weekend, probably in my first year, a group of us went to the movies, leaving three or four brothers in front of a roaring fire. They were drinking and occasionally added some discarded furniture to the flames. The moviegoers returned to the house just as the fireman were packing up their gear to leave.

Apparently, several passersby had run into the house and announced, "Your house is on fire!"

A brother responded, "Sure it is."

Eventually someone induced a brother to walk outside and see the fire for himself, whereupon he exclaimed, "Holy s—t, our house is on fire!"

A spark had ignited the roof, but most of the destruction was water damage on the top two floors. Repairs were facilitated through the benefit of insurance. When the brothers discussed this, the consensus was the fire department call should've been delayed long enough to have the whole house redone!

In football, with a 4-6 record (ACC 2-4), UVA had its most successful season in many years. Coach Bill Elias (the Silver Fox) was named the conference coach of the year for this memorable season. However, the highlight of the season was the Maryland game, when the Hoos upset them on their way to the Gator Bowl, back when there were only a few bowl games. Thousands of us were actually excited about the game and waved goodbye to the visitors in the fourth quarter while chanting "Bye-bye, Gator Bowl, Maryland to the Toilet Bowl," which was followed by the wonderful tradition of singing "The Good Old Song" while swaying arm in arm with one's peers.

That good old song of Wah-hoo-wah—we'll sing it o'er and o'er
It cheers our hearts and warms our blood to hear them shout and roar
We come from old Virginia, where all is bright and gay

Let's all join hands and give a yell for the dear old UVA.
Wah-hoo-wah, wah-hoo-wah! Uni-v, Virginia!
Hoo-rah-ray, hoo-rah-ray, ray-ray—UVA!

Home football weekends were the focal point of all the fall social events, just not the games themselves. It started with parties on Friday nights and was followed by a Saturday brunch at the house, featuring Smith-field ham and plenty to drink. Afterward, Scott Stadium was a pleasant place to spend a lovely fall afternoon with friends. This was typically followed by a down period get-together before dinner, which was a preamble to another series of Rugby Road–Mad Lane combo bashes.

It was a glorious life! This camaraderie is part of Virginia's attitude toward sports. Competing at your best level is what should be done in all aspects of life, but sports are woven into the tapestry of Mr. Jefferson's University, not as a blood sport upon which the integrity and honor of the institution depends.

Another song was in common usage on the Grounds from the early 1900s until it was banned in 2010. Its second verse contained language commonly used in a locker room. In later years additional verses were added, many of which were unacceptable and rightfully eradicated. However, I feel that the first verse, which I've sung hundreds of times, describes the culture of the University I attended and loved in my era of the twentieth century:

From Rugby Road to Vinegar Hill, we're gonna get drunk tonight.
The faculty's afraid of us, they know we're in the right,
So fill your cups, your loving cups, as full as full can be,
And as long as love and liquor last, we'll drink to the U of V.
Oh, I think we need another drink! Heh!
I think we need another drink! Heh!
I think we need another drink! Heh!
I think we need another drink! To the glory of the U. VA.

It was sometimes said The University was so insular as to be immune to or ignorant of the increasingly violent protests beginning to spread across other university campuses regarding civil rights, the Vietnam War, and other social concerns. But an injustice of such magnitude occurred right on our doorstep, and all in Hoo Land were forced to intercede in a way that absorbed all the physical and emotional energy of the community. I'm referring, of course, to the news that the administration would no longer observe Thanksgiving Friday as a school holiday!

For one week pent-up outrage overflowed and large crowds milled around until police reinforcements were called in. Simultaneously, students from elsewhere showed up, which exacerbated a situation already spiraling out of control.

For example, my cousin Chip, always one to be where the action was, showed up from the University of Miami.

Madison Bowl ("Mad Bowl") became a flashpoint, and teargas was used to quell the mob. Chaos reigned throughout that weekend, until, quite suddenly, it was over. Everyone left. And life resumed as if the demonstration had never happened. It was the only experience I ever had with massive civil disobedience, and it was quite remarkable, although the cause had no moral or social significance.

The final event before going home for break was the annual Beta Christmas party, a much-anticipated function that, after a fall full of boisterous carousing, was quiet, relatively sophisticated, and sentimental. Cocktails flavored and colored with grenadine were the order of the day. In late afternoon and early evening, we enjoyed a sumptuous buffet dinner, which was followed by Archie and his quartet singing classic Christmas, gospel, and folk songs. I was transfixed by some I had never heard before: "I Was Seeing Nellie Home," "Telephone to Jesus," and "Let the Church Roll On." It was an afternoon and evening of peace and goodwill toward all.

Shortly thereafter we all went home for Christmas, and my first fall at Virginia was over. I note that currently exams are administered before the Christmas break, but in the early 1960s, they were three weeks after we returned from the holidays. In theory that gave students extra time to prepare, and I'm sure many did. Although I had taken all my books with me for the yuletide, the thought I would spend my vacation studying never actually germinated. I spent my time much as I had in prior years, namely, doing things with friends and family. However, with Dave Coulter dead, Alan Rimer out of town, and a significant interest in Anne who lived close by (in Sewickley) but was out of town on a family trip, I was somewhat at loose ends. So, I did all the Christmas things with my family: buying and putting up and decorating the tree, Christmas morning, and meals together. When I was with my old group, I went to dances and movies and generally hung out. But introduced into this recipe was a powerful new ingredient.

Although many of my friends at both Blair and Virginia had begun drinking in their high school years, in Mount Lebanon the accepted practice was not to do so until college.

The year before, I took a friend in his first year at Middlebury to visit a girl whose mother asked him, "Would you like a beer?" And then she turned to me and said, "I'll ask you the same question next year."

It was next year now! Although I had some minor league experience between Blair graduation and through the summer, by Christmas I'd entered the major leagues at a playoff-level school. Having grown up in a Victorian family, I was, however, quite unprepared for the liberation that was beginning to occur with some females.

One night I took out a girl for drinks and a movie, after which we engaged in some extracurricular activities. While I had always considered making out, sometimes intense, as the normal way to finish a date, the thought that nice girls might want to go further was an unconsidered possibility to me.

When I asked my date if she wanted to go home, she replied in the negative, and we parked in an isolated place I'd been to before. Suddenly I was in uncharted waters, and then she began to emit a series of alarming noises. I was surprised and stopped and asked if she was in pain. She made no response, and I took her home.

That evening was a glimpse of my years at Virginia until I entered holy matrimony. It also was one of the reasons I did not become a Beau Brummell. I was firmly convinced that "nice" girls were not interested in going all the way—and so were most of them. Closely related to this was the certain understanding that if a girl became pregnant, the father was supposed to marry her, leave school, and resign himself to a life of unremitting toil. I also believed all forms of birth control were absolutely undependable. Most important, the life of a partier ("wild man") was far more rewarding.

Years later, after a typical night, my wife observed she was never concerned I would become smooth with her or anyone else.

As to partying, while I had a few beers or a drink or two, not too much drinking went on for me that break until New Year's Eve. The year before, I'd had our group over to the basement rec room at our house.

The next morning, Mom commented on how nice the girls looked and how gentlemanly the boys had been.

I agreed while at the same time being very thankful that (1) we'd taken Roger, a freshman at Penn State, out the side door and rolled him in the snow to bring him around before taking him home and (2) that Mom and Dad hadn't noticed Roger didn't leave by the front door like everyone else.

This year it was time for me to walk in Roger's footsteps, and somewhat before midnight, I was brought home from wherever we'd been. The next day someone told me that this year had a somewhat different twist to it. After they had brought me home, I started to leave, and my friends tied me to a sofa in my bedroom. The unfortunate part was that my eleven-year-old brother, Doug, was innocent to the ways of the world, and he called Mom and Dad to tell them I had been brought home very sick and they needed to come home right away.

After the recent Bid Sunday episode, this additional bump in the road did little to assuage my parents' concerns that, as my mom commented the next day, "It seems that Virginia is like it has a reputation for being."

On that note, a few days later, I returned to Charlottesville, where such actions were commonplace, to complete first-semester exams and live the life of a Beta goat.

# Chapter 5

# A Virginia Gentleman

Many of the events related thus far about my experiences at the University may leave the impression that student life was not all work and no play. While there were many industrious, academically excellent scholars in our community, achievement was not measured in GPAs but by whether an individual could be considered a Virginia gentleman (VG). Such a decision was subjective, capricious, and depended upon which person or group was making the determination.

There were two student self-government bodies that created the boundaries to be considered in making the decision, in addition to a third, uniquely Virginian concept that added considerable latitude: the Honor Committee, the Judiciary Committee, and the gentleman's C. These are my impressions of how the three were woven together to create the concept of the VG as well as my first exams at UVA.

The overwhelmingly dominant influencer of the three was the Honor System and the certain knowledge that a man's honor was the sole standard by which to judge him. No matter what his grades or other accomplishments were, if he could not be trusted to act with honor, he was not acceptable as a member of the community. The

Honor Code was quite simple: "I shall not lie, cheat, steal, or violate my word of honor." On every paper, quiz, and exam, the following honor pledge was written: "On my honor, I have neither given nor received aid on this [paper, quiz, exam]." And the student had to sign it.

Because the code was universally accepted and revered, Virginia was a wonderful community in which about six thousand students could live in mutual trust. The practical advantages of this on a day-to-day basis were phenomenal. A person could leave his property, books, clothing, or whatever and return to get them later, knowing they would still be there. It was never necessary to lock any door, request permission to leave the room during an exam, worry about leaving one's notes uncovered, or countless other things not possible in other dishonorable environments.

My introduction to the Honor System occurred when I was a senior at Blair. The Reverend Foster Doan summoned me to a meeting in his quarters as dorm master of Locke Hall, chaplain, and religion teacher. The Reverend Doan had written my recommendation to the University of Virginia and also created the Chapel Committee (irreverently referred to as the God Squad), of which I was one. He had taken three of us to New York City for a seminar and an incredibly marvelous performance of a Shakespearean play by the incomparable British group the Old Vic Players. During the free time after the performance, the two other fellows had ordered and consumed alcohol. I had not, not because of any moral considerations, but because I had no desire for a drink and was afraid of what would happen if we were caught. Since this occurred during swimming season, I used that to avoid pressure from my peers, because training was considered almost inviolable in our team culture.

Later, the two students either turned themselves in or had been found out. Since I had not been named a co-conspirator, the Reverend Doan was prompted to discuss the incident with me and describe the Honor System in uncompromising and intricate detail. While I was glad for the opportunity to clear the air about the New York trip, the principal advantage, in addition to clearing the cloud of doubt, was seeing the abstract concept of honor become reality.

Upon my arrival at the University, a major thrust of orientation was making first-year men fully aware of the Honor Code as it applied to all events in the universe and that nothing was exempt from it. The full-class assemblies and small-group meetings were conducted by impressive upperclassmen of impeccable standing. In the weeks that followed in a male culture where nothing was sacrosanct and everything was subject to sarcastic, cynical comment, the Honor System was beyond reproach.

Shortly before the incident of the invitation to meals, another occurred on my hall while I was a resident of the second floor at Emmett. One of the residents was missing some money, suspected another, and planned to accuse him of an honor violation. In keeping with the code that called for him to make the accusation directly, he asked several of us to accompany him to investigate the circumstances. Afterward it was clear that, while the money was missing, it was due to an honest misunderstanding. Once the matter was resolved, I recall the two fellows leaving together for a meal or a beer to make sure there were no hard feelings. There was no question in anyone's mind as to whether the code was just or whether the procedures followed had not been absolutely necessary.

During final exams that semester, a person with whom I'd become friendly, since he sat near me in one of my classes, caught my attention. After the exam had started, I noticed him pull out some papers, look at them, and then put them back under the desk. And then he did so again a while later. After the exam I asked him why he had referred to what appeared to be notes during the exam. Startled, he pulled out the papers and showed me that one was his exam schedule and the other related to his travel plans after exams were over. Taking what amounted to a break from the exams, he'd reviewed the time frame for completing his remaining exams to see how much time he had to make the necessary connections for the ride he'd arranged. Nothing in the notes was related to the class for which the exam was being given, so I believed him.

He said, "You would've turned me in, wouldn't you?"

No answer was necessary. I wished him a wonderful break and said I looked forward to seeing him when class resumed.

Over the next three years, I had no further personal experiences concerning the Honor Code. Occasionally there were sudden, unexplained departures from the University, but one of the aspects of the system was that such cases were not discussed.

That changed dramatically in my fourth year, when, as Student Council president, I was told by B. F. D. Runk, dean of students, that a student charged with theft by the civil authorities had to be specifically accused by another student. And he wanted me to be that other student. That was my only personal experience with a trial, which I will relate when this narrative turns to my fourth year.

As I've said, while the Honor System, Honor Committee, and Honor Code were very simple and universally accepted, the judiciary system and committee were quite a different matter. While no one disputed the need for a disciplinary body, there was no requirement for a student to turn in another for a breach of discipline and no consensus on what such a breach was. In my mind, it boiled down to destruction or defacement of public and University property and actions that publicly displayed a negative view of the University.

In fraternities and other personal groups, such matters were dealt with internally. Probably most important, outrageous acts of heroic proportions were apt to induce admiration rather than censure. A few of the incidents described thus far help to illustrate this, as will many, many more to come. After all, Virginia was regarded as proficient in the world of party schools, a title that many and probably a majority of people were content with or even proud of. Many outsiders who had been lulled into relaxed admiration of the handsome young men in coats and ties with overtly courteous and chivalrous manners did significant reappraisals as the hours passed. When they asked about this seemingly Jekyll-and-Hyde dichotomy, the answer was and is simple: they neither lied, cheated, stole, or violated their word of honor. If something was determined to be a prank (the more outrageous the better), the perpetrator was usually home free. As my friend Wooly, who spent a lot of time with the Judiciary Committee, told me, "If you get them to laugh, it's going to be okay."

There was yet another student governing body: the Bad Check Committee. A wonderful thing about Charlottesville and its environs was that merchants accepted students' checks without question, knowing they were good because intentionally writing a bad check was a violation of the Honor System, since a check assumes money is available to cover it. The committee's objective was to determine whether a bad check was fraudulent, a breach of honor, or an arithmetic error. While plastic has now supplanted checks, the idea of the Bad Check Committee is archaic or even incomprehensible, but in the 1960s, student checking accounts were at the cutting edge of consumer financial advancement.

The third leg of the Virginia gentleman concept was the gentleman's C. While there was truly an atmosphere of academic excellence (exemplified by membership in Phi Beta Kappa, the Raven Society, and the Dean's List, which were duly noted and appreciated), there was no stigma on the many students who chose earning a degree as their only objective. Not only that, but a true wild man who was known to have pulled it off with all-nighters at the end of each semester was accorded a good deal of admiration. During Rush, no one ever asked me what my GPA was or how I was doing academically.

There was also a system of quality points in order to be in good standing with the University. This did not consider the total hours needed to earn a degree. In theory, this was a minimum of 2.0 (the number of semesters times 10 grade points). In practice, it worked differently.

Let's say at the end of the first year of school (2 semesters x 10 = 20 points to be in good standing), a person had eight C's (2 x 8 = 16 points), a D (1 point), and an F (0 points). That scholar would have 17 total points, which is 3 shy of good standing (20). However, if he went to summer school and earned one B (3 points) or a C and a D (3 points), those points would be added to the 17, and he would be in good standing; however, he would have less than the necessary C average, or total hours, to take his degree. (At the University of Virginia, one did not graduate; he took a degree, since graduating implies having reached the end of learning.)

Eventually he would have to get enough As and Bs to offset the Ds and Fs, which is why there were a number of great fellows in their fifth or sixth years. Sometimes a person ran out of courses in their major and had to move to another one. I met several men who told me their major was economic geography, defensively adding that it was a very important and fascinating area. While that was possibly true, it was also one of the last branches to grab for before being swept over the Niagara of never taking a degree.

At any rate, the gentleman's C occupied a prominent position in the UVA culture. An example of this was my friend Rusty, who survived two tours as a Seal in Vietnam and later distinguished himself prominently in a major role on Wall Street. At the end of his last semester, he found it necessary to beg a professor to reduce a B to a C, telling the don that not to do so would destroy his four-year quest of achieving a perfect gentleman's C.

When I was at Blair, the return after the Christmas break had always been difficult. For one thing, it was a return to an isolated school, generally ensconced in heavy snow and consistent subfreezing temperatures from which one would not be released until spring break, except for the occasional free weekend, mixer with a girls' school, or an away athletic event. The return to Virginia, on the other hand, was a return to as much obscurity or companionship one desired. It was a place where one could do anything that didn't violate the Honor Code. At Blair, attendance at meals was mandatory, but at Virginia you could eat whenever or wherever you wanted.

Probably the most different aspect was class attendance. At Blair, there was no question that one would go to class. At Virginia, unfortunately, nobody made sure anyone went to class. And I learned more about this later in the coming semester.

In just about all other aspects, however, Virginia and Blair had a great deal in common (and still do in their current state). At both, students were male, wore coats and ties (the former by requirement, the latter by tradition), and each had thought and speech patterns developed and refined through generations on sporting fields and battlefields as well as continued use of men's clubs and locker rooms. My brother, educated at the Lawrenceville School and Princeton University before med school, was an undergraduate during the trial period of coeducation. He told me he'd always considered it a good idea until it actually happened, at which time he decided it was preferable to see girls on the weekends, when they had prepared themselves, and not when they first arose in the morning and were around all the time. All-male surroundings also created in me a perspective of a woman as someone's sister, wife, or date, not a separate individual. (On the other hand, it never occurred to me that I would not be forever responsible for caring for my date and eventually my wife, a concept missing in today's culture.)

Both Blair and Virginia had classes on weekdays and Saturday mornings. This was a new thing for public school fellows but something I had known since ninth grade. And all the teachers and instructors were male. In four years at Virginia, I had only two female professors. Thus, what was considered both restricting and unusual about our environment was, for me, a very comfortable and natural environment.

During my time at the University, approximately 45 percent (later reduced to 35 percent) of the students were from out of state. And 45 percent of my class had come from private schools, a majority of them boarding. Those men had worn coats and ties, had a five-and-a-half-day class week, and were subject to certain codes and practices that had been established at all-male schools for generations.

For the record, I have not confirmed these statistics, but I believe they are accurate based on my experiences in the Class of 1965.

My reflection now is that either by design or by choice, it was a very wise move. Students from private schools, especially the Northeastern schools, tended to have academics that were a little too weak to go to the Ivies but above the Virginia public school averages, and thus increased the academic profile of the University. Moreover, some of students were quite wealthy and even more became wealthy later, which enabled Virginia to increase the endowment, out-of-state tuition, and annual giving, which decreased the need for support from the Commonwealth. The result was that Virginia moved from being a party school of national prominence in the South to its current status as a university internationally acclaimed for academic prowess across a broad spectrum of specialties.

I once remarked to a friend, a doctor who was treating me, "If I were in school today, or if the Bath County school system had been able to test, I would've been AD."

"No," he replied. "You would have been ADHD."

Because of this or in spite of it, I have always been able to achieve significant results in subjects that interested me. I graduated from Blair with the Academy Trophy for the highest all-around achievement, and I took my degree from the University with numerous achievements. My testing prowess was superb, but my grades were often only adequate or below.

My dad asked me, "How can you remember every word of every song you've ever heard but not one word of Spanish vocabulary?"

I said, "I suppose it's because the songs interest me and Spanish vocabulary doesn't."

Over the years, my ability to see the forest clearly but not the trees has served me well. While there seemed to be a lot of undiagnosed ADHD students with me at Charlottesville, a significant number of them achieved very successful and contented lives as they matured. Alas, some remained forever locked in that period.

In the mid-twentieth century, final exams at both secondary schools and colleges were several weeks after the students returned from break. For my grandchildren (and probably my children), a much more practical and humane system has been established. Exams are held before the break, permitting students to have a much more enjoyable vacation without anything hanging over them. While I was at Blair and Virginia, I lugged home lots of books, put them on my desk, and spent my time enjoying the season while spending very little time using them. Moreover, in boarding school I was in the swimming pool for hours, neither smoking nor drinking, getting ready for the season. In college, since I had quit swimming, I didn't do this either and arrived back in Charlottesville unprepared both physically and mentally.

After New Year's, I plunged, like everyone else, into a frenzy of preparation for exams. In that respect, whether a student was going for all As or trying to avoid suspension or expulsion, the end result was the same: from early morning until the wee hours, frantic preparation went on. In addition to using the textbooks and my sparse class notes, I searched out people such as Dick Tucker, an Echols Scholar and pledge brother, who had prepared copiously throughout the semester. When the testing days arrived, I was more or less prepared for all my subjects, that is, except for my great nemesis: Latin III. Some history may help here.

In many high schools, including mine, either two years of two languages or three years of one were required, because it was necessary for entrance to many colleges and also a requirement for graduation from institutions such as Virginia. Since my first year at Blair had been a disaster, I had failed Spanish. Therefore, in my second year I elected to take three years of Latin, which seemed a better alternative to French or German. It was thought (and I still think) a knowledge of Latin was a splendid preparation for many other things. My first two years of Latin (Caesar) were undistinguished but respectable. When I returned for my senior year, a week before the general student body, for early football practice, a new master, Mr. Ritter, approached me.

(We referred to Mr. Ritter as "Tex," after the semi-famous cowboy star of the era. He had an undergraduate degree from Yale and graduate degrees in classical languages from Yale and similar institutions. He was a prep school gypsy, well-prepared academically but a basket case as a teacher of preppy smart alecks.)

He said, "I see you're a football player. Football players do not do well in Latin."

This comment filled me with alarm.

"But," he continued, "don't worry. I understand that and will take care of it."

Since my other subjects included advanced English and history, I thought that was a great idea! And so, before every quiz or test, he would say, "Pay special attention to...."

I would go to those pages or readings and memorize the English out of Virgil's *Aeneid* and do all right on the test. There were six other people in the class, all geniuses, who eventually went to the Ivies and could read Latin and understand it. Then there was me. At the end of the second semester everyone in the class earned an A. I got a C. So, I went to Mr. Ritter and said I didn't think that was fair. He agreed and changed my grade to a B.

In preparing for admissions applications, my other grades were quite good, except in math, where a long line of Cs trailed behind me. Moreover, I had done quite well on the SAT scoring in the mid-700s in English, 600s in math, and the mid-700s in English composition and literature. (These scores were under the old grading system.) After I was accepted at Virginia, I had to take chemistry achievements, which was further proof (if any were needed) that I shouldn't be a chemist.

But no one required me to take Latin achievements. When I arrived at Virginia, I was given a Latin placement exam. Thus, I signed up for Latin III so I would be rid of my foreign language requirement at the end of the year, assuming that my placement exam would determine if that was all right.

As the semester progressed, it was obvious I was in over my head. When my parents visited, I relayed the situation to them and said I would probably drop Latin. But my dad told me a cock-and-bull story about how, when he was at Cornell, he was doing very poorly in chemistry but worked much harder and received a B (the implication being that it was subpar for him).

So instead of dropping Latin before the drop date, I hesitated and cooked my goose. At the last class meeting before the exam, which was a review day, Mr. Coaker, my instructor, said, "Mr. Briggs, you needn't get the feeling that it's hopeless, even though numerically it's impossible for you to pass with your current average of 48 percent. If you score in the high or even in the mid-90s, I will pass you."

Somehow that did not seem reassuring, and after I missed enough questions to be below 90 (which didn't take very long), I handed in the exam and left. Later, I asked Mr. Stocker, chairman of the classical languages department, how I could have been put in Latin III, given how my placement exam must have gone.

He said, "We had a death in my family, and those tests were never graded. So, we placed you based on your high school results."

Which goes to show that justice always prevails in the end.

After I began to write down these recollections, it occurred to me that I'd never looked at my transcript. Once I'd seen them as posted after each semester and determined that I had achieved my objective of staying in school, I never looked at them again. In December 2018, fifty-three years after I took my degree, I decided to look at my transcript before I wrote any further. It showed I'd moved from the best semester I'd ever enjoyed (my final one at Blair) to one of considerably less prominence: a C in composition, a C in general geology, an F in Latin III, a D in math analysis, a C in introduction to military science, and a P in activities. My GPA was 1.44.

But I considered my first semester an overall success. I had pledged a good fraternity, made a lot of friends, and participated in several extracurricular activities, and I was eligible to return for the next term.

# Chapter 6

## Beta Goat

Before I get into the goat period and the following spring activities, I must comment on the means of my transportation home for Christmas break. It was much used in those days but no longer. In short, I hitchhiked.

In 1961, I caught a ride with some students to Harrisonburg, and in Harrisonburg my thumb got me a ride with a woman about my mother's age, who was going to visit her daughter's family in Hagerstown, Maryland. After about fifteen minutes my thumb advanced me to Somerset, Pennsylvania, with an elderly couple, and immediately thereafter I hitched a ride with a salesman to Johnstown (which was a little out of the way but closer to Pittsburgh than Somerset). Even though I wore a coat and tie, it took a little longer to get a ride at night, so when two black guys offered me a ride, I accepted with a little apprehension, which was unnecessary, because they were great fellows and we had a lot of fun. Upon our arrival in Pittsburgh, they announced they were going to the Hill District and asked if I wanted to go with them or be dropped off on the highway. I elected the highway, which caused them a good deal of amusement. (If you don't know Pittsburgh, read between the lines.) I don't remember who gave me a ride after that, but it was over the bridge, through the tube, and I was dropped off on Washington Road in Mount Lebanon. From there I walked a half mile to our house on Navahoe Drive. At eleven o'clock, I was warmly welcomed by my mom and sister, since my dad and little brother had already gone to bed. All in all, my trip probably took about eleven hours, which wasn't much longer than catching a bus or a train and a lot less expensive.

The semester break, like everything else Virginian, did not coordinate with other schools, so there were no friends home from their respective institutions of higher learning. This meant I had more time with my mom, since my sister and brother were still in school; my dad left for work before I surfaced in the morning, and he retired almost immediately after dinner. Mom had been my consistent supporter, confidant, and defender for as long as I could remember, which made those times special, although I took them for granted at the time.

My father was fifty-five when I went to Virginia. He had worked for five years before putting himself through Cornell's School of Hotel Management, and he had reached the pinnacle of his profession. While we loved each other in our own way, we had absolutely nothing in common and could not even begin to understand what made the other tick. This relationship continued until my early thirties (his midseventies), at which time we began to make great progress in discovering each other, until he entered eight years of senility in his early eighties.

The point is that Virginia men increasingly became both my companions and role models when I returned to UVA.

My return from break was by public transportation (probably bus), since return to class required exact timing rather than relying on the vagaries of being picked up by a friendly series of drivers. My first arrival at Mr. Jefferson's Academical Village was as an immigrant, while this time it was for stage two in the naturalization process: a fraternity pledge.

My world was now split into fraternity brothers, fraternity pledges, and everyone else, with one further, enormously complicating distinction in that there were thirty-one houses. Each house was the chapter of a national fraternity, chartered by that entity and subject to its general constitution and bylaws. There were no local fraternities, because the University required each be affiliated with a national, which gave the administration of each some leverage. Because of the tremendously strong tradition of student governance and the reality that a significant number of the administration had grown up in the system, fraternities were allowed for the most part to do what they wanted.

There was an Interfraternity Council (IFC) comprised of delegates from each of the fraternities, which regulated issues involving the Greek community, quite often involving Rush rules and infractions. But it was a loose confederation and had no influence on the operation of individual chapters. In that it was like all things Virginian. Each individual or group was free to pursue their own course as long as it did not become a nuisance to others.

Because UVA was quite small for a state institution, the number of members and pledges of these fraternities was not large either, with memberships running from the forties to the seventies. Looked at individually, it was apparent each one was different from the others and reflected the blended personality of the majority of its membership. From this point, while I will comment on the other fraternities, I will do so from the perspective of a pledge and then a brother of the greatest of all national fraternities: Beta Theta Pi.

The Omicron chapter of BOII pledged twelve men in November 1961 from different locations, backgrounds, and interests. That spring, through the second week of the following fall, ten of these pledges formed an unshakable bond that exists to this day. While every brother shared a common relationship with every other in unquestioned loyalty and support, each pledge class member had the additional kinship developed during the Goat Year. Like all brothers, there were plenty of differences, arguments, and heavy-duty male banter, but an attack on one of us was defended by all of us. In the years that followed, especially in Charlottesville, whatever adversity I experienced in the wider world, I knew the Beta house was there to embrace, comfort, and uplift me, no matter what.

The narration of the Pledge/Goat Year will be straight from my memory and a compilation of events that are representative and not necessarily exact recitations of specific events. Since ten pledge brothers will figure prominently in the coming chapters, I will introduce them now as primary characters in the coming episodes alphabetically:

| Name | Hometown | Secondary | Nicknames |
|------|----------|-----------|-----------|
| Frank Hay Briggs Jr. | Pittsburgh, PA | Blair Academy | "Frank," "Beta" |
| Michael Sherman Cobb | Annapolis, MD | Severn School | "Mike," "Cobby" |
| Robert Hilliard Green-wood | Birmingham, AL | Spring Hill Academy | "Bobby," "[Mr.] Green-jeans" |
| Edward Leigh Hogshire | Norfolk, VA | Norfolk Academy | "Teddy," "Hoggy" |
| Lee Wilson Mather Jr. | Virginia Beach, VA | Woodberry Forest School | "Rusty," "Pony," "Flash" |
| Richard Blackburn Tucker III | Pittsburgh, PA | Episcopal High School–Alexandria (EHS) | "Dick," "Slippery [Dick]" |
| William Hamilton Ty-lander | Fort Pierce, FL | Episcopal High School–Alexandria (EHS) | "Billy," "Willie T" |
| Jonathan George Verity | Middleburg, OH | Hotchkiss School | "Jon," "Cherub," "Minnesota Fats" |
| Hugh Kellaher Wood | Virginia Beach, VA | Virginia Episcopal School (VES) | "Kelly," "Hugh Dog" |
| Joseph Rutledge Young Jr. | Charleston, SC | Woodberry Forest School | "Rutledge," "Rut" |

There were two other pledge brothers, but one did not return after the first semester, and the other drifted away and will not be a part of this narrative. The next year Sheppard Craig transferred to Virginia from the University of North Carolina. He was well liked by all the Woodberry guys and, as soon as the rest of us got to know him, by us as well. He was a welcome addition to the house and our group, although he may have been one year behind us with the transfer.

There is one other member of our pledge class, a fictional character I have named Hickory, who will appear whenever it is appropriate to conceal a brother's actual name.

While I will dwell in some detail on the indignities experienced by pledges, I will start by pointing out that it is a great advantage to be part of a homogeneous family. For starters, the house served three extremely good meals every weekday and on special Saturdays for a very reasonable price. All brothers and pledges were billed $45 monthly for lunch and dinner, with the option of adding breakfast for $10 more. Everyone who lived at 180 Rugby Road took advantage of this perk. While attendance was not required at meals, everyone wanted to be there because it was a wonderfully social time with a close family. Long after each meal, everyone congregated until called to class, study, Mr. Van's Pool Hall at The Corner, or any of myriad destinations.

In hindsight, how and where else could a first-year man spend time every day with seconds, thirds, and fourths who were genuinely interested in him? During that first year, we had many role models. Despite our cohesiveness, I have never been able to remember which person attended which classes other than, of course, my own.

There was a trio from Louisville: Eli Brown, Hoyt Blakely, and Roydon Peabody. Eli had been the Rush chairman. He was effervescent and voluble, with definite opinions on almost everyone and everything. To him there were Betas and everyone else, most of whom were geeks. (Geek was a commonly used, all-inclusive term of distain, but only Eli could make the listener understand it to the fullest depth.)

Hoyt exuded confidence and was extremely reserved, but he had a biting wit. It was alleged, after listening to a date express her innocent virtue and abhorrence of sexual activity ad nauseam (a quaint notion in many quarters these days), Hoyt quietly responded, "That's all right. I'd rather drink anyway."

Roydon was a handsome example of the Kentucky aristocracy, with strong, angular features. He fit dominantly into the culture and everyone listened to him when he expressed his opinions.

Steve Chipman was Eli's close friend, and the two of them shared an unkempt basement apartment at the back of Elliewood Avenue. Chipman was liked and admired by all, including our pledge class, although he was probably the most consistent enforcer of pledge discipline.

Ralph Fraise, svelte and urbane, with French features and matching accent, was a native of Madagascar. He was affable and popular.

Chuck Spence was and still is the brother I was closest to outside my pledge class.

There were several people in the house I knew by rank to be the oldest. The first was President Jim Sommers from Newport News. Another was Jim Brandhorst of Fort Thomas, Kentucky. He was perfect for his job as the neat year's president in that he could, better than most, maintain some order in this anarchic group. Probably six feet tall, in unexpectedly good shape and well groomed, he was a natural leader. Capable of being stern when necessary, but always with a twinkle in his eye.

By contrast, our vice president, John "Soups" Wilder, of Columbus, Ohio, was only older chronologically. While not actually heavy, he came by the nickname honestly. There will be more about him in the next chapter.

Then there was Joe Garland, who was more like an uncle in my mind than a fraternity brother.

Another group was comprised of the few fellows who had longtime girlfriends from home and were subject to a special torment by their brothers.

For example, the girlfriend of Leonard Woolsey Cox of Lexington, Kentucky, received a lot of ribbing. Leonard was a chubby, diminutive man who I remember every day because of a silver-plated hairbrush engraved with his initials that sits by the mirror in my bathroom. I used it so much while living in the Beta house that he told me to keep it.

Another who had an at-home girlfriend was Jim Lanier, who was also the butt of much ribbing and probably took it more seriously. It was generally understood that permanent relationships while at the University were impediments to be avoided at all costs, though there were plenty of exceptions as long as the male participant did not appear to be whipped.

Getting pinned (the practice of giving a girl your fraternity pin to wear) had the double jeopardy of appearing indelible as well as smacking of State U-ism. It was also considered appropriate to wait until Thursday before asking out a girl for that weekend as a proof of one's desirability and freedom from entanglement.

The Beta house had a handful of aviators who occupy their own place in my memories. Richard "Rabbit" Tilghman became a bank president, but I remember him as a pilot who took me on my first small plane rides. When he raised the nose to make the single engine stall, I assumed he knew what he was doing since it always restarted itself. Another flyboy was Lew Seiler, who had difficulty mastering navigation. One day he told us he'd headed toward Lexington, Kentucky. When he landed and said he was glad to be there, the ground personnel informed him that he was at a different city.

Yet another small group were the intellectuals. Although many if not most brothers had good to exemplary grades—several went on to medical, law, business, or other graduate schools—very few chose to be identified as such. Two who did were the Scully brothers, Malcolm and Tucker, from The Beach.

(A noun preceded by the object "The" means that the descriptive adjective *Virginia* is associated with it: The University, The Beach, The Country Club, The Medical College [now University], The High School, The Seminary [Episcopal], etc.)

One more group who took their meals at the house and added a tremendous dimension to the fraternity were UVA Beta graduate students. While Eddie Baird, Brereton "Brere" Jones, Hutch Overby, and others came later, in 1961 my biggest hero was Bunny Benham. He was a lithe, lanky blond from Winchester, then in law school, and he was remarkable for his unassuming, extremely relaxed bearing. Yet he was a competent scholar, a former lacrosse star, an Eli Banana, and universally accepted as a leader on the Grounds. He also dated Julie Enslow, then and is still an object of my awe and admiration.

Some other notable Betas who will appear throughout this narrative, though by no means all, are Jim "Sparrow" Summers, Wyatt "Cowpie" Williams, George Armistead Tyler Browning, Andrew Jackson "Jack" Bowen, Richard "Dick" Tedrow, Jim "Sausage" Morris, and Wickie McNeely.

There were many other advantages to living in the Greek world, a few being which class/teacher to take and what "gut" (easy) elective should I take. The house also had pooda files containing notes and tests from past years.

Upperclassmen were also instrumental in procuring dates through myriad connections at the big three to five women's schools, as well the many other schools within a few driving hours. Counseling on females in general, and specifically on the hundreds of girls known by one or more Betas, was also freely administered. Comments were given, whether sought or not, in a frank, generally unvarnished, and sometimes brutal manner, but typically with the best intentions.

Solace and comfort were also offered during the many adverse occasions that occur in one's life: a death, a divorce, family misunderstandings, failure to achieve a longed-for objective. Most frequently these related to someone who had been dumped on by a female. One thing I was always certain of: the brother was always the aggrieved party and to be fully supported. In summary, the Beta house was where you knew for certain your back was always covered against any external presence.

The full realization that the courtship of Rush was over and that the goat year had started in earnest was at our first chapter meeting. We all happily ascended to the third-floor meeting room, and all of a sudden, we were assailed by a derisive cacophony raining down on us from all sides.

"You stupid goats!"

"You ignorant morons!"

"Get into your places, you dumb goats!"

It was the first of many times in which we were supposed to know something we had no way of knowing.

Goats were never permitted to speak unless specifically called upon, but they were represented by our pledge class president, Rutledge Young, the perfect choice for that thankless job.

I described the meeting room before as a long rectangle, twice as long as it was wide. Around three sides was a single continuous bench for the brothers, and in the center were four benches facing north. Three chairs were set up at that end of the room for the president (Jim Sommers), vice president (John "Soups" Wilder), and the secretary (whose name I have forgotten).

Brothers spoke freely when they were recognized by the chair or, in many cases, whenever they felt like it. At every meeting, some time was directed to pledge development, usually after the report by the pledge trainer, Lew Seiler, who was ably assisted with constant input from the brothers. Generally, the report involved Beta lore or secret pooda, disciplinary matters, and pledge work requirements.

As to Beta lore, the house was ambivalent. On the one hand, there were certain things that were required knowledge. Lew met with us once a week. Always in his hand was the pledge manual, *Sons of the Stars*, for training. He assigned us parts and songs for us to memorize. For example, I can still quickly recite the founding details, including the place, time, day, and names of the eight founding brothers. Quickly was very important, because as the year advanced, the consequences of not being able to recite pooda correctly and in a hurry became more dire. Upon request I can also sing every stanza of at least six Beta songs out of the voluminous songbook. Memorization was an important and easy way to have something as a gauge for enforcing discipline.

The problem with Beta pooda was the great fear university wide, and possibly even more so at the Beta house, of State U-ism: the concept that one might look like a student at any other state university. State U-ism included, but was not confined to, wearing any article of apparel with the school's name on it, unless one competed athletically for the school. The thought of wearing anything with a fraternity name on it was such a mortal sin that I never saw it during my four years at Charlottesville.

Another area that could be considered State U-ism was any overt display of enthusiasm, since Virginia gentlemen were to remain reserved and blasé at all times. A student never spoke to another unless he had been properly introduced. (If in direct contact in class or someplace similar, one could introduce oneself.) For that reason, the idea of learning fraternity lore was both required and ridiculed at the same time, which was no problem for those who were practiced in that art.

I have two final thoughts on State U-ism. Invariably the district representative sent by the Beta General Fraternity of the Miami (Ohio!) Triad were graduates of places like Gung-Ho State and wore fraternity-branded clothing in a very gung-ho manner. When he left the men at 180 Rugby Road, yet another deficiency report was submitted to the general fraternity.

On the faculty of the Law School was an outstanding legal scholar who was one of the leading Betas of all time: A. J. Gustin Priest. One of the most well-known rumors of the early 1960s was that Brother Priest made his first visit to the Beta house during the annual faculty party. He wore a Beta tie and carried a copy of *Sons of the Stars*. These were abominations to the UVA men, so a senior member of the house, who later became a formidable jurist, poured a beer on Brother Priest's head, and so Brother Priest departed the house and vowed never to return. Three years later, Brother Priest and I served together on the 3-3-3 (Student-Faculty-Administration) Committee, but I'll talk about that later.

Certain responsibilities, such as phone duty, followed a specific schedule in which a goat was always at the house for their assigned evening. The house had a regular dial phone for local and incoming calls downstairs and a pay phone upstairs for long-distance calls. The scripted response to a request for an absent brother was, "He's not here, sir/ma'am." And the follow-up was, "I don't know where he is, sir/ma'am. He may be at the library." This response was sometimes greeted with skepticism. For example, Sparrow's father, an old Wahoo himself, countered, "Don't tell me that, son. Wherever he is, I'm certain it's not the library!"

Another goat duty involved work details for a variety of things: scrubbing and waxing, oiling the woodwork, replacing broken windows from the latest snow- or ice-ball battle with the Zetes and/or the DU's, or any of a number of things. The houseboy, Sam Ragland, was above middle age, and he did the general cleaning and made the beds.

A last-minute summons, however, supplanted any previously planned personal activity, except for a scheduled class or tutorial session.

The third facet of goatdom involved spontaneous requests for a goat to run an errand or perform a task for a brother. For example, Steve Chipman informed Rutledge Young and me over lunch that we were going to clean the apartment he shared with Eli Brown, which was a formidable task. During the cleaning, we asked if we needed to change Eli's sheets (the white sheets were yellow.)

Steve responded, "Goat, are you saying you think Mr. Brown is dirty!?"

Rutledge snapped to attention and said, "Sir, no sir!"

Steve said, "I hope not, goat! Mr. Brown would be very offended if you thought he was. If Mr. Brown had wanted his sheets changed, he would have told you."

For the most part, pledges were treated as any other brother, but at any time goatism could lead to discipline. While some brothers ignored the system and others pursued it diligently, all stood behind it regardless of what form it took. Since pledges lived in their first-year dorms until moving into the house the following fall, bonding was not segregated by classes. We went to dinner in groups of brothers and pledges when the house wasn't open or when we attended sports events and other activities. Who went with whom was based upon shared affinities and availability.

One night was especially momentous because it presented me with my first opportunity to meet the dean of the University, B. F. D. Runk. That night, Carlton Abbot and I were going to the railway station restaurant. Since it had been snowing, we threw some snowballs at a billboard across the street. Then, as we were about to enter the restaurant, I reminded Carlton how I had hit the door at the XXX House on Bid Sunday by slamming my fist against the side of a railroad car parked at the station.

Moments later a Charlottesville policeman approached us and said we had been throwing snowballs at him, and he added that I was also in trouble for trying to damage railroad property. We assured him we did not know he was standing under the billboard and that it would be impossible for me to damage a railroad car.

After what seemed like a long time, I realized our arguments were falling on deaf ears. But instead of following Carleton's lead of earnest supplication and extreme subservience, I made a huge tactical error.

Unwisely I said, "Don't waste your breath, Carlton. He's not bright enough to know what you're talking about!"

We were immediately escorted to the police station, where Carlton got us out with the assurance that we would report to court at 10:00 the next morning.

In court, the officer took special pains to say how nice and courteous Carlton had been and how discourteous and unruly his companion was. I assumed we would pay a fine and be free to leave.

(In hindsight I do not recall Carlton thanking me for painting him in such a favorable light!)

The Charlottesville police and UVA students in general did not have a warm relationship. For one thing, students tended to act superior to others, which did not sit well with the municipal keepers of the law. Furthermore, only the University police had jurisdiction on state property, the University grounds, and the Charlottesville police had none. So, if a student could manage to get to the University Grounds, he could turn and laugh at the policeman. If he didn't make it, a much different conclusion followed!

A few days after Carlton's and my day in court, we were invited to Dean Runk's office. As a leader of the architecture school, Carlton was on friendly terms with the dean, but I was unknown (to the extent there was anything he didn't know already from my record). While we always wore coats and ties, we took special care to be extremely well-groomed for this meeting, which was something Mr. Runk always noted.

Carlton explained the circumstances of our run-in with the law, which of course the dean had already read in the police report. Since I had not had any beers before the meeting with the dean, I was more circumspect than I had been on the night in question. I kept my mouth shut while Carlton talked and only responded to the dean's questions.

To my surprise, the meeting was cordial and the dean seemed content with our story. I understood it should not happen again or the outcome might not be as pleasant.

Without revealing any upcoming details, I will say that in my four years at UVA, Dean Runk became one of several individuals who helped mold my character, although it did not reveal itself for some years!

At a chapter meeting someone shouted, "Ball grabber check!"

Somewhat befuddled, the pledges were made to understand they were to stand on the benches and drop trou. So we did.

I don't remember in our class whether there were any Jockey shorts or briefs, but I had recently graduated to boxer shorts when I realized that "ball grabbers" were uncool and beneath the dignity of a Virginia gentleman.

Some of the members of our pledge class knew and dated the senior girls at St. Anne's, a boarding school several miles away, now St. Anne's-Belfield School. As I mentioned earlier while describing Chatham Hall, the term *dating* was a stretch when at any girls' secondary school, because that act involved spending an hour or so walking around a driveway or sitting on a bench in clear view of hawkeyed elderly chaperones (apparently younger, more sympathetic chaperones were never chosen).

In 1962, several goats accepted an invitation to attend the school's spring prom. Thus, when the date of the annual spring Beta hayride was announced, and it coincided with the prom, two or three goats asked to be excused. An incredulous brotherhood could not believe their goats would rather attend a high school prom than be a Beta. So, there was no reprieve, and the prom invitees had to renege their acceptances.

In Army ROTC, I became an enthusiastic member of the Monroe Rifles, a drill team that wore spit-shined jump boots, white puttees, Sam Browne belts and blouses, as well as a chrome helmet liner, white gloves, and carried an M1 rifle.

To induce Wahoos to sign up for the color guard that raised the flag at home football games, a promise of demerit forgiveness was offered.

I volunteered eagerly.

Since the flagpole was at the north end of the stadium, by the walkway to the student section, everyone went past me, and I was proud to be a part of it—until the chapter meeting the following Wednesday.

As soon as the meeting was called order, I was summoned to stand before the tribunal of officers. Twenty minutes of outrage and incredulity ensued. Never had the brothers of the Omicron chapter been so humiliated. One of their pledges had paraded around in a Mickey Mouse uniform, a dweeb military costume in front of the entire student body and alumni.

In that moment I understood I could either be a Beta, or I could be a member of the color guard. I don't remember exactly when this occurred, but it obviously wasn't during Rush!

What transpired had nothing to do with patriotism. Many of the brothers were ROTC cadets, two were captains in Army ROTC, and one was on a full Navy scholarship. Three men in that room later lost their lives in Vietnam, while many others served with distinction, some as career officers.

That being said, we were not to "parade around as toy soldiers." However, I could continue as a member of the Monroe Rifles and march in several holiday parades in different cities in southwestern Virginia, but never at a University event, other than drill.

While each of the episodes mentioned above actually occurred as best as I can remember, I have no memory of physical abuse during the period between Bid Sunday and Hell Week the following fall. Neither do I recall feeling put upon in any way. Like all my pledge brothers, I was proud to be a prospective Beta. I felt wanted and appreciated, and I was eager to do what it took to become one!

# Chapter 7

# Alcohol and Tobacco

Attitudes about drinking and smoking have changed dramatically since the early 1960s, and so I need to describe what influenced my thinking about these behaviors back then. By drinking, I always refer to alcoholic beverages. Until I moved to Atlanta after college, I don't recall ever meeting anyone who did not drink, unless they were either a recovering alcoholic or in training. For as long as I can remember, my parents always enjoyed the cocktail hour before dinner, and they drank appropriately at social events. Whenever any adults who were accepted as family or were club or neighborhood friends drank excessively, it was either ignored or excused through humor. The car that missed a driveway, parents that drove others' children around after drinking heavily (happily never mine), and other besotted events simply were a part of life. Nonetheless, I was never offered or requested a drink at home, although as soon as I was in college, I drank at parties, receptions, and other events with my parents.

At the time, it was understood, in any group I was acquainted with, that minors should not drink until after high school graduation, at which time it was considered acceptable. The drinking age of twenty-one was overlooked unless the person to be served in a public place was obviously underage.

As I said earlier, I had no interest in drinking until several parties after graduation from Blair. The one time I ordered a beer before then was at Penn Station in New York, while waiting for a train back to school to start my senior year. I was sitting at a counter, and when I ordered a chili burger, on impulse, I daringly ordered a five-cent glass of beer. As soon as my order arrived, a large uniformed member of New York's finest sat down next to me, and I immediately prepared myself mentally to be carted off to the clink. The officer inquired pleasantly about where I was going and other conversational items until I realized he couldn't care less that a seventeen-year-old might have a glass of beer.

In the ensuing year, I understood those a year older than I might be offered a beer at someone's house (not mine) while I would not be. Interestingly, had I not dropped back a year, that would not have happened. During the summer after graduation, any date and I, going to or from an event, often stopped at a bar or restaurant and were invariably served drinks without question. It did not it occur to either of us that we would not be served.

When I arrived at UVA, I was fully prepared for alcohol usage along these guidelines, but Hooville moved it up a number of degrees. While I had a few encounters with the law, none of them ever concerned the question of underage drinking. It was evident that the hundreds who were going through Rush and drinking beer at the houses were well under the legal age of twenty-one, yet it was a total nonissue. While it was conceptually understood that drinking too much and driving was unwise, what constituted an offense was conscientiously avoided, both by us and the larger culture.

Once I was stopped in a borrowed MG convertible while rushing my date from Dickinson College in Carlisle to Penn Hall (now extinct) in Chambersburg to make curfew.

The state trooper said, "Son, I'm just an Indian. The chief got you on radar. I just need to see your license and registration."

Since I had no clue where the registration was, I frantically rummaged through the glove compartment and pulled out a mostly empty bottle of rum.

"That's all right, son," he said. "I don't need a drink, just the registration!"

Mercifully the hand of abounding grace showed me where the registration document was, the officer gave me a ticket for speeding, and we went on our way.

And there were a few more examples of the law turning a blind eye to underage drinking. A justice of the peace dismissed a drunk driving charge against an Elmo on his way back to school. The Elmo had rolled a VW Bug and lost the windshield. The passengers rolled the car upright and proceeded for a number of miles before the police pulled them over. Under questioning, the driver admitted to having had a few beers.

When asked how many, the Elmo responded, "About a hundred."

The unamused officer took him and the passengers into custody. But the justice of the peace reasoned that no one could have driven that far in frigid weather and still be under the influence.

And a friend once found a note to himself in his shirt pocket: "Hickory, you ran through the phone booth in the Amherst Square and must appear in court at 10:00 Monday." The court appearance related to the payment for property damage, a non-alcohol-related driving offense.

Stories like this were not uncommon and regularly circulated as humorous.

The liquor laws in effect sometimes helped increase alcohol purchases. Since liquor stores were not open in the early evening or on Sundays, there was a tendency to stock up ahead of special weekends. A rule of thumb was one bottle for Friday night and one bottle for the game and Saturday night. For Big Weekends that started on Thursdays, a third bottle was often held in reserve, commonly referred to as a "three-fifth weekend."

Another common practice around most bars and dancing establishments was the nightly announcement at 11:45 p.m.: *"Fifteen minutes!"* Immediately everyone ordered more pitchers of beer, knowing that no more could be served after midnight. Since places were usually open until 1:00, students didn't have to leave until about 12:30 or as late as 12:40 in order to make a date's curfew, which was also at 1:00.

In lieu of beer, since the Commonwealth was dry to liquor by the drink, patrons could buy a bucket of ice and mixers to brown bag a bottle. Beer and wine could be bought by anyone who wasn't obviously underage at numerous grocery stores, gas stations, and convenience stores.

There were three ways for students to procure bottled liquor. The first was to go in person to one of the stores mentioned above, but since first-year men didn't have any wheels and there was a risk of being carded, this was not the most practical option. The second was to go to the Alcoholic Beverage Control (ABC) store and pay an enterprising wino a dollar to be a go-between for the purchase. This involved a slight risk of being flimflammed or detected. By far the easiest way was to get an older brother who was going anyway to make the purchase. I heard Steve Chipman tell a peer that he knew the difference between pledges by who bought by the pint versus the fifth (there were no quarts back then).

In summary, knowing that this will both date me and create significant controversy, I've always considered that changing the law to permit undergraduates and eighteen-year-olds to drink in close proximity to a recognized establishment is far better than having them travel long distances to do what will happen anyway. Now that coeducation is almost universal, and the need for road trips almost eradicated, it would be much easier to accomplish. This could be done because of the increased awareness by young people of the terrible consequences of driving under the influence, coupled with the acceptance of designated drivers and ride-hailing services such as Uber and Lyft, and strict enforcement of DUI laws. If those under age twenty-one can vote, marry, and fight (and die) for their country, this seems quite reasonable.

It is very difficult for the generation younger than mine and almost impossible for the one after that to imagine the tobacco environment of my growing-up years. I can think of only one place that was nonsmoking: an occasional passenger car on a train. Movie theaters often had only one area for smoking, but that was for fire safety. Any place not specifically for those high-school age and younger—restaurants, college classrooms, hotel and dorm rooms, airplanes, sports venues, non-school locker rooms, hospitals, and workplaces—was open territory. Waitresses, airline stewardesses (flight attendants), office workers, bank tellers, nurses, etc. were all free to smoke on duty. My boarding school had butt rooms for students sixteen and older. While there must've been some personal residences where smoking was not permitted or even discouraged, I don't recall ever being in one. Virtually every living room in the country had ashtrays, lighters, and often stocked cigarette boxes. Often the invitation was heard from the lady of the house to a visitor, "Come on in and have a cigarette!"

Most fraternity houses at Virginia had hardwood floors, which were somewhat safe during the week. On big party weekends, with people dancing and drinking, these floors became no different than sidewalks for stamping out smokes. In looking back, around 50 percent of my male friends and many more females were smokers. It was a strange world in which an adult, while smoking a cigarette, would tell someone under sixteen how it was bad for that person to smoke. However, many people didn't care how young a person was and offered weeds to youngsters.

Smoking had always held a great fascination for me and many of my peers. My parents smoked several packs a day, until my dad quit, cold turkey, at the age of sixty-five and subsequently lived to age eighty-eight, while my mom died at age eighty-one from the effects of tobacco.

However, my dad often railed against the evils of smoking, particularly for young people, by which I think he meant younger than midtwenties or himself, whichever occurred later. As a child, I remember being with my dad and seeing a teenage girl smoke a cigarette. Dad proclaimed it was clear by her smoking that she was a bad girl. Thus, my first impression of girls who smoked was that they were all fallen women, a view Dad unintentionally reinforced over the years.

The first time my dad's pronouncement came under scrutiny was when I was in second grade. We were in a drugstore on Main Street in Hot Springs. To my utter shock and amazement, there sat my second-grade teacher, Miss Ryerson, to me an example of beauty and feminine perfection, smoking with friends. Other examples occurred of teenage children openly smoking in front of their parents, something I could not imagine doing. In fifth grade, we were visiting my grandparents, and everyone went out. My sister and brother and I were left for the evening with a high school babysitter, presumably vetted. To my astonishment, she calmly took out a cigarette and smoked it. If she were a fast woman, she didn't look the part, and my parents had let her take care of us.

Finally, in seventh grade, I took the plunge with my best Houston friend, Robert Robbins. We pilfered a pack of Pall Malls and often puffed without inhaling. I proudly started to inhale after my ninth-grade year, at age fifteen. Only my dedication to swimming prevented me from indulging regularly, until I quit the UVA swim program in my first year.

When I finally summoned enough courage, after my first year, to tell my parents I'd started smoking, my dad said, "Don't ever do it in front of me!"

Mom responded, "For goodness sake, Frank, just because you couldn't do it in front of your parents is no reason to say he can't!"

Dad made no further comment, but I almost never did smoke in front of him, and then only if peers in the room were doing so.

Over the years there were only two girls I dated for more than a month who didn't smoke, and one of them is my wife of fifty-five years and counting. That, combined with the increasing hostility toward the vice, growing awareness of the health hazards, and a decreasing number of people to indulge with and places to do so led me to a pipe, and then to abstinence. Occasionally, however, I remember how pleasant it was.

# Chapter 8

# First-Year Spring

My first-year winter leading into spring is more a kaleidoscope of im-
ages in my memory as opposed to a chronological progression. The
second time one takes a journey and thereafter, the waypoints become
increasingly familiar, but during this period, each point of interest was
brand new, with no prior experience by which to evaluate it. Therefore,
while it was an exciting and fun period, my maturity level was not well-
enough developed to process it particularly well. For one thing, I actually lived at 180 Rugby Road while sleeping across the Grounds,
about a mile away from the Beta house, at Emmet House.

From my room I went east on McCormick Street, which
crossed the Emmet Street–Route 29 bridge, and curved sharply to
the left at Clark Hall before coming to the Law School. If I were
going to class, I went straight ahead, between Bryant Hall and the
amphitheater to New Cabell Hall, where most of my classes met.
Bayly Museum, which held geology, was a half mile farther, which
was not a boost to my already troubled academic career.

Very utilitarian, ugly New Cabell was immediately behind and
cleverly concealed by lovely Old Cabell Hall, which sat at the south

end of the Lawn—a wide, grassy area flanked by student rooms and faculty pavilions several hundred yards from the Rotunda at the other end. From there to the Beta house was another four-tenths of a mile. Had I been going straight to the house, I would've continued along McCormick Road with the West Ranges, Gardens behind them, and the Lawn to my right side. To my left were several buildings, including Newcomb Hall and the Alderman Library.

The other reason for classroom mediocrity was that, between Beta pledge activities and being privy to the inner workings of Rugby Road, Madison Lane, and other strongholds of the Greek environment that dominated university activities, I forgot to put academics in perspective.

I began to hear stories of outrageous exploits, such as the student on his way back with his group from down the road, who stopped to board a construction crane parked by the highway. He started it and drove it down the road a short but significant distance, and then he disappeared into the night before the authorities converged.

Such tales I believed to be true throughout my four years, and I was fortunate enough to participate in similar mischievous adventures without negative consequences, which I'll reveal when we get there.

The most spectacular stunt of the period concerned the great train theft. One of my all-time favorite eating establishments was down at The Corner (and still is): The White Spot Restaurant. While that hole-in-the-wall's most famous entrée, long since immortalized, is the Gus Burger, my favorite was always the bacon-cheese dog. The dog was filled with cheese and wrapped in bacon, and then deep fried. I prefer it with liberally added mayo. The White Spot is situated almost immediately under the railroad trestle over West Main Street by the University Hospital, and thus a favorite spot for train crews to take a break.

One fateful night, while a train crew was on break, a few enterprising scholars boarded the train and drove it about twenty-two miles to Crozet, where they left it somewhat short of the station. It was a deed of such remarkable military precision that it was a topic of conversation for days. While it was widely rumored who the perpetrators were, no one knew for sure, and they certainly weren't talking. The deed has remained a standout in the annals of history with no one ever having been apprehended. After all, who really wanted it to get out? Certainly not the train crew, who had permitted it to be stolen, or the railroad, if they ever knew, or the powers that be at the University, for a variety of reasons.

That winter I experienced my first bus roll, which was very popular with the fraternities but definitely not with women's school administrators. Jim Brandhorst and others dated girls at Hollins, so a bus was chartered, kegs were purchased, blind dates were procured for those who had no contacts, and off we went for the two-hour trip. The whole thing was great fun. But as the trip progressed and the line for the sole toilet lengthened, the situation became increasingly anxious for pledges who had to make way for brothers, unless some kindly soul took pity on a hapless goat.

After a boisterous trip of beer-drinking camaraderie, we reached Hollins, on the outskirts of Roanoke, and disembarked. The next act was something like my junior high days at Mrs. Putman's dancing class, in which Jim and his girlfriend, Carol, paired the pledges with their dates. It might have been more like mail-order brides getting off the ship from Europe or a train from back east, in that we had never set eyes on each other before. Blind dates in these instances, and most others for that matter, were often dormmates well liked by the girls but seldom recipients of dating invitations. ("You'll love her! She makes all her own clothes!")

Since I remember nothing about my date, I believe this was my case, and as I never heard from her again, I assume she was no more taken with me than I was with her—and probably less so.

We boarded the bus with our dates while some of the older folk drove in cars to a spot with lots more beer and a live band. As the evening progressed, things became a little hazier until, probably around midnight, in order to get our dates back to their cloister's halls before curfew, we boarded the bus yet again. We dropped off the survivors at Hollins and started the long trek back to Charlottesville. As all but the most nonworldly must surmise, the trip home was tremendously less inspired than the earlier trip, and a sleepy band of brothers arrived back in Charlottesville around three o'clock.

The last thing I remember is that I must've had a lot more fun than my date since the next day I wrote several meek and penitent letters, under stern direction, to the fair Hollins damsels, bemoaning my over-exuberance and lack of attention the prior evening.

As I've said, my second semester was the second steepest flight of steps in a gradually flattening learning curve, and the blind date and bus roll were each one more in the process. As with anything worth mastering, continuing progress required extensive practice and additional experience, with the goal of perfection moving ever closer but never quite being reached.

Finding dates during the first year was difficult but became increasingly less so as time passed, since inroads to women's schools went from extremely limited upward.

First-year men were not permitted to have automobiles within Albemarle County, and thus could not interest dates who were beyond their first year, while upperclassmen had access during all four years. Joining a fraternity was the most efficient way to deal with those problems, as well as the procurement of alcohol.

Dating, girls, and academics were the most discussed subjects at any male gathering (along with athletics). In many ways the conversations resembled talk about golf: overall handicap, technique, difficulty of various courses and holes, results of the last round played, significant achievements, advice, and a lot of minutia. Certain players were acknowledged to be superior; others were known to exaggerate significantly while describing their results, and their advice was often wrong.

Concerning golf, a friend once told me that, as he aged, his decrease in power was compensated for by finesse and experience. By the end of my first year, during the thirty-three weeks school was in session, I'd probably had no more than fifty actual dates, while by the time I took my degree, I estimate the number had grown to almost four hundred. As with most of my friends, by that time my former lack of confidence and contacts were replaced by a calm self-assurance in my ability to foster relationships, which I believe to be a vital component of my Virginia experience.

The next big happening was Midwinters Weekend, which even more fully convinced me that I had chosen my university correctly. While I cannot remember who my date was, I do remember the glorious experience on Friday night of standing between the huge speakers near the combo (I believe it was the Rockin' Rifts), a large red cup of Rebel Yell bourbon and ginger ale in hand, and letting myself be drowned in the music's roar amid the sea of collegiates filling the living room. But more than that, I recall leaving the Beta house and visiting the same scene in as many other houses as I wanted to visit.

While Openings Weekend had been in the early stages of Rush, which preoccupied most first-year men, Midwinters had no such restraint. It was on party weekends (the big three and numerous others) that the student body separated itself into several distinct groups: the lovers ("ass bandits"), the wild men, the athletes in training, and the rest—a throng of enthusiastic partiers. It was only after leaving the University that I learned some people didn't drink alcohol by choice, but I don't recall knowing that at the time.

The Beau Brummels were beyond my comprehension, for they were seldom in sight, choosing instead to woo their dates at quiet dinners and in secluded places. While there were a large number of guys who were permanently on wild-man duty, anyone could occasionally rise to that standard. I know of a noted judge who is still relieved that an arrest for public urination was never revealed as well as a lion of Wall Street spent a few weeks with his skull encased in bandages for showing how he could head-block the steel-mesh-encased window in a fire door. In many other ways, we truly benefitted that there was no such thing as social media in the early 1960s!

Although they occurred only at Openings Weekend in October and the greatest of all weekends, Easters in April, a highlight of Thursday evenings for me was observing the raucous marches of the two ribbon societies: TILKA, led by its guru with an enormous original loving cup, and Eli Banana, who wore flowing robes of assorted colors with the Grand Banana and a loudly booming drum in front. The marches lasted for hours, tapping new members by stopping at their houses to call them out to their new brotherhood. By then each society had existed for almost a hundred years. As my mentor, Chuck Spence, a TILKA, explained to me, the purpose of the groups is to march around the Grounds several times a year, drinking and tapping people who would march around in the future, drinking together and tapping people.

My eldest daughter, Margaret Carolyn ("MC"), whose class ('89) was twenty-four years after mine, called me after witnessing her first march and said, "They just kept marching until some people were falling down, and still they kept going!"

The groups continued strong, through my daughter Barbara's time (Class of '91) and my son Bo's (Class of '95). In recent years, with the need for everything to have a socially redeeming reason for existence, TILKA and Eli Banana have begun to lose their appeal since they were specifically created to have fun and not necessarily facilitate good deeds.

While many dedicated scholars studied or went to class on the Saturday of every Big Weekend (and some of the lesser ones), the festivities began at the Beta house with a traditional brunch, which highlighted thinly shaved Smithfield ham with all the appropriate side dishes. Iced tea, water, Bloody Marys, and screwdrivers were also served, although some preferred bourbon or beer. The men wore nicer jackets and ties than they did during the week, while their dates all looked as if they had just modeled blouses, skirts, shoes, and accessories at an upscale boutique! The thought of a woman in pants or a gentleman without a coat and tie was unthinkable.

At Openings this wardrobe was suitable for heading off to football games at the world's largest cocktail party at Scott Stadium. At Midwinters, it was in preparation for the concert at Memorial Gymnasium. One thing I always found amusing was that the dates tried to be in the know with Beta terminology, especially "grunt" and "growl." The former referred to a meal while the latter alluded to defecation. Thus, at mealtime, when a hapless date asked, "Isn't it time to go in and growl?" she received a great many amused responses!

Mem Gym, a multipurpose facility, is one of the most remarkable structures on the Grounds. At that time, it accommodated the required physical training classes, all indoor intercollegiate competitions (including swimming and basketball), training and rehab facilities, and the Athletic Department offices. Any other large indoor University function was held there as well.

It was here that the PK and German dance societies combined to sponsor concerts featuring internationally famous entertainers. Each of the two dance societies was comprised of several members of each class from every fraternity, although a few fraternities actually ran each, as was true of all extracurriculars. All students in the University community and their guests could buy tickets and bring blankets or other padding to spend several hours on the hardwood court and be enthralled. Mem Gym, classes, and academic venues were the only places where the open consumption of alcoholic beverages was neither permitted nor considered a right.

After a game or concert, it was quiet time until around eight, when Friday night activities were repeated. It was a time when small groups had cocktail parties or dinner together. On Sunday morning, "not a creature was stirring, not even a mouse," until at least nine or later, and after-lunch dates began to be packed off, and life, very slowly, returned to normal. Many people deferred the ending until after such things as the polo game, where the remains of the kegs were emptied. Easters was the exception, which lasted all Sunday afternoon, until the infamous SAE-ZBT grain party eventually collapsed by dinnertime.

As winter gave way to spring, my fascination with Anne Gwaltney didn't falter, and we continued to write each other (a strange concept in this day of smartphones and texting). Then she excitedly told me that a group from Chatham Hall was planning to take a field trip to Natural Bridge. I said that I would meet her there.

On the day of the event, I hitchhiked out Route 250 to Staunton and then down Route 11, past Lexington, to Natural Bridge, about eighty miles from Charlottesville. A vibrant Anne came to meet me under the admiring and somewhat envious gazes of the other girls. For about five or ten minutes, we had a wonderful time, until she was summarily summoned by one of the chaperones and had a brief conversation with the very serious woman, after which she came back to tell me in a crestfallen manner that I would have to leave.

After considering I might point out that Natural Bridge was a public park, reality asserted itself. I realized the enormity of what might happen to Anne, told her I hoped she could get permission to come as my date to Easters, and hitchhiked back to Charlottesville by midafternoon, with sadness weighing on my heart.

As expected, I was supported and reassured with the false bravado prevalent at the Beta house dining room. As resident members in the system of separate-but-equal gender education, though, we all understood the futility of challenging the authority of those entrusted with the protection of women at their respective schools.

Another memorable event was the annual Faculty Tea, which in reality was a no-holds-barred drinking affair. In preparation for the tea, several brothers were dispatched to Maryland for large quantities of alcohol, because the retail prices were significantly lower than the ABC stores in the Commonwealth. This required some stealth, because carrying so much booze across state lines without paying the Virginia taxes constituted bootlegging, even though it was a very common practice in many states and counties because of the patchwork quilt of liquor laws and dry counties.

The Saturday before the tea, a local Beta mom (Fred "Doc" Twyman's mom), assisted by some brothers, directed the pledge work groups to make the living and dining rooms absolutely spotless. This included cleaning every window, polishing every bit of the considerable amount of wood paneling, and waxing the floors. The cook, the kitchen and house boys, and one or two of their recruited friends prepared to help with the hors d'oeuvres and act as waiters and bartenders at the soirée. Naturally a silver tea service was borrowed from the Twymans, although I don't recall anyone availing themselves of its contents.

As midafternoon arrived, so did the first guests. One of those was Mr. Ellison, my geology teacher, who remarked upon entry, "I was balled by the Betas at Penn State!" which did not seem like a propitious start. But more guests arrived, the drinks flowed, the initial stiffness of the gathering evaporated, and the party came to life. As the afternoon turned to early evening, the older, more sedate faculty departed, leaving only the younger set, who had come to enjoy themselves. While the inviolate bar between students and others remained, it became almost invisible during the party. During each of the four years I was at the University, the Beta tea was a highlight of the spring social season.

While weekdays, including Saturday mornings, were devoted to academic and extracurricular pursuits, on many if not most weekends in the spring, one or two houses would have a party with a jukebox or a local combo, to which the members of peer fraternities were welcome. The rest of the Greek community was either down the road or, for the more studious, involved in school projects and papers.

Saturdays were a time to relax and hang out with friends, mostly one's own fraternity. We would often walk to one of the nearby restaurants, such as Buddy's (where the neat meet to eat), almost across the street from Frank Kessler's Cavalier, which was at the intersection of Routes 29 and 250. More generally we headed toward The Corner to one of the four or five places there, particularly the College Inn, University Cafeteria, or University Diner, to name some of the better known. Never do I recall eating at Newcomb Hall (University Union), except for counter snacks while taking a study break from the nearby Alderman Library.

One other place I frequented more and more was the Parish Hall at St. Paul's Episcopal Church. If you went to the five o'clock service, there was a fried-chicken-and-biscuit dinner afterward for fifty cents. In hindsight, it was much like the union mission or the soup kitchens at St. Luke's Episcopal, Central Presbyterian, or Sacred Heart Roman Catholic in downtown Atlanta, where, for the price of going to church, one could be physically and possibly spiritually fed.

Sunday mornings, when applicable, the jukebox would be placed on the front porch, which led to a traditional activity. Right across the below-grade railroad tracks, with the Beta Bridge spanning Rugby Road over them, was the First Presbyterian Church, whose windows were invariably open (this was before widespread air-conditioning). Like clockwork, a delegation of dark-suited ushers would come over and politely request the volume on the jukebox be turned down. Then followed a brief but heated discussion, initiated by a brother observing, "We don't tell them to turn down their [effing] organ while we're trying to sleep, so why should we turn down our [effing] jukebox for them?"

Invariably, after the ushers' visit, the jukebox volume was significantly reduced.

Since the jukebox was not picked up until Monday, Sunday afternoons were spent on the front porch, drinking beer with dates and others who happened by.

If you asked a Beta if he was religious, I'm fairly certain he would have responded "Christian." Followed by, "but not a very good one."

To us, one's faith was determined by birth. But very few of us attended services on a regular basis. Some went to St. Paul's Episcopal Church, and I later became junior warden of the student vestry. This included serving as an acolyte (altar boy), and I occasionally came almost straight from partying to serve at the eight o'clock communion service.

Other frequent churchgoers were Chuck Spence, Ted Hogshire, Jack Williams, and a few others at the eleven o'clock worship service or the five o'clock gathering. Episcopalians constituted the largest body of students, followed by Southern Baptists. The only people I knew were like me, but there were Presbyterians, Roman Catholics, and a few Methodists. Had you asked me if I was devout (I was not familiar with the word *committed*), I would have responded with appropriate humility, "Yes." It was only much later in my life that the reality, "You will know them by their fruits" (Matthew 7:20) opened my eyes.

First year many Sunday afternoons, some of us would visit St. Anne's girls after church and, as noted before, walk or sit on benches under strict supervision. The school also had a mixer, where I remember an obese fellow lying on his back while someone, a St. Anthony's Hall pledge, danced on his stomach in sync with the music, encircled by a clapping crowd of onlookers. Since I recall no intervention, I assume that as long as young men occupied themselves without endangering the school's damsels, all was well.

Although both the Beta hayride and St. Anne's prom had occurred, and all pledges attended the former, I can't remember much about that, possibly because the next two years were so momentous, as you will see when we get there. Memories of St. Anne's that spring remain with me, and several girls from that senior class—Jeanne Sims and Vicki Elsas (their maiden names)—remain friends fifty years later.

All of a sudden, it was early April, and spring erupted in central Virginia, bringing with it Easters Weekend, a college happening unrivaled in the country. And for the occasion, Anne Gwaltney arrived at the Greyhound depot downtown. I can actually use the old cliché my heart leaped at the sight of her to describe how I felt when she descended from the bus. I also remember that, as we waited for her bag, one of my pledge brothers—a tall, gangly fellow immaculately clad in a perfectly pressed gray suit, white shirt, rep tie, and big-boy (laced) shoes—suddenly appeared.

When he saw me, he said, "Hey, Frank. I'm going (I can't remember where now). Do you want to go?"

Proudly I said, "Rusty, this is my date, Anne." And then I invited him to join us for the taxi ride to the Beta house.

Rusty seemingly noticed Anne for the first time. He stood perfectly erect and announced with magnificent chivalry what a tremendous pleasure it was to meet her. As he turned to depart, he went sprawling over her suitcase. Undaunted, he stood and, with superb dignity, announced his departure, as if the stumble had never occurred.

Thus, Anne stepped through the looking glass and into the wonderland that was Charlottesville at the beginning of the country's most famous party weekend, where the events were often unpredictable, but the revelers were always impeccably attired as befitted gentility.

After dinner at the Beta house and a few dances with our combo, Anne and I set out to explore the other houses, starting at the easternmost fraternity on Madison "Mad" Lane, and we partied ourselves from house to house until we reached the path next to Mad Bowl and back to Rugby Road. Each house had a party to remember on its own, and the combined result was outstanding. Everywhere we went, the rooms were full of dancing, smoking, and drinking in glorious abandonment to the overwhelming roar of bands, each with a male and a female singer, booming out the popular music of the era. To do so with a perfect date participating enthusiastically on her first major Virginia weekend made it a truly spectacular start to the second night of Easters. (Thursday was mostly a warmup session, with Ribbon Society marches and many fewer dates.) Around eleven o'clock, after brief visits to the three Quad places and the Zete house, we arrived back at the Beta house for the final hours, until a taxi took Anne to her approved housing in time for curfew.

Saturday dawned and another glorious day began with the festivities starting at the traditional Beta brunch. While Openings and homecoming had football games and Midwinters had the concert at Mem Gym, Easters had a variety of afternoon party venues, including a large open-air gathering at Mad Bowl that continued throughout the afternoon. This aspect of Easters grew even larger in the decades to come, from a disorderly mob affair by the mid-1970s to a completely unmanageable situation in the 1980s, when Easters was discontinued. But in the era of the Old U, this was not true. While there was certainly extensive, nonstop partying, it observed a certain decorum and had well-known but undefined boundaries for acceptable behavior. For one thing, the dress code—with men in coats and ties and women in spring party apparel suitable for fashionable garden parties—did not lend itself to mob disorder, and certainly not sliding down Madison Bowl on mud slides. The Honor Code and the concept of Virginia gentlemen, unruly as Easters may have been, were incompatible with the hostile incivility and civil disobedience of many colleges and universities, especially Berkeley and up east. These actions and thought patterns were unknown and alien to us. The U was a place where outside storms were not permitted to interfere with almost a century of hallowed traditions.

In between parties, Anne and I explored my world at Charlottesville: the dorms (from the outside), the Grounds (including Scott

Stadium, Cabell Hall, and the Lawn), and The Corner, with institutions such as Mincer's and Eljo's. It was a tremendously fun-filled weekend and probably the best of many until the spring of my third year and beyond.

After we had dinner with my Beta friends on Saturday, the parties resumed where they had left off the night before, only this time we ventured to the houses to the north before returning to the Beta house, where we rocked until closing. Those were the final years when the outside crowds were still friends from Washington and Lee, Hampton Sidney, UNC, and like universities. By my fourth year, University policemen manned the doors of the fraternity houses, in uniform, when the barbarian hordes began to increase their sorties onto the hallowed ground.

Gloriously, unlike all other Big Weekends, Sunday was another party day, dubbed the Grand Finale. As I recall, we attended the 11:00 a.m. service at St. Paul's, lunched at The Corner (perhaps at the White Spot), and returned to the house for the final hours. The living room furniture was removed, replaced by a combo and outsized speakers. In daylight the get-together was a totally different experience, with our dates still dressed to kill in their third or fourth or fifth outfit for the weekend.

Finally, the time to leave for the bus depot approached, and the very special weekend drew to a graceful end. Knowing that I would see Anne again at her Chatham Hall graduation after my semester ended, as well as being her escort for the deb party and activities, made the end of Easters easier. After all, all good things must come to an end.

As April turned to May, I continued to live a carefree life, but it was becoming apparent that a day of academic reckoning might be drawing nigh. For one thing, I met with Conrad Warlick, the senior counselor and faculty advisor for Page-Emmet. (He turned out to be a wonderful friend over the years.) As I learned during my time at Virginia, no one was summarily summoned. Instead, they were courteously invited to come by at their convenience. During my first week, I had met with my association dean, the legendary T. Braxton Woody, for the ten-minute meeting each of us was required to have with the other. After that, I assumed no academic system had me on its radar. My meeting with Mr. Warlick, however, revealed that some people were paying attention to who showed up for class. I was on attendance warning. But Mr. Warlick said he would look into it for me.

I recently found a letter from me to my parents, explaining that they would be getting a letter about this academic warning and that Mr. Warlick was going to take care of it. I also found a letter to them announcing that I had been downgraded to academic probation, but this one had no rebuttal from me. In those days there was no question of privacy issues, so grades and other correspondence went directly to those who were paying the tuition bill.

(Exactly thirty years later, my son, Bo, told me he didn't have to show me his grades. I assured him that was certainly true, but I didn't need to pay his tuition, fees, and other expenses either, after which there were no further comments about privacy.)

Conrad Warlick's personal interest generated an increased resolve on my part to attend classes regularly and stay at the geology lab the full two hours rather than leave after thirty or forty-five minutes. However, time was shortening.

A week before exams began, Soups Wilder, a fourth-year man, asked me if I would like to get a date at Mary Washington and go with him and another fourth-year brother down the road. I reasoned that we would be leaving by midafternoon and returning later that night, which would give me time for a break before getting back to my books four days before my first exam. I agreed and asked Soups to have his date tell mine that I would pick her up at her dorm.

On the afternoon of the trip, I filled a large jar with rum and fruit juice and settled into the backseat for the hour's ride to Mary Washington.

Upon our arrival, I proceeded to the dorm and asked for the girl. As she came downstairs, my smile was banished by the intense fire emanating from her eyes. Her demeanor told me something was very amiss before she even said a word. But talk she did!

I was told in no uncertain terms that she had no intention of going out with someone who would not even spend a quarter to call her and ask her out. In fact, she already had a date with someone who actually had spent a quarter on such a call.

Chagrined, I returned to the car and told the brothers what had happened. They struggled to contain their dismay at the thought of a third wheel—and a pledge—accompanying them to Georgetown with no date. Since the prospect was no more attractive to me than it was to them, I told them not to worry and that I would head back to Charlottesville. Torn between the conflicting choices of the very bad idea of leaving me to my own devices and the thought of my tagging along, dateless, led them to choose the former.

Clad in a seersucker jacket and tie, with my rapidly diminishing rum-and-juice potion on my arm, I walked off campus and onto a main street in Fredericksburg. Along the way, a serious-looking dark-haired girl approached me.

"I saw you," she said, "with your parents at the opening of school in Charlottesville, having dinner together. They looked very proud of you."

After I mumbled an appropriate response, she continued the conversation with the fervor of evangelical concern in her eyes and inflections.

"And what would they think of you now?" she said. "Wouldn't they be ashamed?"

I increased my pace in an effort to escape, but this empowered crusader was not finished and continued to follow me down the street.

"Do you know how much Jesus loves you? Would you like to invite him into your life?"

Not knowing what she was talking about, but realizing I had a real nutcase on my hands, I broke into a trot. I think this drew the attention of a squad car that happened to be cruising in the area.

After a very short chat with the policemen, I found myself in the backseat of their vehicle. I was taken to the lodgings the city of Fredericksburg generously provides for people such as I was thought to be.

When we arrived at the lockup, I was treated courteously, although indifferently, and ushered into a two-person suite, decorated throughout in early concrete. Two narrow steel bunks were attached to the wall, and a toilet adorned the end of the cell. The entire front of the roughly six-by-ten-foot room was a very avant-garde set of ceiling-to-floor bars. I don't remember going through registration at the front desk, and there was no mug shot taken or fingerprinting involved in my processing.

My roommate, a forlorn middle-aged fellow, had arrived before me, and, as it turned out, was a regular at the facility.

From what I had seen in movies and on television and read in books, I knew a phone call was an entitlement of the incarcerated. I requested one and was granted access to the phone.

Looking back, in hindsight, I made the terrible error of calling my father instead of the Beta house. As you might have already deduced, Dad was not pleased and suggested, since I had gotten myself into this mess, I needed to find a way to get myself out of it.

For the next hour or so I proceeded to do just that, but to no avail. First, I tried to explain that I really shouldn't be there, I had a lot of homework to do, and I should be released and allowed to go my way. Next, I threatened the officers, telling them I was a close friend of Harry Byrd III and promising serious repercussions if his grandfather (a US senator) heard how I was being treated.

Neither approach proved fruitful, so I lay down on the upper bunk and listened to my roommate explain how things really worked in the Fredericksburg jail. His primary concern, which I heard several times, was that his employer would not bail him out this time, and he would wind up going to court on Monday. This would be a significant problem since, as this was his third offense, he was liable for a ninety-day vacation at the county farm. Other than the fact that this was my first offense, I found nothing he told me to be reassuring.

Around ten o'clock, we both drifted off, that is, as well as possible on a metal frame with a mattress that was about a quarter of an inch thick. Sometime later we were awakened by the opening of the cell door and the arrival of our third roommate. He was a veteran Marine, in splendid shape, who had pulled over on the side of the road to sleep off his night of drinking, and then he was awakened to join our happy little group. Since there was no other bed in the cell, he lay down on the floor and fell asleep on his back. I expected him to wake up and tell me to trade places with him, but he never did.

The next morning dawned bright and sunny, with me feeling some-what less so, wondering what was going to happen next. An unkempt trustee arrived at the wall of bars and slid metal plates of eggs, grits, and biscuits through a space beneath the bars while he picked up cigarette butts at the same time. Somehow this serving method did not excite my appetite, and I declined. My first roomie eagerly claimed my plate.

After some desultory small talk, we quietly thought about our fates until, all of a sudden, at about ten o'clock, I was summoned. I was escorted to the front desk, and an officer looked up and pleasantly said, "You're free to go."

Momentarily at a loss, and not wanting to ask why or how, I just stood, needing a moment to collect my thoughts.

"Where do you go to school?" he asked.

When I told him, he asked, "When you finish, what do you plan to do?"

I quickly replied, "I plan to go to law school and be a lawyer."

He seemed to find that news to be quite amusing. The officer wished me good luck and nodded toward the door.

I headed out to the highway and stuck my thumb out, around twelve hours later than I had planned, but with another of life's learning experiences under my belt.

When I reported my experience to the Beta house, there was great consternation and angst, mainly directed at Soups for leaving me to fend for myself. The general consensus was that leaving me was akin to abandoning a wounded comrade under fire. Nonetheless, I did not escape criticism for calling my dad rather than my fraternity. After all, that's what fraternities are for. There was some concession, however: the two other brothers had not left me with much confidence in the dependability of brothers.

So now, with three days left to prepare for exams covering three months of coursework, I started a series of all-nighters.

My sojourn in Fredericksburg occurred before the age of computers, which meant that information was not quickly transmitted from one jurisdiction to another unless it concerned major crimes. If my episode had occurred in recent decades, I suspect things would have happened a lot differently. Some years later I asked several attorneys, graduates of the University Law School, what I should do, if anything, if I wanted to look into the long-ago incident. They all recommended I do nothing. They reasoned (1) the case might have been dismissed, (2) if I had been charged, it was probably not done correctly, and (3), pragmatically, don't look where you don't want answers when there are probably no readily available records.

# Chapter 9

# First-Year Finale

The best thing I can say about my second-semester exams is that they could have been worse—but not too much worse. I will go course-by-course in the order they appear on my transcript.

Once Mr. Warlick let me know that someone was genuinely interested in what I was not doing, I began to pay more attention to what I needed to do. But by that time the finish line was too close.

The first course was physical education. I had been exempted from this in my first semester, because of my swimming commitment. Actually, it was a Virginia requirement that anyone taking an undergraduate degree had to prove he could swim before he could receive the degree.

My first job for the Athletic Department, which was to be my PE credit, was to stand shoulder-to-shoulder with other swimmers around the pool, ready to pull out those who tried to swim but couldn't. I had never known that anyone couldn't swim until that day. However, during the second semester, I didn't rejoin the PE class. Eventually I realized the Athletic Department wasn't going to forget about it, so I went to the department to find out what I could do to satisfy the credit. They said I was to go a certain number of laps for each class missed, so I spent a few hours each day for a week running and walking them off. Because of the Honor System, I could just tell them when it was done, with no need for supervision.

(I may have forgotten to mention that Mr. Jefferson believed everyone in the Academical Village should be on an equal footing, without titles to impede the free transfer of ideas. Thus, everyone was referred to as Mr. or Miss or Mrs. or, later, Ms., regardless of how many degrees or titles one had. No teacher or administrator ever referred to a student by his first name unless they had a personal relationship and it was a social setting. The only exception was the title *dean*.)

From here things began to go downhill. The next stop was geology. In the final review class of the year, Mr. Ellison made the somewhat ominous comment to me, "You are a perfect example of what the Beta house can do to a person." I spent a whole day and night reviewing all the coursework, since 25 percent of the final grade was based on the lectures and 25 percent on the lab work.

On the day of the exam I could not believe my good fortune: the test was one hundred multiple-choice and true-false questions. As I progressed into the test, earlier questions began to provide clues for the later ones and vice versa. The result was a score of around 90, placing me in the top 10 percent of the one-hundred-plus-person class.

The lab exam was somewhat more complicated, but I managed to score in the 80s. My cumulative result was an overall grade of D (*almost a C*).

For those who say, "Just think how well you could've done if you had applied yourself all semester." I say, "Just think of everything I'd have missed doing if I'd spent that time sequestered in study!"

Now we reach Latin II. While I did much better than the 48 I received in Latin III the previous semester, a score of less than 70 was an F.

There's not much else to say, except that I had the choice of repeating Latin II and III or taking three years of Spanish, for the requirement at that time was two years of two languages or three years of one. I chose the latter.

My calculus class was one of the two semesters of math required for everyone in the College, the other being trigonometry, which was first semester. This was the course that separated the mathematicians from the rest of us. I knew some people who were still taking it two years later when, happily, the University changed the course numbering system. Thus, they could take trigonometry again and graduate.

My section was taught by a nice, unassuming soul, Mr. Lemon, a pale graduate assistant. Had I been a casting director for Charles Dickens's *David Copperfield*, I would have chosen Mr. Lemon to play Uriah Heep. While I'm certain Mr. Lemon was a brilliant mathematician, occasionally a numeral out of context would appear on the blackboard. Whenever that happened, a very distinct "Wrong!" would erupt, because there was in the class a particularly arrogant pledge, a graduate of a significantly elite New England school, who had perfected the art of the condescending, caustic put-down.

While I have always liked and talked to almost everyone I've gone to school with, there were very few classmates with whom "Arrogant" would converse. In hindsight, it was a reminder that there was a deep moat between fraternity row and everyone else. For that matter, in the Greek community, some houses were more equal than others, much like neighborhoods and boroughs in a metropolitan area. This was taken for granted as part of life and certainly on the Greek side.

It now became even more apparent why divine providence had chosen Charles Hudgins Spence, later president of the Engineering School, to be my hall counselor. The night before the exam, he spent several hours helping to get me at least minimally ready to sally forth into the arena. When he recognized my scant knowledge, he said, "If the letters, numbers, and symbols look like this, you do this. If they look like that, you do that." Thus armed, I had a good night's sleep with the belief that I could survive because of my wits and not knowledge.

On the morning of the exam, I arrived early, opened my information, and again memorized the definitions, since we'd been told that would account for 15 percent of the test. That being done, I went into the classroom, grabbed a test and a bluebook, and answered all the definition questions. Thus, being assured of a score of at least 15, I started to do what Chuck had told me as best I could. I was reassured when at least three students looked at the exam, signed the honor pledge on the bluebook, turned in the test, and left.

For those of you who may not know what a bluebook is, it was a slim pamphlet of empty lined pages stapled into a blue cover sheet. Bluebooks were used for everything other than specifically designed multiple-choice tests. For many liberal arts classes, the exam could require two or three of them.

I met my objective of passing math—with a D. Many years later, my wife told one of the children, "Daddy didn't get really great in math until it was about dollars, other business things, and when he wants to use it for something he needs to do."

In my last class, I was in for a significant shock. As the semester progressed, I became more and more certain not only was I going to get a B in English composition but perhaps an A. When the grades were posted, I was astonished to see a C next to my name and immediately scheduled a meeting with my teacher. In addition to teaching one class, Marvin Perry was also the dean of admissions, the one who had admitted me.

"Mr. Perry," I said, "there must be some mistake. I didn't have one grade below a B, and I had the highest score of any of the exams your grader did!"

He said, "I do not give above-average grades for below-average performance. You attended very few classes during the semester, thus providing very little to the classroom discussions. I grade on the whole body of work and not just on the numeric grades themselves."

In my best penitent manner, I said, "I know I've missed some classes, but since I've read all the books we were going over, I guess I spent too much time on some less-interesting courses that were giving me more trouble."

"That's exactly what I'm talking about!" he admonished. "You entered the University having taken Advanced Placement English courses in an excellent secondary school, and yet you registered for basic composition English, which is designed for less-prepared men from smaller public schools."

Although I pleaded my case a little longer, in my heart I knew the hearing was over, and for many years I believed the outcome to be totally unjust. Interestingly, some years later, when Mr. Perry became the president of Agnes Scott College, I had the opportunity to consult with him on that school's pension program. During the meeting I reminded him of our conversation over my grade.

He smiled and said, "Oh, yes. I always was an SOB as a grader!"

And so, after a second semester at the University, I managed to lower my cumulative GPA from 1.442 to 1.39. In addition, I had the dubious academic distinction of being on two types of probation: academic and attendance. Finally, the registrar's office advised my parents and me by mail that, if I wanted to come back in the fall, I needed to have more quality (grade) points than I had. As I said, it could have been worse.

Since I was in no great rush to discuss my academics or my Fredericksburg trip at home, and because of my dad's concept of going to work the Monday after I got back home, I resolved to have a little vacation before I headed to Pittsburgh.

A few days after my last exam, I hitchhiked to Chatham for Anne's graduation. After Mr. Yardley and I exchanged somewhat guarded greetings and I said hello to Anne's parents, the ceremony commenced, nestled in the beauty of central Virginia in the late spring. Shortly after it was over and Anne and her family had vanished, two Chatham alumnae gave me a ride back to Charlottesville.

As I mentioned in Chapter 6, Bunny Benham was a great hero to me. His girlfriend (fiancée), a PE teacher at Saint Anne's, was packing to move back home to Huntington, West Virginia, to prepare for their wedding. To me, no female was more vivacious and stunning than Julie, whose darting hither and yon was in striking contrast to Bunny's relaxed, easygoing manner. Since I was planning to ride to The Beach with Bunny after Julie departed, I welcomed the opportunity to accompany him when he helped pack her accumulation of furniture etc. from several years in residence there.

One amazing thing to me was when Julie, while cleaning out a drawer, said "Oh, look. Here's my paycheck for March. I guess I never deposited it."

I tried to imagine my not noticing the loss of a month's funds!

Because it took longer to pack than we thought, Bunny decided it was too late to leave for The Beach. So, we didn't leave until several days after I returned from Anne's graduation.

This trip remains a very fond memory for me more than half a century later.

We started in the early afternoon, heading down Route 250 toward Richmond, long before there was an interstate. Along the way I talked about my Uncle Red, who lived in Richmond. He had been decorated for his action in the OSS in Burma, and he was a great guy. When Bunny said he would like to meet him, we headed to the Charles Smith manor. Uncle Red happened to be home, along with Aunt Sam and my two gorgeous cousins, Elaine and Melinda. After a couple of beers and a wonderful time, Bunny and I got back on the road, heading toward Williamsburg.

While we cruised along, the conversation turned to friends who went to William and Mary, and lo and behold we wound up spending some time with my old Blair pal Mickey Taylor and some people Bunny knew. This visit showed me how glad I was I'd gone to a school with fraternity houses rather than one with nonresident bungalows or dormitory sections.

When we got back on the road, the sun had set. As we came close to Norfolk, we saw the Ocean View Amusement Park and its vintage roller coaster.

"Bunny," I said, "wouldn't you like to ride a roller coaster?"

He said no, but since I wanted to, he would pull over so I could.

I recall it was as great a roller coaster ride as any of the dozens I've ridden, and it was a blow to civilization in 1979 when they tore it down.

Around midnight we arrived at Malcolm and Tucker Scully's family home, right by the water, on Seventy-eighth Street. There we were with many other Betas there who had been in happy companionship for a day or so. Since I was a pledge, I slept in the front seat of Bunny's convertible. I woke up the next morning about ten o'clock, with at least four hours' sunbathing already accomplished.

I had planned to stay at my pledge brother Ted Hogshire's house on Sudeley Street in Norfolk, but as it turned out, while I went there to visit and get something to eat, I wound up staying on the beach itself (a fact noted by Teddy's mother, who wondered what to do about an almost nonexistent houseguest).

We enjoyed the local haunts down where the town starts, like the popular Jet, a bar and a restaurant on a pier over the water, where they dumped hard-shell crabs on newspaper and served plenty of beer. (At that time Virginia Beach was a popular oceanside town, and then it merged with Princess Anne County to become the sprawling assemblage of hotels and urban mediocrity it is today.)

A day or so later, Bunny and I headed back to Charlottesville, by a more direct route this time, and I began to prepare for my return home to Pittsburgh.

Several Betas traditionally lived in the lower level of a house on University Circle, about a block from the Beta house, if one went behind the faculty apartments. It backed onto Lambeth Field and was accessed directly through a side entrance. I called it Ralph Fraise's apartment, because that's where Ralph lived during my first year.

The next morning after Bunny and I returned from Virginia Beach, I called my mom (collect) on Ralph's new speaker phone. This turned out to be a mistake, because Mom was not happy, and I didn't know how to switch the call from the speaker to the receiver, all to the amusement of everyone listening in the room.

It turned out that Mom knew the semester had ended and was concerned about what had happened to me. I apologized and explained I had a few things to do before I could catch the train home by the next day. It turned out I could leave that afternoon, so I took my already packed suitcase and headed for the station.

The train ride to Washington went through some lovely countryside, and I alighted in the architecturally significant Union Station. My fellow travelers in the integrated coach were largely black women and children headed north, which caused me to reflect that the railway was no longer underground. Realizing I had some time before I boarded the next train, I checked my bag and walked to the National Mall and reflection pool, marveling in the glory of our national capital along with the other tourists.

When I returned to Union Station, I retrieved my bag and caught the train for Pittsburgh, via a change in Philadelphia that was scheduled to arrive early the following morning.

At some point I joined a conversation with several passengers, probably salesmen, in the club car, and they invited me to their Pullman suite for a drink. After an hour or so, they were ready to retire, so I headed back to my seat. On the way there, I noticed the stairway to the observation dome and decided to take my bag there. The vistas I glimpsed as we sped across the moon-drenched countryside with the occasional twinkle of farmhouse lights, punctuated by the little hamlets we flashed through, created a surreal experience of flying through time. The experience eventually lulled me into a sound sleep.

When I awoke, we appeared to be entering Pittsburgh along one of the rivers, and I prepared to exit the train. As the minutes passed, signs of civilization seemed to diminish, and we entered the open countryside.

I went downstairs and asked a conductor when we were scheduled to reach Pittsburgh.

"Pittsburgh!" he exclaimed. "We left Pittsburgh forty minutes ago! Were you supposed to get off in Pittsburgh? Did you change cars?"

After I responded with a meek yes, he took out his schedule and began to plot a solution. He turned to me and said, "We'll drop you off at the State Line station. The station manager can flag the Eastbound to pick you up an hour later. You're in luck, because the next train would be six hours later."

And so, a mighty passenger train made an unscheduled stop in State Line, Pennsylvania, to drop off a screwball student.

For several moments after I alighted from the train, which thundered off, trying to make up for a few wasted minutes, it appeared that the town of State Line was deserted. And then a fellow in the dark blue pants, white shirt, and blue hat of a railroad official appeared out of the depot. He was the station manager.

"You got off the train!" he said with incredulity, which led me to believe this was not a regular occurrence. "The conductor didn't get you off at Pittsburgh?" he added with amusement.

Suddenly he became animated.

"I'll have to flag down the Eastbound."

And off he went.

While I waited for the train, I encountered three old men who were sitting in front of a small store, the only open establishment in town. I purchased a filling breakfast of a chocolate soft drink and pastry. Shortly thereafter the Eastbound ground to a stop, picked me up, and deposited me at the station in Pittsburgh.

I will say that, quite unnecessarily, the conductor stopped by my seat at least three times to remind me to get off. He apparently thought this was funnier than I did.

And so, I called my mom to pick me up. I was glad to see her, and she was relieved to see her somewhat wayward but much-loved eldest child. I was thankful that my parents were not well versed in train schedules. After all, if no one knows *when* you're supposed to arrive, you'll never be early and never be late!

I was home now. My first year was over. But one more thing was needed to bring closure to all of this, namely, a meeting several days later with my dad. I went to his office to discuss summer school, but he pulled out a piece of paper with a list of companies and two numbers next to each. He placed it on his desk and asked, "Do you know what this is?"

I did not.

He said, "This is a list of investments I've made. Column one shows what I paid for each, and column two shows their current value. What does it show you?"

"You've lost a lot of money," I responded.

"No," he said. "That's not what it shows me at all. It shows me that each of these is worth less than I paid for it. However, the only way I could lose money is if I sold one of these investments. And for you to go to summer school at the University of Virginia, I would need to sell something off this list. Right now, each investment on this page shows me more promise than you have at the University of Virginia."

Looking back over all these years, I believe this to be one of the most significant concepts I have ever learned. It also caused me to find out about the University extension program, where an undergraduate could take up to twelve hours of extension courses and have the results count toward his course load.

That summer I enrolled in History 21, Colonial Virginia, and earned the second B of my college experience. I returned to Charlottesville in the fall with nine quality points added to my cumulative GPA.

# Chapter 10

# Hell Week

In those happy days when summer vacation lasted from before Memorial Day until after Labor Day, returning to the University was always a fun time. The summer had started with Anne Gwaltney's coming out party and other social events of that season. Once done, however, she went on a Grand Tour of the Continent, I returned Mr. Putman's dinner jacket (he lived across the street) and my father's shirt, cummerbund, etc., put the dress pants I'd purchased from a tux rental store in the attic, and went back to the life of a summer construction laborer.

One more thing germinated that was to make a significant difference, though. Joan, a girl I had pursued with little success for over a year, now became enamored with me. As the summer progressed, we became inseparable. On weekends we'd go to Cheat Lake in West Virginia, where her family kept their small motorboat. There we wiled away the days waterskiing and drinking Iron City beer. By the end of the summer she was my new girl.

I was firmly ensconced in college life as I returned with pledge brother Dick Tucker to 180 Rugby, my residence for the next few years. Nestled within all my other thoughts, however, was the dark cloud hanging over each of us. Hell Week was starting soon!

Our entry into the Beta house residence started with each of us as members of a heavy-duty work crew tasked with cleaning out the house, which was gross after being dormant for three months. We believed our overseers had studied the Egyptians of Moses' day and/or the harsh masters of Harriet Beecher Stowe's novel. (It was not really that bad, but it was intense.)

Bill Tylander and I roomed together in arguably the worst room in the house, directly off the main living areas on the first floor. But then we were probably the least academically interested students in our class. Someone gave us a gallon or two of battleship gray paint, and we painted the room, walls, and woodwork, creating the effect one might imagine.

We took time off to participate in the monstrous lottery called registering for classes, and this was many years before computerized registrations became widespread. The affair was held, like everything else that required large, open spaces, in Memorial Gymnasium. Registration was much like the Oklahoma land rush, with hundreds of students vying for the choicest classes. Once the starting bell rang, everyone was on his own to get to the line of the class he most wanted, then the next, and so on. Maybe there were blocks of spaces held for gifted students (who really acted like that), but no accommodations were made for someone with a cumulative 1.51 GPA.

This year, other than the feared foreign language (Spanish I), I finally got to choose the courses I wanted: principles of economics, public speaking, English and American literature, American history, and military tactics.

After registering, it was time to head down to The Corner to purchase books and supplies at the University or Anderson's bookstores, since there was no bookstore at Newcomb Hall.

Then we tried to enjoy the final weeks before Hell Week began at 6:00 p.m. on Sunday, October 12, much like liberty leave before going into combat.

There were two schools of thought on preparing for Hell Week. One being to drink a lot in order to alleviate the initial shock, while the other was to go into training and abstain. I was concerned (scared) enough to choose the latter.

Bob Barron, a somewhat obnoxious Zete pledge from across the street, whose father was a Beta, kept telling us that he knew the secret Beta pooda and recited a few Greek words and phrases at us. Since I had no idea whether this was or wasn't pooda (but if it was, we shouldn't know it), his bull continued until we knew better.

There are three things that need to be said up front about Hell Week.

First, I have never borne any ill will to anyone who harassed me. To the contrary, when it was done, I felt a bond to those who'd gone through what we did and then passed it along to us. Any pangs I might suffer come from some of the things I did to others, but I never felt any animosity from them, by which I concluded that they felt the same way I did.

Second, Hell Week was a series of experiences that transformed a group of friends, formed by a series of pledging decisions, into a close-knit band who are still loyal to each other and talk regularly almost sixty years later.

Finally, I will exclude two types of Hell Week experiences. Some things are better expounded in a locker room. The other is anything that remains secret.

To prepare us for Hell Week, our pledge master itemized several things we were never to be without. Each member of the class was to wear a burlap undershirt during the day. It was suggested there be a second that was cut more like a toga, for wearing during the evening festivities, since those would quickly become unsuitable for wear under a shirt and tie. Since burlap is unpleasant next to the skin in any circumstance, and even more so in the late summer heat of central Virginia, each of us washed them many times before we ever tried to wear them.

The other items were a small sheep's bell and a piece of yarn, the latter to tie the former to one's manhood. (Because of the strenuous nature of the evenings, the bells could be removed as I recall.) We also understood that, under no circumstance, were we ever to miss any classes, under threat of severe repercussions. And so prepared, we assembled in the meeting room at 5:55 that Sunday evening.

The first several minutes were pleasant enough, with kindly President Brandhorst telling us how nice we were, when all of a sudden forty voices screamed, "You stupid goats, get your ugly asses downstairs. Faster! Faster!"

Stumbling from the third floor to the basement by way of the back stairs (goats were not allowed on the front stairs that week), we arrived at the dining and television rooms. These had been stripped of all furniture but contained a few galvanized garbage cans and a water hose. We were told, "Scramble, goats, scramble!" which we were made to understand meant spread-eagling on our stomachs, swimming the frog stroke under never-ending streams of water, and yelling, "I'll rush my ass off for Beta Theta Pi."

The first night may have been the worst, because all the brothers participated. But as the week progressed, the number of tormentors reduced significantly, mostly to those one year removed from goatdom themselves.

Finally, in the early hours, we were sent to bed together in the furnace room, with the ugliest dog our elders could find at the pound as our mascot. There were dark implications as to the dog's future.

The next day was spent, hands in pockets, trying to mute our bells, especially in economics class, which met in the Old Cabell Hall auditorium, with over a hundred students, many of whom were listening for the Beta bells. In fact, since the old U was an insular community, many of the teachers knew about both the bells and the burlap.

All of us delayed as long as possible before showing up for the next night, which started with a special goat cocktail hour featuring Westin oil cocktails and Crisco crackers. On this night the games began, a large collection of which had been assembled over several generations, with new ones being created on the spot. One favorite was called fire truck. The pledges filled their mouths with alum water, ran up three flights of (back) stairs, spit on a trashcan fire, and ran back to the basement for more water—all the while trying to make siren noises. Another, called martini, involved ice and an olive. There was also an elephant parade and a game involving a large pile of peanut butter.

Pledges constantly committed offenses that were known only to the accuser, and the guilty were required to "Assume the position!" which meant bending over, hands on knees, to receive a swat. After each blow the goat responded, "Thank you, sir! May I have another, sir?"

Another way fellowship was established was to have the pledges smoke cigars as a group but under a rug. In between the game, the time was filled with scrambling, scrambling, and more scrambling. Every task was accompanied by constant deprecations.

The longer it went on, the more I relied on the company of my enduring pledge brothers. One of my most vivid memories concerned Ted Hogshire. He was a short fellow the brothers nicknamed, for Hell Week, "Teddy the Toilet," because his metal-rimmed glasses gave the appearance of a seemingly drowned small animal. At the command, "Flush, Toilet!" Ted would pull on his earlobe and corkscrew himself downward. Finally, when the last brothers tired of this, the pledges were sent back to the furnace room with our mascot, now dubbed Beta, the forlorn mutt.

On the third night we were assembled in the meeting room and told, since we'd done so well, that Hell Week was over! We received congratulations and, scarcely believing our ears, began to thump one another's back.

And then President Brandhorst announced, "There's just one more thing, of course. *It's not over*, you stupid goats. *You're not fit to be Betas. Back downstairs!*"

As we lunged for the stairs, the president shouted, "Freeze!"

After a moment, he told us, "Go down to your rooms, dress in dark clothes, and reconvene in the living room in *five* minutes."

When we reassembled, we surrendered everything in our pockets except cigarettes and lighters or matches. Then we were blindfolded, loaded into different vehicles, and driven randomly for a while. Eventually we stopped meandering and settled down on a particular route for what seemed to be around thirty minutes. After a while the cars stopped and let us out, one at a time, with strict instructions not to remove our blindfolds until we no longer heard the car engines.

After I was released and after the sound receded into the distance, I removed my blinders and found myself on a deserted highway in the countryside, with nothing in sight in the dim moonlight. I started walking with no clue whether I was moving in the right direction. A few minutes later, out of the darkness emerged a figure that turned out to be Rutledge Young. And then two others came into sight.

As we approached the second group, the sound of an approaching vehicle made Rut say, "Quick, into the ditch!" We threw ourselves into the drainage ditch. After the dark shape crawled slowly past and receded into the distance, he surmised that, had it been the brothers coming back to check on us, we would have been collected and then separated again.

We decided two pairs had a better chance of avoiding detection, so we split up. Rutledge and I resumed walking in the direction we had chosen earlier. After a while we spotted a sign that said "Entering Albemarle County," which was a relief. The other side announced we had been in Fluvanna County. Rutledge said we were considerably south of Charlottesville, on the road past Ash Lawn, Monticello, and Michie Tavern.

As the late evening turned into the predawn and then dawn, we passed each of these landmarks and entered the southern outskirts of Charlottesville, approaching Main Street shortly before ten o'clock. Rutledge had clearly proven to me that he was our squad leader, because as I headed toward the house, he said, "We're not going back there yet.

We're going to check into a hotel, get some sleep, and let them wonder what happened to us."

With that great idea in mind, we checked into a small hotel on Main Street, near the Sears Department Store. We explained we were students, so there was no question of payment. We were exhausted. As soon as we got into our room, we fell on the beds and slept deeply for the first time since the prior Sunday morning. We left a wake-up call for five o'clock.

When we returned to 180 Rugby Road we were met with great relief, although the brothers tried to disguise it and feign anger and nonchalance. One of them said, "We're going to have to punish you for disobedience, but we're very proud of the way you thought for yourselves."

We received our punishment and went back to the rigors of scrambling. And that was how Rutledge, who I had known only slightly and was not sure I even liked, and I started a lifelong friendship. He was in my wedding and I was in his. To this day we still visit each other.

Meanwhile, Kelly Wood—he had the mindset of a practical engineer, which is why he later became the head of engineering at the Norfolk Naval Base—followed his instincts and went to the first farmhouse he saw with its lights on and explained why he was there. It turned out to be the residence of the executive assistant to the dean of the University, B. F. D. Runk (previously introduced as the most powerful man at the U in terms of day-to-day operations).

In today's world I suspect this treatment of a pledge would cause a major brouhaha, with lifetime expulsions, suits by the ACLU, and on-the-ground reporting by CNN, opinion pieces in *Rolling Stone*, and investigative segments on PBS. But in the 1960s, this was a nonissue.

Although Kelly was chastised by the house for not using more initiative, there were two reasons why this was a not a problem. First, students at the University were self-governing. Activities were not interfered with unless there was an occurrence deemed to be detrimental to the University. Second, Dean Runk was a card-carrying member of the traditional Old U way of doing things, and he proudly wore his Zeta Psi brand on his forearm. As Joel Gardiner's excellent book *From Rebel Yell to Revolution, My Four Years at UVA, 1966–1970*, reveals, much changed with Dean Runk's retirement as the last dean of the University several years later. I believe—having had two Kappa Kappa Gamma daughters and a Kappa Alpha Order son (before Beta Theta Pi rose back from the ashes like a phoenix) from 1985 to 1995—by 1970 the University had outgrown the Greek community. After 1970, fraternities and sororities remained healthy and intact but increasingly insular.

One more incident worth mentioning is the paint affair. Thursday night a trash can of ice and water was poured on my head. Involuntarily and instinctively I clenched my fists and teeth, whereupon I was accused and convicted of clenching my fist at a brother, which was a treasonous and rebellious act. My sentence was to be paddled from one side with a wooden Coke case and a switch on the other, the result being a number of welts on my backside.

Later that evening, while all of us were scrambling to the brothers' commands, Wicky McNeely threw a gallon of paint onto us. It was supposed to be water-based paint, but it turned out to be oil-based, which required mineral spirits to remove. Around 2:30 a.m. another person I had scarcely known, Rusty Mather, painstakingly cleaned the paint out of my welts, one stripe at a time. Such action can create no closer bond with another individual, and Rusty has since been an integral part of my life.

The next night we were told to dress in our best clothes for our ultimate hurdle. This was to be our final test.

When I entered the room, I noticed two officers flanking a distinguished-looking older man, probably in his forties, who was to administer the test. I later learned that each year an outstanding alumnus, who himself had gone through Hell Week and the ritualistic procedures many years before, was brought in for the end of Hell Week. I won't say more about it except that it was a challenging and emotionally draining experience, after which I was sent to a room alone. After a while, the door suddenly burst open and I was surrounded by Beta brothers, all assuring me as well as the other initiates that we were all now one in Beta Theta Pi.

It was one of the most rewarding times of camaraderie imaginable. A loving cup was passed around until the wee hours, with the stern elder statesmen reverting to the day he'd entered the special brotherhood himself.

Eventually we all headed off for some sleep before classes (for those so inclined) and for Rush, which started the following Saturday and would go on for the next twelve months!

# Chapter 11

## A Beta Brother

What a difference a year makes! In September 1961, I had been a new boy all over again in a school dormitory with no real contacts. This year I was living in the Beta house amid people I could trust, with my meals, housekeeping, and house maintenance all taken care of. In my eight years of boarding school and college, my bed had always been made and my room vacuumed and bathroom cleaned. Someone had always picked up my laundry and dry-cleaning, at least weekly, which was a vital function for those who wore coats and ties, especially before no-iron 100 percent cotton shirts were even considered. But the massive difference was that it was now fraternal, not institutional, so I now had a voice and vote, although small at first, in how my housekeeping was governed.

Other changes occurred. In addition to being a reporter and features writer, I was promoted to assistant city editor, or day editor, of *The Cavalier Daily* (*CD*), with the responsibility for ensuring all articles and pictures fit and were submitted to the printer on time on my day. As the sports and features editor of *The Blair Breeze*, a smaller weekly paper, I'd received my training in this labor-intensive task. While great strides had been made since Johannes Gutenberg had invented the printing press, the process involved counting column inches, type size, and typesetting, all of which has since been made obsolete through technology. However, without today's almost unlimited ways to get news and opinion, the power of the press was vast and had little real competition. The opportunity to play a significant role was exciting to me and I enjoyed the challenge.

In those years the *CD* was controlled by the KAs, with Joe Gleason and then Guy Tripp as consecutive editors in chief (if memory serves almost sixty years later). However, by the time I was fourth year, the chain had been broken, and Dick Carlton became editor in chief. And when that happened, he and I lived next door to each other.

One night I was approached by a disheveled middle-aged black man who related the sad tale of his family on the verge of starvation and asked for a little change. When I replied I had none, only bills, he responded, "I got change!" and proceeded to pull out of his pocket a fistful of change and bills. He was known as Carwash George, and how he came by this name is a Charlottesville legend.

One day George approached a group of fellows on the porch of St. Anthony's, which overlooked Mad Bowl on the other side of the street. He offered to wash the cars parked there at a relatively low cost. Word quickly spread on Mad Lane, and soon he was washing most of the vehicles parked there. When he was finished, Carwash pocketed his pay and took off. Only later, when people began to get in their rides, did they realize he'd cleaned only the sides that faced the houses. Since a truly clever con that causes no damage is generally appreciated, no attempt at retribution was ever tried.

Sometime in my third or fourth year, Carwash disappeared. It was rumored that he'd entered the tuberculosis sanitarium in Staunton. When he returned, we were a little wary of getting too close to him for fear of being infected, although he did go back into business.

Another regular in the community was an even worse case. He was known as Lightnin', probably because he resembled the character on

*The Amos n' Andy Show*. Lightnin's headquarters appeared to be beneath the broad wraparound porch of St. Anthony Hall (the Hall), although he could be seen around the neighborhood quite often. In cold weather he was permitted a trash-can fire to keep warm. At mealtimes, the kitchen help would, under orders, feed him. They typically served him using a metal pan and left it on the porch, since the servers considered him to be a sorry soul.

Lightnin' had a withered hand. Some said it was the result of a combat injury, when his hand had been caught in the detonation cord of a land mine. While the proper procedure would have been to carefully disengage from the device, Lightnin' allegedly panicked and ran. For many reasons I've doubted this story. At any rate, Carwash and Lightnin' were part of our community, and they were provided for by our social services safety net.

During my stint with the *CD*, while I reported many different stories, I favored features more because they allowed me to personalize my column, as opposed to factual reporting. One of the articles I wrote that year greatly affected my understanding of a journalist's ability to color the truth. At lunch one day, someone announced that a guy at the Zete house alleged that a local Catholic priest had denounced all fraternities. Since I needed an article that afternoon, I went across the street and questioned the person who'd supposedly said this. It turned out the fraternity comment was a passing reference and not the subject of a particular homily.

Nonetheless, since my deadline was fast approaching, I went to the Newman Center and interviewed the priest. He was a very likable Jesuit, and the gist of his message had been on accepting all people. As an illustration, he'd noted that fraternities didn't accept everyone, but that didn't mean they were wrong. His point was that the Catholic as well as the general Christian view needed to be larger. Afterward, I headed to the *CD* office and wrote up the interview into what could be regarded as very readable muckraking, gave it to that day editor, and headed off to dinner.

The next morning's edition of the paper generated two emotions within me: exhilaration and dismay. The former because my article had been chosen as the lead, and the latter because it appeared under the headline "Catholic Priest Assails Fraternities."

At the end of the month, I received the award for the month's best feature article, which included a thirty-dollar cash prize. All I could think about was that it was the same price Judas Iscariot was paid for betraying Jesus.

Never again would I write a piece that wasn't either truly accurate or clearly labeled opinion or fiction.

While the newspaper was not a literary magazine, it was sometimes given to heading off on a lark. At no time was this truer than in the days immediately preceding a Big Weekend. At the end of this chapter is one of my favorite contributions to the *CD*: "Ode to Mid-Winters Weekend," which appeared in the February 15, 1963, edition.

An enormous change occurred in my life in 1963, when Virginia hired a new swimming coach, Ralph Law, who then recruited me to rejoin the varsity team in the fall. It is almost unimaginable how much college athletics, particularly at UVA, have changed since the 1960s. Other than the two revenue sports of football and basketball, which provided only a modest profit to the University for the support of the other programs, I don't believe there were any other scholarships given.

Also, there were no special dorms or eating facilities. College athletes lived the same lives as other students. (Other than the less than 1 percent of athletes who eventually turned professional, that part was undoubtedly good for their general preparation for life.)

After their first year at the dorms, amid the general student population, many outstanding football and basketball players pledged and were active in the fraternities. One of my best friends was Pat McFalls, an interior lineman, who became an SPE. He and I went to parties in Natrona Heights, Pennsylvania, at the house of another great, wide receiver Larry Molinari, and his Sigma Nu brothers, who included fullback Charlie Hart and offensive guard Bob Kowalkowski.

The Zete house also had revenue sports players, such as forward Mac Caldwell, who was the leading scorer on the basketball team. Caldwell was nicknamed Gerald Giraffe by his younger brother Joe Brown, and it was a name he bore good-naturedly. The Zetes also had football players such as offensive lineman Paul Rogers, center Chips Longley, and tight end Ed Carrington, but also many guys who never dreamed anything beyond the required phys ed courses. Lacrosse, baseball, swimming, track and field, tennis, polo, and others were all represented in the Greek community in most of the chapters.

Finally, the sports facilities were shockingly bad. All indoor sports were played at Memorial Gymnasium, where the basketball courts also served as an all-purpose facility for concerts, registration, and similar events, as well as housed offices and abysmally basic training facilities. If that weren't enough, all physical education classes were held there. With the exceptions of Scott Stadium (which was half its current size and tremendously more basic) and the Lady Astor Tennis Courts, the outdoor facilities were equally bad.

While I hadn't actually missed a year of eligibility as a collegiate swimmer, I still had a lot of catching up to do in the pool. The first thing the trainer did was send me to the student health athletic physician for a weight-loss program, and a doctor there gave me a bottle of eight-hour Dexedrine tablets, with instructions to take one a day three hours before dinner. The pills worked quite well for weight loss, but practice began fifteen minutes after I took the medication, and so, as the afternoon progressed, my heart rate advanced as well. By the end of practice, my heart rate was so high as to have no pause between beats. It also became part of my routine to periodically put away a few pills for exam time.

Many years later, someone asked me, "Do you know what Dexedrine is? It's Speed!"

I can honestly say I never participated in a meet after taking any medication, even though there was no consideration of performance-enhancing drugs at the time. I didn't because I thought of the tablets only in terms of weight loss (and keeping awake), so I could not imagine why anyone would take it recreationally.

While I swam the 100-yard individual medley and butterfly and the 200-yard freestyle at Blair, freestyle was by far my best stroke. I was not competitive in the other strokes at the 200-yard collegiate distance. For that reason, I was moved to the 500-yard and sometimes the 200-yard freestyle and freestyle relay.

As I noted earlier, the swimming pool at Virginia was antiquated. It was replaced not long after by a splendid natatorium, which was replaced (much as it was at Blair) after I took my degree.

Nonetheless, it was gratifying to be back in competitive swimming, where I could compete against the clock and against the other distance swimmer, Jep Doley, a Hallie who had been a swimmer at Deerfield Academy. The old ACC was a diverse swimming conference, with two dominating schools (Maryland and UNC) who awarded scholarships. The University of South Carolina was at the other end of the conference, and I earned more points against the Gamecocks than any other adversary in high school or college. Duke, Wake Forest, and Virginia filled out the middle. I have no memory of Clemson. We also swam against some nonconference teams, and I specifically remember one of these being William and Mary.

The most notable event for me occurred during our first road trip, which was at UNC. The night before the meet, I was shown a copy of *Intercollegiate Swimmer*, which featured Harrison Merrill, the 500-yard national champion, on the cover. I was going to swim against him the next day, and that was a sobering thought to sleep on. Carolina's visiting team accommodations were first rate, and the pool water was so much clearer than ours, we had to account for turns appearing closer than we were used to. All in all, Jep and I did quite well, entering our twentieth and final lap before Harrison (now a longtime friend) finished.

By contrast, the next day was striking. For one thing, I left my UVA meet swimsuit at Carolina, and I had to borrow a friend's car (Alan Rimer's) to go the twenty minutes between the two schools to get it before Coach Law found out. Duke put us up in rooms that were quite substandard at the top of an old gym, and then they did something unimaginable.

During the meet, Doley and I were preparing to enter our stances. The starter (a Duke employee) was obligated to start the race fairly, but the race began with both Duke swimmers already entering the water. This unjust event, coupled with swimming against the national champ the day before, produced an adrenaline surge that propelled me as never before, and Doley and I finished first and second, respectively.

The bad start was the sort of thing that's contributed to my Wahoo lifetime mistrust of the Blue Devils, with a few individual exceptions. At our fiftieth reunion, Doley said, "[Coach Law] had us swim the 500 because he liked making fat guys work hard."

Looking back at that year, probably Brereton "Brere" Chandler Jones's return to the Law School for that one semester did more to shape my next two and a half years than anything else. Over the several months he was there, he convinced me that I could be elected to the Student Council and then elected president of the council. Not only did he give me a conceptual goal but also a map to follow.

Brere was a Beta who took his bachelor's degree in 1961 in commerce, started every football game during his three varsity years on a team that never won a game, and was a noted figure around the Grounds from a fraternity that was largely inner-focused. He left Virginia at the age of twenty-four, became a member of the West Virginia

House of Delegates at the age of twenty-six, and floor leader at twenty-eight. Then he left politics and moved to Kentucky, where he reentered public service and became a highly effective governor there at the age of fifty-one.

He was quite a mentor for me, though he did not know it until many years later.

Student politics at Virginia at the time was built on two foundational blocks. The first was the intelligent assumption, derived from the republican form of government, that students didn't know enough to self-govern before they gained some experience to do so. Thus, first- and second-year men enjoyed only the privilege of voting. Third-year fraternity men who'd proven themselves (and/or were good politicians with strong connections) held appointed positions of leadership, secondary elected positions, and became eligible to run for offices to be held in the last half of their third year. The Student Council and other organizations elected their own officers, often for two-semester terms.

The second foundational block was the efficient but somewhat undemocratic two-party system at the University. The two political parties were Scepter Society (Tweedledum) and Scull and Keys (Tweedledee). Membership was determined by each fraternity, which sent eight members to each party's caucus. Thus, when a brother was ready to run, he'd round up the eight brothers to support him. At that point it became somewhat more competitive, based on which persons or groups liked or disliked which other groups.

A nonfraternity member, an Independent, could run for office by petition. The prospective candidate petitioned a significant percentage (I believe this was 20 percent) of the students in his school: arts and sciences, architecture, engineering, and education for undergraduates. (Nursing, an all-female group, did their own thing.)

Platforms, if they could be called such, had one common theme: don't change anything considered traditional. Within that general category were some key components, several of the most important included the following:

The infallibility of the Honor System.
The inviolate right of University students to self-govern.
The University was, is, and will always be all-male.
The fraternity houses are private property and not subject to University jurisdiction.
The student activities fees are too high, no matter what they are.
Anything that happened outside of the University community was of absolutely no consequence to anyone.

In fact, each year the Student Council declined to join Who's Who in American Colleges and Universities because if people knew what they were doing in Charlottesville, what difference did it make if anyone else did?

Finally, while it was important to appear interested in being elected to a position, it had to be without appearing eager to do so less the expected reserve of Virginia gentlemen be compromised.

The Rush experience from the inside was a great deal different from that of being a rushee. From the week after Hell Week ended in early October until the first or second Sunday in December (Bid Sunday), Rush was omnipresent. At first it was a simple matter of open houses, meeting first-year men, and making some basic cuts. After a few weeks those who were given initial consideration were invited to meals and further culled. Trivial comments or actions could help someone along (such as drinking a bottle of catsup), having friends in common, being liked by brothers at a former school or hometown. Opposites of the same things (such as drinking a bottle of catsup) could cause a person to be culled or being disliked in any of the prior situations. The heavy-duty job of the Rush chairman was to make the initial lists from recommendation letters, friends, dorm counselors, girls, and frankly anyplace. Letters to the house penned by unknown Beta alumni from other schools could be a death knell if they described unconventional attributes when read aloud to the brotherhood by a gifted ridiculer.

Much of each weekly meeting was devoted to Rush. In the early weeks, lists of names were read with the following responses: keep, drop, and no comment. Unless there was an objection, the latter two categories were removed from the Rush list. If a name had been left with reservations, the brothers discussed it. Once that phase was complete, when a name was called, it went around the brothers seated on the benches around the room, and each member was required to say yes, drop, pass, or ball.

As Rush progressed, more and more names were dropped without being balled until drops outnumbered passes. People who were known to be going elsewhere were dropped to avoid being bumped by another house. Sometimes a brother would say, "We shouldn't be influenced by ego" (a distinctly minority opinion). Others had done something that irked someone. The overriding philosophy in a one-ball system was, even if one person felt he could not live happily with someone, he dropped his black ball. Once this happened, it was over for the rushee, and there was no recourse. For that reason, those who advocated a candidate would prevent his name from getting to that point, until they felt it was time to call the vote.

At one point, Rusty Mather checked the beer can or cup of each departing rushee, and if they hadn't finished it, they received a black mark. Rusty claimed not to want anyone as a brother who would waste beer.

"You mean the guy who plays with trains?" spelled doom for the rushee who told the wrong person about his hobby. Another wore a tux on his way to Glee Club, one asked a brother's casual date to go out some other time. Certain people rose in popularity because they had pledged two or more houses and sparked a competition between the chapters.

On another occasion, Teddy Hogshire, who was given to passionate endorsements, concluded (not for the first time), "He's a good man with his feet on the ground, and he knows where he's going in life."

In response, Rusty Mather said, "I'm not a particularly good man, my feet are not on the ground, I have no idea where I'm going in life, and I don't want to be around people who do. If you ever say that again, I'll ball the person on the spot."

When Bid Sunday was a week to ten days away, and only seven or eight out of an objective of twelve and a breakeven number of ten or eleven rushees had been passed through, an annual liturgy was enacted.

"Hey, y'all, we have to agree on more pledges or we'll go in the [financial] hole."

The reply, delivered in a grave and sonorous tone, was always, "I never thought I'd see the day when we made decisions about who we'd bid based on finances!"

After that was done, we'd get back to the business at hand, much like a legislative body agreeing on a bill. As a rushee was discussed, a small group would do most of the talking while another kept quiet. Then the majority delivered selective input. Thus, the outcome was never certain.

One night, after twenty minutes of positive input about a popular rushee, and it looked certain he would be a pledge, his name started around the room. After twenty or so quick pass votes, Wicky McNeely, who hadn't said a word, pronounced, "Ball."

After a moment's stunned silence, we went on to the next name, because a ball was irreversible. Eventually, at the ninth hour, a class was put together and preparations were made for delivering the invitations to the individual rooms.

The final weekend, designated as Formal Rush, was more structured than the prior six to eight weeks, and certain requirements were observed. For one thing, fraternity visits were assigned specific times, for example, St. Elmo from 8 p.m. to 9 p.m., Beta from 9 p.m. to 10 p.m., etc. But there was no requirement to make a rushee leave by a certain time, and there was every reason to keep rushees fully enthralled so as to stay around into the following hour. On several occasions, using upperclassman aggressiveness and status, I went to another house to escort a guest back to our house. Those moments were not without tension. It was a calculated risk.

Solidly committed first years were enlisted to continue the Rush process in the dorms, acceptable best friends were promised bids as part of a package, female friends and alumni of various ages from home were enlisted in the final all-out blitz.

I was told the Beta house had been on social probation the year before I pledged because they had taken someone out to a farm in the country, kept him happily inebriated until Bid Sunday was over, and then pledged him.

Tom Rue came not quite certain to the Beta house, and he was magnanimously sent downstairs to make sure he was certain of being Beta with the thought that he was secured in our house. But as soon as the KAs found out what we were doing, they kidnapped him through our back door to their house and pledged him.

Such shenanigans were not uncommon on Bid Sunday weekend. But once it was over, there was no backtracking. Pledging was complete and not revisited, and normal life resumed the following Monday as it had for generations. Second-guessing was not permitted, and remorseful boys who attempted to retract were told how much they would enjoy whatever choice they had made. Everyone was tired of Rush that year.

> Ode to Mid-Winters Weekend
> Hark now! Have you all heard the cheer?
> Mid-Winters weekend is already here.
> The bottles have broken, the combos have begun,
> Hurry up now, lest you miss all the fun.
> Down at old Sigma Nu, some fellows howl,

Maybe it's because their dates are so foul.
While up at the Zete house, the story's the same,
Where someone called Lunchbox will go down in fame.
A view of the KA house, where all's prim and proper,
Shows young Mickey Callahan in his shiny new topper.
Wait! here comes one now, a Madison pig,
She seems to be trying to snare Terry Sieg.
And now the sweet strains of The Brothers Four,
While old Wally Rhodes is passed out on the floor.
Those Brothers Four now, they sure can croon.
So it's worth all six dollars to make your date swoon.
Back from the Law school for a mid-winters sip,
Bunny Benham, Ken White, Scotty Sykes and Guy Tripp.
Look over there now at the fellow's pant,
They're purple clam diggers on sly Bobby Ganz.
Now out of the crowd a young damsel yells, "Spooks!"
Is it Hootman, or Cudlip, or that fellow Luke?
But now then, readers, don't knock the Hall.
With their fifty cent combos they have a ball.
Now all of the guys up at old SAE
Appeared to be starting a forty-hour spree,
When out of the darkness, like three or four bells,
Came the melodious voice of the Reverend A. Wells.
Now there a cauldron of purple punch
That Marshall Coleman brewed after lunch.
Alas, none but he will drink the swill,
Except Nicky Bacalis and Pete McGill.
And there a young maiden spies a man for her bower
Now curses her luck, for it's only Guy Tower.
Ric Moore, Santarelli, Leventis, and Hogshire,
My what a quartet of great balls of fire.
Over at the Kap house, they're twisting in flight,

While giving poor Lawder a horrible fright.
This gallant captain and his IFC crew
Will punish offenders, be it me or you.
Then there's Bradley and Nixon in one Sigma Phi.
They must be real sharpies to make their dates sigh.
At the Pi Kappa Phi house, the old Alpha Mu,
They're serving cocoa and good cookies too.
Old Freddy Hughes will come on by later
Watch out now, girls, he's a confirmed woman hater.
In Bornhauser's company will be John Omwake,
Between those two wolves, they'll make the girls quake.
MacKensie, Paul Beeker, McNeely and Moss
Have their wives with them, to show them who's boss.
Those sterling fellows from the diamond ring set,
Dare not attempt a secret tête-à-tête.
Fred Hilton and Maull, down at old Delta U
Are cutting some capers, although it's past two.
Dave Tucker and Bill Orr are out at the lodge.
It's a two-hour drive in their shiny new Dodge.
All in all, things are swinging from Phi Delta Theta
Way over to Brandhorst and Spence down at Beta.
Tom Adams and Mather and all our stout crew
Are busily turning themselves pink and blue.
And now, regretfully, this poem must close
As my small tribute to our friend, J. Booz
Now if you all don't think me a bore
Perhaps then, someday I'll write you some more.

# Chapter 12

## Living at the House

Although I don't know when Beta moved into the Rugby Road house, the Omicron chapter was chartered by the General Fraternity in 1855. The similarities between the Betas today and those of the early 1960s and earlier are many, since, as the song says, "We all drink from the same canteen in Beta Theta Pi." Nonetheless, the history is far more complex than that.

For example, while present-day Betas occupy the same residence I did, right next to the Beta Bridge, from the mid-1970s until the early 2000s they were exiled both from the house and, for a few years, from the University. Adding insult to injury, the house itself was taken over by Delta Upsilon (the DU's), a disdained group that had lived immediately next door and to our south and across the street from the Zete house.

Shortly after the Betas' eviction and before their return, 180 Rugby Road, the DU house was damaged by a fire of unknown origin, giving rise to the famous "flaming arrow" myth. The story goes that an old Beta or Betas, enraged by the desecration of their house, fired a flaming arrow into the roof to protest their occupation of Beta sacred ground.

From 1985 to 1995, while my three children were enrolled at the University, I was occasionally asked by other students whether the tale was true. I always replied, gravely and honestly, I had no knowledge of the affair.

During the almost forty years of exile, the brotherhood inhabited the old Zeta Beta Tau (ZBT) house near Scott Stadium.

There are a number of distinct differences between the old and current Betas. I noticed the last GPA average was 3.51, which was either the highest at the University or close to it. I don't think many academic records were kept by the chapter in my day, and they certainly had nothing to do with who was bid. In fact, I noticed in the meeting minutes that our representative to the Interfraternity Council (IFC) had been sent back with specific instructions to vote against a motion that called for chapters with GPA's below 2.0 to be placed on probation. The motion was defeated overwhelmingly because a fraternity's grades were no one else's business! (This was always the general sentiment shared by the fraternities.)

There are sixty-one current members whereas our numbers were usually in the low to midforties. The current fellows, to their credit, take great pride in their philanthropy and intramural sports achievements. We did almost neither as a house, unless joining a touch football game with another or there was a small per-head assessment for an IFC charity drive. Generally speaking, none of these things were even on our radar.

Another minutes entry from that period noted that our volleyball team had won our first game in two years. (It didn't specify whether it was only in volleyball or any sort of competition). However, we're all brothers and share a common bond deeper than superficial generational differences.

While many brothers chose to live elsewhere after their second year, staying at the Beta house suited me to a T. Not only did I live with my best friends, but room, board, and living arrangements were all taken care of and in one place. Had it not been for some specific circumstances during my third year, all three of my upper-class years would have found me there, so I'll concentrate on some of the more significant aspects and events of that experience.

Every school night during my first year, my roommate Billy Tylander would say, "Tomorrow you really need to make sure that I get up for class."

And I would always respond, "I try to do that, but you're very difficult to work with in the morning."

Billy would promise, "Tomorrow I really will get up if you keep on me."

And then he never did.

Pulling his sheets off, rat-tailing him, pouring water on his head, and other harassments would only anger him, and he would charge at me while I escaped toward the bathroom.

Others might shout words of encouragement to him to get up, but he would always lumber back to his rack and say, "It's too late now. I'll never be ready in time."

Willie T eventually graduated with honors, but not until after he'd spent two years as a swabbie in the Navy.

Teddy Hogshire, on the other hand, was always ready to go in plenty of time, but he had the misfortune of giving some of us a ride to New Cabell Hall since he had a car.

"Come on guys," he would plead. "We're gonna be late!"

Eventually he'd threaten to leave us, but we knew he was too tenderhearted. And so he'd drop us off on time, but then be late himself, as he had to park. Thirty years later I was in Charlottesville to see my son, and Ted offered to drop me at the airport for a 6:30 a.m. flight to New York. When I remarked to my wife that I felt bad to take advantage of his kind nature, she said, "I don't see why. You've been doing it since y'all were eighteen."

Judge Hogshire, I plead guilty.

A great thing about living at the house was there were always kindred souls around, ready to chat away the hours in happy indolence. Dick Tedrow and I were particularly good at this, but there were many others as well.

On the other hand, Hogshire, Rutledge Young, Verity, Dick Tucker, and Kelly Wood had the wonderful ability to go to their rooms, shut the door, and concentrate for hours at a time. The rest of us, not so much. Some were great at heading to the library, books in hand, but there were many temptations along the way. For one thing, Newcomb Hall was right next door, with goodies galore, and televisions offered popular shows such as *The Fugitive*. Also available were several bowling lanes. Especially deceptive were rooms in which checked-out music tapes could be listened to. For many, music was undoubtedly helpful as a background for concentration, but not if the sounds became primary and distracting. There were always the ever-present press gangs making up "Flick Teams" to head off to a theater for a break.

To really study, I had to go alone to one of the library carrels, way back in the stacks. (If you're Generation Z or later, google what those are.) I did most things with Rusty Mather (aka Pony and Flash) than I with of anyone in our pledge class during the two years I lived in the house. It was wonderful fun, but not the best way for either of us to achieve academic greatness. After lunch we frequently visited the tables in Mr. Van's Pool Hall, behind The Corner, working diligently to improve our skills.

During swim season, things changed dramatically for me, since I realized the need to apportion my time and actually accomplished more than I planned. At times I would stop by The Cavalier after swim practice to gather friends and head to dinner. On those occasions that hallowed institution and its customers always seemed a lot different through the eyes of an athlete in training and presented no impediment to academic advancement. At dinner, under the effects of Dexedrine until I made weight, I would eat meat and vegetables with iced coffee to prepare for several hours of study that needed to be over by ten o'clock, or else swim fatigue could overcome the concentrative effects of the drug. Moreover, when the eight hours a tablet lasted were up, my ability to avoid thousands of calories evaporated, and I was apt to fall prey to massive caloric temptation. However, participating in intercollegiate Division I athletic competition made undirected leisure time more difficult for me to achieve and academic pursuits more achievable.

My chance to leap ahead academically occurred after Christmas break, three weeks before the fall semester exams. While I was home, I had a nose operation (submucosal resection) to reduce sinus infections that occurred every swimming season. The plan was, since there were no meets during this pre-exam period, I would miss none of the season but be unable to practice, thus creating additional study hours. Unfortunately, it left me with the notion that time was limitless.

Each day, right after lunch, Rusty and I left our books on the front steps of Alderman Library and then bowled a quick game or two at the Newcomb Hall lanes. Suddenly it would be time for dinner, and we'd head over, promising each other nothing would keep us away from our books—except for one more game to even things up. Not many people can say they bowled almost ninety games over three weeks.

While I didn't spend enough time in study to be as successful in my academic pursuits as I was in my extracurriculars, I enjoyed my classes and went to many of them. In the two semesters of principles of economics, I acquired a grasp of how economies functioned, and that has been of value to me ever since, especially since financial advisory subjects became my vocation. Public speaking was a little boring because of its lack of imagination and fixation on what I considered unnecessary detail.

The second year of American history was taught by Mr. Bernie Mayo, who was the best teacher I ever had. He made topics such as the presidential election of 1884 come alive by transporting us there with the anti-Republican chant of "Blaine, Blaine, James G. Blaine, the continental liar from the state of Maine!" countered by the anti-Democrat mantra of "Ma, ma, where's my pa?" which referred to a paternity scandal involving Grover Cleveland.

I found military science to be an adjunct to history, both semesters, history and military tactics, although the teacher of the former, a major and former University of Tennessee football player, continually mispronounced such place names as Antietam and Shiloh, which were common knowledge to us.

English and American literature, one each semester, were not much different than advanced English at Blair (hence Mr. Perry's irritation with my choice of basic English composition my prior year) and enjoyable, although there were more reading assignments than I could handle.

In Spanish, Señora Blankenship, a voluble, chain-smoking Cuban and the first female teacher I'd had since junior high, was a ray of sunshine for me in a dreaded subject.

Almost all of the College of Arts and Sciences classrooms and offices were in New Cabell Hall, which had been built in 1950 and vastly improved since I was there. The architect brilliantly concealed this incredibly drab and ugly building from view at the end of the Lawn by placing it behind lovely Old Cabell Hall, which had been designed by Stanford White and finished in 1898. From the back, New Cabell looks like a red-brick-veneered four-story educational factory placed on a sharply descending slope. Inside were four floors of un-air-conditioned, lightly colored cinder-block rooms with brownish tile floors. Between the two Cabell Halls was a large, old-fashioned break room with nondescript sofas, chairs, tables, coffee, soft drinks, and doughnuts.

Since Mr. Jefferson's concept had been to keep the southern end of the Lawn open, so as to permit a panoramic view of the hills and countryside, closing it off with the first Cabell Hall had been vigorously protested. Eventually it was decided, if the school was to grow beyond several hundred students, additional classrooms were necessary, although considering the Virginia thought process, there were plenty who favored restricting growth rather than the view.

As a sop, the first Cabell Hall was originally referred to as the Academical Building. As the institution grew and the vista disappeared, the need for additional classrooms was satisfied by the addition of New Cabell Hall. The architects, however, focused on making the new building as efficient and effective as possible but keeping it hidden. Thus, while it was an esthetic mess, it was remarkably practical and utilitarian for the post–World War II era.

While my third semester failed to produce the GPA bonanza originally anticipated, it was a great improvement over my first two semesters. For the first time I passed every course, even a foreign language, albeit with a D. It was also the last time I ever earned a grade less than C. Had I not had the nine hours of Foreign languages (which resulted in a total of three grade points), my GPA would have been .2 points higher. On a positive note, for a 4.0 student the result would have been far more catastrophic, turning his 4.0 into a 3.3!

This was the beginning of a phoenix-like ascent from the academic ashes of my first year, and each succeeding semester was an improvement on the one before it. Indeed, I spent so much effort on passing each year's Spanish classes that everything else seemed inconsequential.

One major expense in our house budget, and probably in most of them, was windowpane repair, which also resulted in each pledge becoming a proficient glazer. While the causes for these repairs were many, probably the most significant was snowball battles. After every heavy snowfall, the fraternity houses became outposts to be attacked and defended, with the fiercest occurrences unfolding in the densely populated Rugby Road and Madison Lane areas.

As I noted earlier, the Beta house had Delta Upsilon (DU) immediately next door, with Zeta Psi (Zete) directly across the street from DU. Evidently no one at DU was familiar with the theories of the renowned Prussian genius Carl von Clausewitz, especially not to attack superior forces on two fronts from an indefensible position. If it was due to a thirst for recognition from the haughty neighbors, who scarcely acknowledged their existence on most days, they succeeded, but the cost in broken windows from the two sides was immense.

After the second or third round of damage that year, Rusty had enough and, knocking on the front door of the DU house, he announced his terms. He explained if they knocked out even one more window in our house, he was going to knock out every ground-floor pane on theirs. They apparently didn't take him at his word, for they sallied forth again. Methodically donning his heaviest boots and thickest gloves, the Beta champion marched across no man's land and worked his way down the side of the house, fulfilling his promise, amazingly unchallenged by the defenders. It was an awesome sight, and it ended that scourge for the balance of our time in the house.

For one who was an acknowledged leader in our class, Jon Verity was not immediately perceived in this role. He was a mild-mannered patrician, perhaps five-feet-ten, and nicknamed Cherub. Jon was always impeccably dressed, never ruffled, and spoke in a calm, sincere manner. Nonetheless, concealed within that misleading exterior was a sharp mind, a keen wit, and a highly competitive spirit. The first time I fully appreciated this was after a chance walk by Newcomb Hall. He knew I considered myself a pretty fair bowler, so he asked if I'd like to bowl a few games. I was surprised by the invitation and eager to get to know Jon better. After several games, with each of us scoring around 200, Jon noted he had time for one more game.

"Would you like to put a little money on this one to make it more interesting?" he asked.

I agreed to an amount somewhat higher than I normally would. And twenty minutes later it was all over. Jon's score was close to 300. He smiled at me and stuck out his hand. I paid up with great admiration. Not only had our friendship increased, but I realized I'd received a valuable lesson for a very acceptable outlay.

Not all gambling in the University Greek community was low stakes and an adjunct to fellowship. There were some high-stake ventures that occurred nightly, moving from house to house from one night to the next, with Beta on the route. The participants played each other so frequently that sometimes they just folded all the hands, knowing the rest as if reading a script.

One night a Jaguar convertible was lost for a short time, but then the car was totaled at Dead Man's Curve on the winner's way back from Sweetbriar. The driver and passenger were unscathed, but it's astonishing how few car fatalities there were each year. At the time it never occurred to us eighteen- to twenty-three-year-olds that anyone could ever be hurt.

There was also football and other sports gambling headed up by a fellow from a Mad Lane house, who went to a bookie (or the bookie's representative), rumored to be in Lynchburg, to handle the money transfers. For me, a son from a reasonably prosperous family, I was expected to earn my spending money by working construction or occasional part-time jobs. I had neither the means nor inclination to participate.

One night Rusty and I came across a mystery. We were headed to The Corner and we found Kelly Wood lying in a bed of leaves next to the Beta house.

We paused and Rusty asked, "How you doin' partner? Everything okay?"

Kelly said he was fine, so we left him. We knew that if he felt like lying there, that was his business. Later, on our way back, we passed by the spot, but no one was there, so we went on to bed. The next morning, we mentioned the incident, but Kelly, always taciturn, said nothing except that his arm felt a little sore.

Later that afternoon, at the start of an intramural touch football game, Kelly seemed lethargic, said his arm was still sore, and doubted he would play. But we needed him as a receiver. And so, he played the whole game, after which he disappeared during the customary post-game camaraderie.

Several hours later Kelly reappeared, but his arm was in a cast from forearm to shoulder! Since his room was on the second floor, two and a half flights above his cozy leafy nest in the yard, the question has always been how it happened, not whether it happened. No one ever explained it, not even Kelly himself.

Dick Tucker was the academic standout in our class, entering as an Echols Scholar and then joining Phi Eta Sigma and Phi Beta Kappa. Since he, too, was from Pittsburgh, we shared many adventures there and in transit between the Steel City and Hoo-ville.

For example, I backed his old navy-blue Buick into a parked car when we traveled to Midsummers our first year. And Tucker and I were traveling to school when, in Hagerstown, a girl across the aisle invited me to sit with her. We made out until the bus reached DC, where she disembarked.

Since Dick's dad was a Hoo and they lived in the socially prominent east side, Dick was familiar with many of the 'Burgh's most attractive debs. I spent many nights at his house. Significantly, it was he who introduced me to one of the most interesting and fascinating women I ever knew: his cousin, Bebe Gordon, who played a prominent role in my years at the University.

Dick was focused on academics (not to the exclusion of revelry) and less so on mundane matters. One day he returned to the room he shared with Hogshire to find all his neckties connected into a chain and crisscrossing the room. In the middle of the display was a sign announcing the "Vinegar Hill Tie Sale." While he feigned amusement, I sensed his feelings were hurt, and I regretted I'd originally enjoyed the prank.

Characteristically, his roommate, exhibiting the righteous call for justice that was to define his life's work, expressed significant indignation about the tie joke. I don't recall him ever accepting responsibility for the endeavor, but all fingers pointed to third-year man Jack "Foggy" Williams.

No matter what generation or culture we're in, there are certain codes to observe or ignore. Idealistic philosophies aside, books as well as people are judged by their covers. While sometimes unnecessarily brutal, it is almost always better to be aware of what others are thinking, even if eventually a decision to ignore is made.

Of all the schools in the country, it is possible the Old U ranked number one in rigid conformity regarding attire. The basic daily uniform was a cotton button-down shirt, necktie, sports jacket, khaki pants, brown belt with brass buckle, over-the-calf socks with garters, and Bass Weejuns. For more elaborate functions, a conservative suit and big-boy (lace-up) shoes were donned. Each item had to meet certain standards: conservatively cut jackets and suits, proper belt buckle, shirt color, and the design and width of ties.

All items were subject to limited choices. Clothes were purchased at one of the few establishments that fell under the category of traditional men's clothing and catered specifically to the UVA market segment. In Charlottesville it was and still is Eljo's Traditional Clothes, where the basic styles have not varied much since my grandfather's time, who used the same man at Brooks Brothers in New York from the 1930s on and who thought collars stitched onto shirts (as opposed to being attached with a collar stay in the back) was a passing fad.

There was another, less popular store at The Corner that was closed after it was bought out by a large Richmond department store. Langrock's on Nassau Street in Princeton, New Jersey, was another popular store. And there were others.

The most radical departure from the norm during my days at the U was when a Mad Lane student wore blue jeans with his jacket and tie instead of khakis. That was widely talked about, which was an indication of the impregnable nature of the supposedly voluntary coats-and-ties tradition.

My second year was also my Penn Hall year. Originally a women's school, Penn Hall is a now defunct junior college in Chambersburg, where Wilson College (founded 1869) was situated as well. Rusty and I each dated a girl at Penn Hall. He went out with Sharon from Smithfield, and I dated Joan from my hometown of Mount Lebanon. Actually, Joan and I had dated off and on since the summer I graduated from Blair, but we didn't become an item until Anne Gwaltney left for Europe, after which we were inseparable. Joan even had my fraternity pin, which was considered State U faux pas by the Betas. As a consequence, once or twice a month we made the two-hundred-mile trip, usually hitchhiking or catching a bus to do so.

Those trips alone could constitute a chapter by themselves, but I'll keep it short. Since Rusty and I didn't start back to Charlottesville until Monday, teachers would ask, "Why aren't you boys in school?"

A popular tag line of the time was "Every day is apple day in Virginia," and so that is how we responded.

As a result of my relationship with Joan, I had a date for every Big Weekend, as well as providing Penn Hall girls for other Betas who wanted dates. And one of those big events was the Midwinters Peter, Paul, and Mary concert at Mem Gym.

As the year progressed, however, my interest in Joan began to wane. It bothered me that the brothers weren't overly impressed with her whenever she was around. And it also struck me there were some third parties who were more anxious for Joan and me to be together than we actually were.

The Beta hayride was only a few weeks after Easters, and I remembered a girl I knew at Southern Seminary, another women's college. My second most eventful hayride started with her arrival at the bus depot. After lunch at the house, which was accompanied by the usual lethal punch, we climbed aboard the hay-laden truck bed for the trip to Blue Hole on the Rivanna River, and she nestled up to me. I had a milk bottle of punch. After we disembarked, she wrapped herself around me in the water until people began kicking water on us. So, she took me by the hand and led me away from the group. Once we were isolated, she took off her clothes and asked me if I had protection.

But as soon as this theoretically perfect situation presented itself, it rapidly deteriorated. First, I didn't have protection because it never occurred to me that I'd have a use for it. I was too embarrassed to even ask for such things at a drugstore counter, and I imagined my mother would eventually find the evidence of such a purchase. Second, I had an ever-present fear of getting someone pregnant. And third, I'd had at least three bottles of punch. The result was a complete failure and enormous ego diminishment from an undergraduate view, although an unrequested deliverance from a Christian vantage point.

Interestingly, my date viewed the result as the effect of something she'd done wrong!

As the evening moved on, so did she, and I was left to finish the early morning hours morosely nursing a beer and listening to the jukebox.

Academically, my second year ended on a much more positive note than my first did, which was not all that hard to achieve. For one thing, I had been removed from attendance probation earlier in the year. I earned no below-average grades: four C's (including Spanish) and a B in military tactics.

# Chapter 13

## Third-Year Fall

After a summer of working on an affordable housing project for a mid-size masonry contractor (bricks, cinder blocks, and chimney flues), I was in great shape. I had never worked harder in my life, and as the only white laborer from Union Local 26 of the International Hod Carriers and Common Laborers of America, I worked with an otherwise black gang from Local 76 as well as masons who only conversed in Italian. It was my first extended look into another world, well, actually two of them. While I was treated courteously by all, every day for the first few weeks was a test to see if I would break and quit. After that I was given grudging respect for sticking it out, but I remained a non-Italian-speaking white college student. Thus, while I felt a great sense of achievement and had fun at night on my home turf, it was great to be a student back at the Beta house for a week of preschool cleanup.

At the Beta elections the prior spring I'd been elected kitchen manager. This was a significant job since it involved all facets of restaurant management: personnel, bookkeeping, purchasing, sanitation, and customer service. My primary task upon opening the house was to be ready to serve three meals a day for more than forty brothers by week's end. The job, however, had actually started the prior April, to give Chuck Spence, my predecessor and mentor in many things, time to train me. Since Chuck had just fired longtime cook Archie for sanitation reasons, both personal and institutional, the new cook he hired, Annie, and I started working together immediately. The only other staff member was Gus, the kitchen boy, who had been around a while.

After Annie had been working at the house for a few weeks, she told me a close relative had passed away, and she asked for an advance amounting to a few week's pay. Chuck advised me to say yes. He said the result would either be a certain sum of money lost or a loyal and faithful employee. The latter proved to be true. Annie was a valuable and faithful key to the success of my kitchen duty.

I found it gratifying to supervise goats rather than be one, and I enjoyed my work in getting the kitchen and dining room ready every day. Soon I realized I was looking forward to Hell Week, not as a pledge, but as a brother.

The previous fall we'd pledged a wonderful group: Marshall Coleman, Walter Hooker, Rick Shepard, Henry Warner, Ray Burger, Archie Peter, Billy Abbuehl, Buddy Nolan, and Doug Kincaid. Upon the completion of Hell Week, they were all initiated and became part of the chapter and my experience. After that, my major objectives were to improve both my academics and swimming abilities while also pursuing political office.

Toward the end of summer, I'd met and been captivated by Dick Tucker's cousin Bebe, who left an indelible impression on my life by introducing me to the civil rights movement. Bebe went to Goucher College in Towson, Maryland, which was 168 miles from 180 Rugby Road, but in a different universe in terms of worldview. Bebe was the first person I ever knew and one of the few ever who burned with a white-hot fervor for a cause, in this case social justice. In all candor, I became interested in civil rights because of Bebe in the same way I would have been in dance, an art form, or field hockey. Nonetheless, she introduced me to the Virginia Council on Human Relations and one of the Law School's several black students. They educated me on the details of the University's token acceptance of integration to mask a policy of segregation.

Since Bebe was Tucker's cousin and my girlfriend, her eccentricities were regarded with good-natured tolerance, but all her causes were vitally important to her. Thus, when asked if she wouldn't rather eat in the kitchen with Annie and Gus or sit on the end-zone hill with the blacks at football games, Bebe would intensely retort, "I certainly would like to every bit as much as being here with you people."

When I said, "I'll be glad to go with you!" she gave me a conspiratorial look of gratitude.

For road trips I skipped Chambersburg, Pennsylvania, and headed for Towson. I usually traveled with Sandy "Shriek" Sierck, a fourth-year Beta from Manhattan. He had a Mercedes, which was several steps up from hitching!

A highlight for Bebe and me, for different reasons, was dinner in C'ville with three of my friends whose dates were all Richmond girls at Hollins, via a prominent girls' secondary school in the capital. Their conversation went like this:

> Bebe: "My roommate is from Richmond."
> Hollins date: "Who is she?"
> Bebe: "Evelyn Powell."
> (Puzzled looks since the Hollins dates knew everyone who was anyone in Richmond.)
> Hollins date: "Are you sure she's from Richmond?"
> Bebe: "Of course I'm sure! She's my best friend."
> Hollins date: "Where did she go to school?
> Bebe: "She went to Maggie Walker."

(More puzzled looks.)

Hollins date: "She couldn't have gone to Maggie Walker! That's a colored school!"

Bebe: "Of course she could. Evelyn's black."

(Thunderstruck silence.)

Hollins date: "Would you invite her into your house?"

Bebe: "I certainly would. She spent ten days at our house last summer."

Since this was so beyond the accepted mores of the day, and certainly not just in Virginia but also in Bebe's native Pittsburgh, further conversation became stilted with "that girl from Goucher" being the only happy and relaxed female at the table.

Since I had lived in New Jersey, Virginia, Texas, and Pennsylvania, I was well aware that the Jim Crow laws in the South were a reality of life, but the realities of segregation in the North were more subtle. When my family moved to Mount Lebanon after Virginia and Texas, a transplanted eighth grader from Oklahoma pointed out that things were no different in Pennsylvania than they were where we'd come from, even though our civics teacher had just been disparaging the Deep South.

"There are thirty-six thousand students in this school district," he said. "How many colored kids do you see?"

Then he answered his own question. "Three from a family that works on an estate."

The first and last time I ever went to school with African Americans was at Blair, where there were two scholarship students my senior year. From Bebe I learned the cause of desegregation in practice where one lived as opposed to viewing it as a concept for someplace else. Changes of staggering proportions were beginning to occur in race relations since the early 1960s, but not at the U for another few years.

All in all, my fifth semester fell into place quite nicely. My study habits, swimming, and entry into political activities were all under way when several events altered things forever. The first was personal and the second was international.

My parents decided to come to Homecoming weekend with their friends, the Ortners, and since Bebe couldn't come, I invited Anne. Everything started out well with Anne, who I hadn't talked to since being her marshal, at the airport in Washington after her flight from Wheaton College in Boston. It continued in high gear through dinner with my parents and borrowing their car for the evening.

As the night progressed it became apparent that Anne of Chatham Hall and my first year's Easters Weekend had matured considerably while I had not. When she wanted to return to her lodgings, I took her there and then went back to the party. Unfortunately, it didn't end there.

Sometime later Rusty and I decided it would be fun to take a speed run to Staunton. We were accompanied by Meg, a Hollins girl from Dallas. We made a pit stop on the side of Route 250 and got stuck in the mud. Contrary to the opinions of several folks who stopped to help, I powered the car out of the mud, and we resumed the run—for about fifteen minutes.

As we approached a bend to the left, a car came toward us in our lane, which forced me to veer off the road. This time there was a ten-foot embankment with no return to the roadway. Meanwhile the other vehicle disappeared into the night. (Later insurance company exams revealed skid marks that supported our account.)

Once we determined we were all fine, we realized the car definitely wasn't. We climbed the embankment, knocked on the door of the only nearby home across the highway, and explained our plight. Our first call was for a taxi to get Meg home before curfew, and the second was for a tow truck. Both vehicles arrived simultaneously. It was then that, in addition to being all right (which twenty-year-olds take for granted), a sliver of good fortune appeared in the person of the tow truck driver.

"Do y'all know Joyce Collier?" he asked.

While Virginia was a men's school, women from Albemarle and its contiguous counties were permitted to enroll. Joyce was in one of my classes, and I knew her reasonably well.

With that bit of news, Mr. Collier called his cousin in the sheriff's office, gave him the necessary details for the police report so he wouldn't have to drive all the way out there, and our account became the official story.

As Mr. Collier took Rusty, me, and the badly disfigured convertible back to town, I realized my right knee had started to swell (there were no seatbelts in the early 1960s) and could no longer support me. It took a while to convince poor Pony, who had to break the news to my parents, that I really was hurt. As a result, I was in the relative safety of a treatment room at the hospital, about to be admitted for a few days, when my parents appeared.

The last I saw of poor Anne, who'd come with them to say goodbye, a resident was telling her, "You better hurry. I'm about to stick this needle in his knee, and he's gonna throw up all over you!"

That afternoon in the hospital I dozed off and awakened to see my swimming coach and team captain sitting solemnly at my bedside. Of the things I've screwed up, that's the one I feel the most remorse for. Today, orthopedic surgery could have had me back in the pool quickly, but back then I was put in a cast for a month. Even then, that didn't fix it. I had surgery instead of helping the team.

My parents had to rent a car to get themselves and the Ortners home, and then they had to replace the car.

And Anne had a horrible weekend.

At the time, my major objective was to stay in the hospital long enough for my father to leave Charlottesville, especially after Rusty said, "When I took your father to see the car, there were lots of rednecks talking about it. Your father said to them, 'You should see the damn fool who was driving it.'"

As for Meg, every time I saw her for the next two years, she happily and proudly told me, "I've still got the scar!" And then she'd joyfully exhibit it just below her knee.

When I was released from the hospital several days later, and since I was not required to attend swimming practice every day, I devoted my energies to my political aspirations and being the kitchen manager at the Beta house. Regarding the former, it started poorly.

Of the two political societies run by the fraternities, Scepter was mine. I wanted to be nominated for Student Council, and the Betas had an agreement with the KAs that we would back their candidate for something and they would back me. But after their person was nominated (with our backing), they chose not to vote for me.

When that happened, Hutch Overby, a formidable Law School student who'd joined us so we had the maximum eight votes, rose to his feet and said disgustedly, "Let's go."

We exited as a group.

My next effort was more fruitful, and I became the chairman of the Finance Committee for the Interfraternity Council (IFC) (without the KAs interference). As time progressed, that experience and being a kitchen manager served to aid each other.

Hutch's presence at the Scepter Society meeting was an indication of how beneficial it was to have graduate school Betas continuing to take their meals at the Beta house. As I mentioned earlier, two of my heroes, Bunny Benham and Brereton Jones, were among them. In addition to them, the immediate past president, Jim "Sparrow" Sommers, now enrolled in the Darden School of Business, took his lunches at the house, and he frequently brought classmates with him. After some jovial hellos, they usually sat together and practiced their skills on being big deals on each other, which was an inherent ability for Sparrow, who later became a very big deal.

Dick Moss was married, and if he was with us at Lambeth Field for baseball and a few beers, he'd have to leave by a certain time, along with the other married guys, to pick up his wife from work.

Bill Porter and Teddy Webb were also in that group. Virtually all the houses had graduate student brothers, and those groups provided significant mentoring in maintaining the University's traditions. Phil Heiner, a ZBT law student, and I served together on a University committee. We became close friends, which lasted after we each moved to Atlanta until his tragic death from cancer around 1980.

There was one law student whose presence at the Beta house was irreplaceable. When Edward "Eddie" Baird returned from several years in the Navy, he was already a legend to our pledge class. For one thing, as an undergraduate, Eddie's ancient MG convertible had a starter that wouldn't work. As a result, in the parking spot reserved across Rugby Road from BOII for him by general agreement, his automobile ran 24/7 for at least three months during his fourth year.

Although Eddie became a highly competent attorney, he always gave the appearance of a lovable teddy bear. The first time I saw him at breakfast, he asked the pledges, "What's the best kind of pie there is?"

Since they had been clued in ahead of time, the pledges would answer, "Apple! No! Peach!"

"No, no," Eddie said. "Come on, goats."

They'd suggest others until eventually, with great frustration, Eddie said, "No! It's *Beta Theta Pi!*"

Other Eddie stories abounded, and none of us were ever sure whether he was actually that innocent and clueless or if he was having the last laugh on all of us. He was, however, one of the most guileless, respected, and loved individuals I ever encountered.

When I became kitchen manager, my predecessor gave me the following admonitions:

1. The house will continually try to move funds away from the kitchen account to the social account. Always *refuse* to be persuaded. The kitchen surplus anticipates the need to replace a major piece of equipment.

Many times during my tenure, I was reviled for refusing to transfer the kitchen money to the other account. On the other hand, my successor took the nice-guy approach, and the house owed him $2100 by February (an enormous amount in those days) after four months. The required two meals a day for undergraduates was $45 a month and three meals cost $55.

2. When someone gives you input, look at them, smile, and say, "Thank you very much." Then do exactly what you think is best.

Often, I did just that, but at other times I'd say, "Sure, we can have steak more often, but not at $45 a month!" Of course, we always have things that I like. Why in the world would a kitchen manager serve things he didn't like?"

The Beta shepherd's pie was unequaled for lunch topped off with a PB&J sandwich from the ingredients that were permanent fixtures on the lunch tables.

I greatly encouraged the dove hunts Rutledge and the other guys had at Woodberry Forest. Annie would prepare their game, and we reduced the amount of other food being served that night.

Ham and chicken were always great buys, which caused Rick Shepard to remark, "Ham and yams! Ham and yams! That's all we ever have around here!"

Occasionally, anarchy reigned, as it did the night Ted Hogshire, one of the waiters (actives who wanted to have discounted meals), felt I had overstepped my bounds. Suddenly, I felt a significant serving of chocolate pudding being dumped on my head. I momentarily forgot that I was in charge of the kitchen domain, which included cleaning up the dining room. So, I reacted in kind, hurling a bowl of the clinging, sticky stuff at my assailant. Within seconds the battle was on, and approximately forty bowls of pudding were hurled across the room (some

more than once). The result was an awful disaster, with walls, caricatures, fixtures, and tables covered in goop. It took more than an hour
for the goats to clean it up, but everyone felt it was time well spent!

All in all, the brothers were happy with the fare and the prices, and
Annie was a great cook. I learned that those who had a limit to their finances tended to be conscientious and paid their kitchen bill on time.
But some of the well-heeled brothers, unaccustomed to any kind of ac-
countability, often overlooked theirs. Whenever they saw their names
on the delinquent list I posted prominently around the house, they
would angrily demand the list be taken down, because finances were a
confidential matter. But I left the lists posted until the bill was paid, after
all, Chuck taught me, "An account receivable does not pay a bill due!"

Each week a wholesaler named Whitey came by to sell his best entrée offers. Then Sam Ragland, our house boy, would drive me downtown to buy the specials at grocery stores or High's ice cream at the
Barracks Shopping Center. These trips always passed through Sam's
neighborhood in Vinegar Hill, so he could proudly display he was driving one of his students on an important matter.

Sam had one answer to all questions: "Yassa, Mr. Frank!" And it would
take a little time to finally get him to answer whatever question I had. Sam
was a wonderful friend. We were very close, and I took up his cause when
he needed it.

Let me share a few anecdotes to illustrate the difference between those
days and now. During my time as kitchen manager, Gus resigned as
kitchen boy, and I had to interview several candidates for his replace-
ment. The kitchen boy was paid $35 a week. He was to be at the house
by 7:00 or 7:30, he had two hours off in the morning and afternoon,
and his day was finished when the dishes were washed and put away,
around 8:30 p.m. Given that hospital orderlies were paid $.90 or $1.00
an hour, depending on race and seniority, the kitchen boy salary was
considered a fair wage.

When Annie asked me to interview her friend Fannie, I pointed out that house boy was a man's job. But she assured me that Fannie could handle it, and so I hired her. When I told her I needed to order a uniform for her, I asked what her size was.

She answered, "Foty-fo'."

And she repeated it when I asked her again. She was not a small woman.

Things went very well, and Fannie performed at least as well and probably better than most men. We had an ice maker, and one of Fannie's jobs was to carry buckets of ice across the street to the Zete house. This was a revenue source created by my predecessor, Chuck.

A few weeks later, the Zete cook, who was also president of the local NAACP chapter, reproached me for making Fannie carry the heavy buckets of ice. I pointed out that she had been advised of this before she took the job.

He then asked me, "Would you make your mother do that?"

My honest reply was that, if that was part of the job I had hired her to do, I certainly would. This ended the conversation, and Fanny continued to haul ice to the Zete house.

In my position as finance chairman of the IFC, a fraternity complained that another house had hired away their cook by offering seventy-five dollars a week instead of the customary sixty-five dollars. After concluding we couldn't have that sort of thing going on, I made a motion to set a maximum salary for the position and limit it to sixty-five dollars. The motion passed unanimously. While it seemed like an obvious solution at the time, I don't think it would pass muster today.

The Old U had its reputation as a professional party school for good reason, and even the most dedicated academics were capable of outrageous acts. One night I came across a larger than usual group of revelers in front of the SAE house, and they were surrounding a Charlottesville police car where a mini drama was playing out. Sitting in the back of the car were Alex and Chris, the latter accompanied by a full-grown rooster. A confrontational dialogue was going on between an officer in the front seat and Alex in the back, with Chris carefully explaining everything to the rooster.

Finally, the exasperated officer turned around and began to choke Alex, who responded as the bull-necked Mid-South wrestler he was, "You're the weakest son of a bitch I've ever seen!"

The result was as expected, but Alex and Chris became "Woolly Neck" and "Rooster" thereafter. Yet another scene in the rich, bacchanalian tapestry that stretched back almost a century.

One night Joe and two friends decided to leave a bag of cherry bombs on the front porch of the president's mansion on Carr's Hill. Joe was to run up the hill, light the fuse, return to the getaway car, and disappear into the night. In fact, a U cops car picked that moment to come up behind Joe's special ops vehicle and wave it on. The result was that, after Joe lit the fuse and raced down the hill, he threw himself into the back of the police car just as the cherry bombs exploded in several huge discharges. That famous prank was the last straw, and Joe returned to be in our class after serving two years as a marine.

When the world was rocked on November 22, 1963, everything changed, even in Charlottesville. I had just finished lunch and adjourned to the living room when Sausage Morris announced, "The president's been shot!" The room reacted in disbelief and anger. We all went downstairs and watched Walter Cronkite tell us about the shooting in Dallas and desperately hope that President Kennedy was still alive. But he wasn't. Just writing this takes me back almost sixty years, and my eyes fill with tears when I think about what followed.

That afternoon I went to evensong at St. Paul's, which was packed to overflowing as I had never seen before.

The next morning the Greek community had to decide what to do about Bid Sunday, which was scheduled for the following day. The issue was hotly debated at a hastily convened session of the Interfraternity Council. A passionate vocal minority insisted it would be disrespectful to revel while the slain president's body lay in state at the Capitol. We then learned that Germans Weekend had been canceled at Carolina. In the end, a pragmatic Wahoo majority decided, with sufficient gravity, the president would want us to carry on and that what UNC did had nothing to do with us. As a gesture of solemnity, we determined, after the bid process was complete, parties could be held, just not at the houses.

As a result, our party venue was at the Beta University Circle Apartments, where we drowned our sorrows with the traditional artillery punch–filled trash cans purchased for the occasion.

My last memory is of Henry Warner and several others, clothed in Beta ceremonial robes, hitchhiking along Route 29, headed for the president's funeral the next day.

Monday was spent glued to the tube, with every coherent student watching the most catastrophic event of our lifetimes conclude with the state funeral of the thirty-fifth president of the United States. More than ninety countries sent representatives to the Requiem Mass at St. Matthew's Cathedral, which was followed by interment at Arlington National Cemetery. With the assassination of our country's first Roman Catholic president, a grandson of Irish immigrants, the world entered a period of uncertainty.

At the U, however, it was time to get back to life, which we assumed would continue forever, and off we headed for Thanksgiving break.

# Chapter 14

# Expanding World

While some time was lost to medical distractions, Rush, and the assassination, even with Spanish as an albatross I had to deal with, I believed I would have an enjoyable academic experience this year. In addition to Spanish, for English I'd chosen a two-semester course on novels and American poetry and prose. For electives I chose Christian theology and a two-semester art history course. My principal objective in selecting these courses was they didn't start before 9 a.m. and they were over by 1 p.m., and they sounded like subjects I would enjoy.

In selecting my major, I decided on English with the thought that more people passed English comprehensives than history. At that time the University required both third- and fourth-year comprehensive examinations. Third-year exams were based on the Bible and Greek mythology, since most of English literature is based on those two sources. Fourth-year exams spanned the full body of knowledge one had studied in those two years. I've always liked exams of that sort since they test huge amounts of information at a cursory level. Since I have a gift for retention, but often not in depth, they're my forte. Nonetheless, all of this played a part in my choices.

Something I didn't choose, however, was the letter I received the preceding summer from the Army. My eyesight was not up to the required standard, and so I was not allowed to proceed with advanced ROTC. I immediately appealed the decision, but I did not hear back from the Army until June 1966—a year after I had taken my degree.

At any rate, the Wednesday following the president's funeral, I rode off from Richmond with my cousins Elaine and Melinda, their parents, Uncle Red and Aunt Sam, and their other grandmother, Mimi, to the New Jersey shore.

The trip was to honor my maternal and their paternal grandparents' fiftieth anniversary. It was a splendid time to be with family, and especially all nine members of our generation, who ranged from Elaine and me at twenty down to my godson, Stuart, who was three or four. After dinner, while the older people gathered, the rest of us who were old enough went to see *Lawrence of Arabia* in Asbury Park. We returned to Brook Corners, my grandparents' place, where I packed to reunite with some Beta brothers in Manhattan.

On Saturday the great adventure began when my dad dropped me at the Allenhurst station to catch a train to Penn Station in the city, where I met Katie, a girl out of my past. Between my graduating from Blair and entering Virginia, Katie had come to Pittsburgh from Connecticut, to visit her friend who had just moved to the Steel City. Later I visited her in Connecticut, and it was a forever relationship—until I'd been in Charlottesville for about six weeks. But by five o'clock that afternoon, our relationship was reestablished.

From her friend's uptown apartment, we had gone down to the Sallee family's residence on Fifth Avenue, by Central Park, to meet a half dozen guys who were there. Shep Craige, his date Allison Dwyer, Katie, and I went to the Stork Club for our first visit. It was midafternoon and we were the only people there, except for an elderly gentleman who was having a small birthday luncheon for a granddaughter.

After we ate and were getting ready to leave, the waiter said, "Your check has been taken care of by the gentleman over there."

When we asked who our benefactor was, we learned the older man was Sherman Billingsley, the legendary owner of the club.

From there we went for drinks at the Bull and Bear in the Waldorf Astoria, and then down to the Staten Island Ferry (five cents round trip). It was a frigid ride, and since they'd run out of coffee, we had to drink Irish whiskey directly from the bottle to combat the cold.

While we moved steadily forward throughout the day, it was on that ride that Katie and I realized that forever was back on! By then I was running out of money and my knee, which had slipped out of place while I was getting on the subway that afternoon, was beginning to malfunction. We went to a place in the Village, where she slipped me some cash to make it through. After a cab ride uptown to drop her off, I realized my knee might not make another subway run. So I used the last of my funds to make it back to the Sallees' by taxi.

During the evening, it was established I would come to Connecticut, for New Year's, and Katie would come to Charlottesville for Midwinters. After we said a passionate farewell, I spent the next six hours on the way to Charlottesville in the back of Shriek's car with a throbbing knee. Nevertheless, it was a great road trip.

Since the New York trip came right before Bid Sunday, it was just in time for us to pledge John Sallee, but not for that reason. In addition to his place being a great base camp in New York, John became a classic feature in the house. That year we also pledged Charles "Chuck" Wood, an engineering student from Louisville, who was an outstanding scholar. He went on to become a TILKA, King of the IMPs, and recipient of the coveted Algernon Sydney Sullivan Award. After Virginia he moved to Atlanta and has been a lifelong friend.

Other pledges from that year and the next were Flip Viles from Norman, Oklahoma; Hugh Ilgenfritz from Shreveport, Louisiana; Macy

Wall, a noted polo player from the Pacific Northwest; his polo playing pal, Hunter Smith; Davey Jones; Harold Block; Chris Ellis; Sidney Morris; and Marshall Coleman.

By my fourth year, as I entered fully into University-wide social and political activities, one-on-one relationships with the Beta pledges diminished. One, however, is worthy of special note because he became a beloved brother only after a significant threshold was crossed.

During the blackball process, a name had to pass around the room three times and over three weekly meetings without a ball being dropped in order to receive a bid. It was a long and perilous journey. On the second pass someone said, "But we can't pledge him. He's Jewish!"

Quick as a wink a formidable, respected brother responded, "You dumb ass! Don't you know anything? Can't you tell a Cajun when you see one."

With that, the sought after rushee, whose family owned a department store in southern Louisiana, was pledged. In fact, he was the brother I trusted to escort my younger sister when she came for a Big Weekend from Wells College in Aurora, New York.

After a Christmas season with my family and Bebe, closed out in Connecticut with Katie, I returned to school for my exams.

In the book *From Rebel Yell to Revolution*, Joel Gardner discussed grade inflation. While I certainly spent 80 percent of my college work time in student government and other extracurriculars, his book acquainted me with the reality of grade inflation, which led me to do a little research. I don't know if this is accurate, but some reports estimate that 81 percent of the students at the University of Virginia made A's or B's due to grade inflation. But another study found there was no grade inflation in the 1960s. Between then and now, however, grade inflation has proliferated to such an extent that it borders on the absurd. I don't know what my grades would have been with grade inflation, and it certainly makes no difference to me if everyone's C's are now B's.

I found the first semester of my third year to be extremely reward-ing. I received a C in American poetry and prose, a C+ in the course on novels, a B in Christian theology, a C in Spanish, and a C- in art history. As I mentioned earlier, I particularly liked my chain-smoking Spanish instructor, Señora Blankenship.

While I had as much trouble concentrating on Flemish and Ital-ian names and remembering who had painted what as I did with Spa-nish vocabulary, art history was more interesting to me than Spanish vocabulary. But there were two significant problems with the art his-tory class. First, the class met twice a week from noon until 1:15 p.m. (lunchtime). And second, the instructor was a very nice but drab-looking woman who spoke in a monotone, with absolutely no hint of inflection in her voice, which made the class seem much longer than seventy-five minutes.

I remember once asking Rusty, who also was in the class, "What time is it?"

He said, "It must be about four o'clock."

The two of us had signed up for the course because it was supposed to be a Gut taught by a doddering old teacher who gave only A's and B's (which may have been why he was replaced). Pity.

In addition to the value of learning to distinguish between impres-sionist, traditional, modern, pastoral, etc., students were also required to visit the National Gallery of Art in Washington twice during the se-mester. Road trip!

As my third year moved on, my friendships expanded. By the time I took my degree, I probably had several hundred friends. While I can't go into detail about all of them, I can describe a few, and I'll start with the houses I knew best on Mad Lane. In Phi Gam, Fiji, the first house off University on Mad Lane, there was Bill Schenck, a great guy from Pittsburgh who became president of our class. John Sakalaris was elected to the Student Council from the Engineering School. Charlie

Dunlap was a year behind us, but our paths crossed in unusual circumstances. The same could be said for Lew Haden and Carl Matthews.

Next was St. Elmo, with whom the Betas had an especially strained relationship. But one of the finest people at Virginia was Bill Debutts. Other laudable Elmos included John "Beetle" Bailey, Dick Debutts, and Mike McGehee.

Two other people, both from Mad Lane, ranked among the least admirable in our class. One was a stuffy, little, curly haired fellow, who seemed to look down on others for no good reason. He frequently bragged about throwing away all his jackets, ties, etc. each year because it took too much effort to pack them. He'd just replace them in the fall. The other was a heavy, loud fellow, who drunkenly took off all his clothes at a deb party and stood naked on a lake float and shouted continually. Wild behavior was one thing, but tasteless displays of arrogant privilege were another.

More humorous was the fellow who started to saw off a baby grand piano leg. He was accosted by an ancient house mother who admonished him to stop being so naughty.

"That's all right, Mrs. B," he replied cheerfully. "I'll just buy us another."

As I recall, the piano leg remained intact and attached.

Between St. Elmo and St. Anthony Hall was another great group, Sigma Phi Epsilon (SPE), several brothers of whom made lasting impressions on me, although this didn't happen until my fourth year. Pat McFalls, a Western Pennsylvania Interscholastic Athletic League (WPIAL) football player from Moon Township near Pittsburgh, was one of my best friends and a political helpmate. Dick Carleton became the *CD* editor in chief and a next-door neighbor. Hunter Hughes and I became close through a letter I sent to Longwood, a women's college in Farmville.

St. Anthony Hall was regarded as a haughty and patrician house, but it was actually one of the nicest groups of all. One morning, after a party at the Hall, I woke up with fuzzy vision and no glasses on my bed-side table, an indication I had lost my contact lenses. But there was a contact case nearby. One of the most thoughtful and certainly percep-tive people at the Hall, Pat McSweeney, had realized my contacts were beginning to irritate my eyes. He convinced me to take out my lenses, provided a case, and called to make sure they made it home with me. One nice guy over there had aspirations to be a physician, but he lacked the academic prowess to be admitted to medical school. He applied to Tuskegee in the hope that his race (he was white) would secure a posi-tion in the historically black institution.

George was called St. Anthony, Polo Pony George or Pseudo St. George by the Betas who had been at Woodberry with him. The polo references were real since he was frequently in his riding boots, with a polo mallet over his shoulder.

Jep Doley capably represented his Eli Banana membership status, and his ability to appear fully confident while always demonstrating a caustic wit never ceased to amaze me.

Eastern Shore patrician Emerson Polk Kellam and I found com-mon cause in our fourth year. But that story will come later, since I fol-lowed him as Student Council president.

Other notables at the Hall include Lee Booth, who I met during a first-year trip to the EHS-VES football game; Joe King, an Eli and eventually the head of several entrepreneurial enterprises; Peter Boehm; Bucky Gage, who I got to know better after UVA; George Pet-tiway; and Jack McCauley. George and Jack were part of the Chatta-nooga–Lookout Mountain entourage.

Rounding out the row of Mad Lane fraternities was the venerable Phi Kap house, founded at the University in 1850. Member Ben Ackerly was president of the college and chairman of the Honor Com-mittee. A Richmond native, after law school he returned home and later became a senior partner at a renowned firm. Roz Wentz, whom I met on my first-year trip to VES, was also at the house. He and Donny

Moses were known to team up at the front door at parties. Whenever an unfamiliar girl entered, the two would stare at her, sphinxlike, to see if this unnerved her. Others I particularly remember are Edwin Copenhaver, Cam Bogan, and Charlie Rose.

In addition to meeting some non-Betas in classes, at parties, and through extracurriculars, I also made friends among those who were going down the road. Spending two or three hours in both directions with someone was an excellent way to find out about each other. Some I looked forward to spending more time with, and others I learned to avoid.

There were actually three types of road trip: first class, coach, and economy. Trips to Washington, where the dates were generally from posh women's schools and the entertainment was in Georgetown, were definitely first class. In this group were the art history field trips, individually planned with a few classmates, which began when our dates rendezvoused with us, now all erudite art devotees, for an afternoon at a museum. This was an advantage for me since my dates invariably knew more about art than I. After roaming the galleries for an afternoon, the meter really started when we went to dinner, and then visited some of the capital's most interesting sights. These were great times, but I had a tight budget.

My favorite DC date was Hope, a cousin of Dick Tucker. After an elbow-bending evening, she joined me for the ride back to school in an open car trunk, locked in a passionate embrace as we rode through the streets of Georgetown.

A coach-level road trip was the most common, where the Wahoos rolled together to one of the better-known women's colleges: Sweetbriar (Sweets), Hollins (Hollie Collie), Mary Baldwin (MDC), Randolph Macon (Randy Mac), or Mary Washington (Mary Wash). After we picked up our dates, everyone went to one of the hangouts that thrived near each of those schools. On the way there, we found a major diversion to be attempts to hit road signs with empty beer bottles or cans while we discussed the relative merits of the dates awaiting our arrival.

By my third year, everyone knew who his date would be or her group of friends. The students at both UVA and the women's schools were beginning to know each other just as students at coeducational institutions knew each other. But we had at least one great advantage: if anyone tired of the company of another, there was a significant distance between the two schools that precluded the possibility of having to see the other again. One just switched schools for a while.

After three hours of partying and the rush to get back by curfew, the return trips were quieter. Before leaving the visited campus, there were always a few confrontations with house mothers, security guards, guys from other schools, and occasionally the local constabulary.

For example, there was a one-armed security guard at Sweetbriar who wore a holstered handgun and carried a billy club in his hand. Bob, a Zete, was generally obnoxious, and he always tried to goad the gendarme until the sentry threatened to shoot.

Bob would shout, "Draw, One Arm! Draw!" and laugh.

The security guard would put his stick under his stump, and then he would unclip his holster.

By the time he was done, Bob had moved away and turned to yell, "Next time, One Arm. Next time."

At Mary Baldwin, a Wahoo who later became an attorney of national repute, discovered that public urination was a misdemeanor in Staunton.

While first-class road trips were well-planned in advance, and coach trips were devised by the Wednesday or Thursday before the weekend trip, economy rolls were mostly impromptu weeknight affairs. Occasionally a bar was involved, but more frequently the only necessary equipment was a blanket, cigarettes, and plenty of beer.

Once I was sitting in a backseat with two guys and a girl of questionable reputation. I saw two hands advance slowly up the inside of a pair of legs until they met at the apex. While the two guys were somewhat surprised, the girl laughed heartily.

One night I didn't have a date, so I walked across a campus and asked each reasonably attractive student if she'd like to go out. The third one I asked accepted my invitation. The car was only crowded for a few miles, until we reached a field. We had four blankets, four dates, and plenty of beer.

At another time my date had a plastic cigarette pack holder inscribed "Buy your own, you cheap bastard!"

Economy road trips included trippers such as Woolly Neck, Jep Doley, the Rooster, Fox, and virtually anyone who happened to be standing around at takeoff. After contacting our prospective dates, protocol often included being told, "I don't usually do this sort of thing" or "Just so you know, I don't go all the way!" The answer was always, "I know that! I would never do anything you didn't want to!"

Road tripping was a well-practiced institution on weekends and not infrequently on weeknights. They accounted for many anecdotes I've relived with my brothers over the years. Often overlooked is that these adventures robbed only a little time from most Wahoos' academic and cultural pursuits. In addition to study, weekday evenings on the Grounds also had an overwhelming number of academic and cultural opportunities. There were always concerts, plays, art exhibitions, and club and organizational meetings that represented myriad student interests. In addition, there were as many athletic competitions, both intercollegiate and intramural, as there are species of animals or vegetables. On the national scene, all these activities were dwarfed by Virginia's reputation as a world-class professional party venue.

The largest turnout that winter was not for basketball (our classmate Mac Caldwell was the leading scorer), the glee club, or any other normal collegiate occurrence. The largest turnout was for two lectures in an annual series. George Lincoln Rockwell, founder of the American Nazi Party, and Gus Hall, president of the American Communist Party, two of the most hated people in the country, were invited to speak at Old Cabell Hall.

While both were considered to be nutcases, when legislation was introduced in the Virginia General Assembly to prohibit them from speaking on state property, that action changed these nonevents into a cause célèbre for free speech. Repugnant though each political cause was, political censorship violated Mr. Jefferson's concept of the Academical Village as a place where they could be openly discussed.

I arrived at the auditorium thirty minutes early, but the auditorium was full. Speakers, however, were being set up in a variety of rooms in New Cabell for the overflow crowd.

Rockwell wore a Nazi naval officer's dress uniform when he gave his hate-filled lecture. His audience was scornful but polite, although all their fathers had fought twenty years earlier to eradicate Nazism.

Gus Hall's lecture drew an overflow crowd as well, with the same result. His ideas and his answers to questions seemed absurd to an audience comprised of 100 percent committed capitalists. Some of the questioners were openly skeptical and hostile, as were the audiences, but the remarkable attitude of the University community was on display.

In hindsight, I believe that any concept that violated the traditions and lifestyle of the University population were thought to be so conceptual that they were dealt with in the abstract, as if such things could never occur in Charlottesville.

In early February, the weekend before Midwinters Weekend, something happened that changed my life, although I didn't realize it for several years. St. Paul's Episcopal Church sponsored a kind of soup kitchen. For students who attended the 5:30 service, they offered a fine dinner, prepared by the women of the church, for just fifty cents a plate.

When I entered the church, I saw Ted Hogshire across the aisle, and he was sitting next to an absolutely enchanting young woman.

After the service, as we walked to the dining hall, I asked Teddy, "Who was that girl you were sitting next to?"

"What girl?" he said.

"The one right next to you, dumbass!"

"I don't pay attention to who I'm sitting next to," he said self-righteously.

At any rate, this five-foot-one, ninety-eight-pound medical technology student from Atlanta, Georgia, enraptured me.

After dinner Jack "Foggy" Williams and I took her for a beer at the Rathskeller, until she had to leave for an eight o'clock date. She may have walked out of my sight that night but not out of my mind.

The following weekend was Midwinters. This was Katie's first visit to a University weekend, and it was a major one at that. When I picked her up at the airport, she was filled with the same devotion we shared when I visited Connecticut. But after so many weeks and against the backdrop of Charlottesville, Katie lost the luster she had at Thanksgiving. We still had an incredible time because it's impossible not to enjoy yourself at a Wahoo Big Weekend.

After the Saturday night party at the Beta house, we went down to the Ralph Fraise apartment on the lower level. Around one o'clock Katie wanted to leave, but that wasn't what I had in mind. We left, but since I was both hungry and the kitchen manager, we got something to eat.

Then she said, "Let's go up to your room."

I didn't think this was a good idea for several reasons. But I couldn't possibly refuse like some celibate geek, so we went up.

I left her in my room and took a cold shower, attempting to bounce back after twelve hours of bourbon and fun. When I returned, Katie was ready, but it turned out, either because of her Catholicism or with some ulterior motive in mind, she didn't practice birth control.

This added another concern to my list of worries, and although I did my best, I'm not sure how it wound up, because she awakened me to say someone, or maybe it was several people, had opened the door of the room (I'd forgotten to hang a tie on the doorknob), and she'd slid out of sight between the bed and the wall.

The interloper said, "They's fo' feet in that baid," and I instantly knew that Doug Kincaid (aka the Woog or Wooglin) had been roaming the floor.

After this interruption, Katie departed for her approved housing by cab.

I picked her up the next morning to go to mass at the Newman Center. I was quite impressed with the way the line for confession went down one side of the room. After being absolved, the communicant went across the room to a line to the Communion table. Having some knowledge of what Katie and the confessor might have chatted about, and unable to contain my curiosity, I asked her what he'd said.

"You're old enough to know exactly what you're doing," she said.

After the traditional Sunday brunch at the house, we departed for the airport and bid each other a lengthy adieu. After the plane took off, the story of Katie (part 2) ended as abruptly as it began.

And I determined to find out more about Margaret Ann Craven, the woman who had captured my attention the week before at St. Paul's and the beer garden.

Weekends at Virginia, as I said earlier, and especially the big ones, transformed the houses into a large neighborhood, where everyone was welcomed into everyone's home. By this time the friendships I'd made over the past two and a half years assumed a new dimension, as my thoughts turned to the Scepter Society caucus, which was about six weeks away in April, and I sought a nomination to the Student Council. Happily, I didn't need to assume a false persona because relationships came easily to me, and I certainly didn't do it because I forced myself.

I loved it! Even so, these were the people who would vote, and the real struggle would be getting a nomination. Once that was done, the next job was to canvas the dorms, which was a much easier endeavor for me since many fraternity men wouldn't bother to vote.

# Chapter 15

# Bahamian Sun

Of the many events in the spring of my third year, three stand out: the rise and fall of my relationship with Margaret Ann Craven, my campaign for and subsequent election to the Student Council, and something totally unexpected just before exams.

Several weeks after Midwinters, the Beta house decided to have an off–major weekend party with a combo, so I invited Margaret Ann to join me.

"It's Thursday," she said, "and I already have a date." (She seemed amazed I didn't know that.)

"Who is he?" I asked.

"John Bailey!" she answered.

I didn't know him, so I asked, "Is he in a fraternity?"

"He's an Elmo."

"Do you mean Beetle?"

"His name is John."

Immediately I knew, since the Betas were providing free entertainment, Beetle would be interested. So I asked her to bring him. And they came.

During the evening I danced with Margaret Ann at every opportunity, which caused Beetle to ask her how she knew me.

"He's my friend from church," she said, which caused a great deal of amusement when Beetle told everyone, "Beta is Margaret Ann's friend from *church*!"

The more I saw Margaret Ann, the more I liked her. She was always active and never downbeat. From Atlanta, she had come north via the University of Chattanooga to complete her bachelor's in medical technology at the Medical School.

When I learned that she and Beetle studied together at the library, I started studying at the library and sat next to her, opposite him. Although this increased my library time, my focus was on her.

I brought her to some meals at the Beta house, and she invited me to a party hosted by her Law School friends. Since they were all males and older than I (almost all law students were both at that time), I did not find the party to be relaxing—until Margaret Ann wanted a Coke, and they didn't have any. So I walked down Lewis Mountain Road to the gymnasium to get her one, earning a burst of affection for my chivalry.

And so, when we left for spring break, Margaret Ann was the one for me, and I was one of a number for her.

In the mid-1960s spring break trips to Florida, and particularly the Fort Lauderdale area, were approaching a peak, and for that reason, we chose to go to Nassau. The day we left, Rusty Mather was eligible to get his driver's license back, but the Charlottesville office was closed that day, so he went without.

I had saved $131 for the trip, which was reduced by $5 to pay a parking ticket on the day we left. Margaret Ann accompanied Rusty and me to run an errand, and she stayed to watch the car while we went inside. When we came out and I saw the ticket on the front window, I asked why she hadn't moved the car.

"Oh, I can't drive a stick shift," she responded.

In today's terms, the amount wasn't much, but at the time $5 was almost a day's income for an average college student. Nonetheless, out of that had to come a $28 round-trip ticket, gas, rent, beer, rum, five fifths of duty-free liquor to bring home, everything else, and hopefully enough to last until we returned to Charlottesville.

We knew the currency of Nassau was the British pound and its various denominations, but American dollars could be used just as easily. And it was important to keep track of the exchange rate when using U.S. money to pay for services and items priced in pounds (quids), crowns, shillings, etc., lest the merchant make more on the conversion than the sale.

The first leg of our trip was to Greenville, North Carolina, where Rutledge Young dropped Rusty and me off to ride with George Fitzhugh, who attended East Carolina Teachers College (now known as East Carolina University). Rut continued on to his home in Charleston. George, Rusty, and I arrived there around ten o'clock.

We were warmly greeted and entertained by his parents. His father was a prominent attorney and a councilman, and his mother was a winsome, vivacious lady with a commanding personality. After a late dinner, we resumed the trip.

By this time I'd done more things with Rusty than anyone in my pledge class, with the possible exception of Dick Tucker, a fellow Pittsburgher. In addition to and because of our escapades together, I knew a lot about Rusty's family and especially his father, a captain in the Navy.

As a Harvard (not Annapolis) graduate, Lee Mather recently had been promoted from executive officer at Naval Air Station Oceana to command the aircraft carrier *Wasp*, flagship for the eastern fleet. Thus, for me, the Cuban Missile Crisis, two weeks of tense global fear in October 1962, became much more personal when the captain called Rusty to tell him to take care of his mother and two sisters, should the need arise.

Given that the U.S. fleet was ordered to intercept a Soviet convoy laden with nuclear missiles for Cuba, where they were to be installed less than a hundred miles from the U.S. mainland, it was a sobering call.

"Are you going to Cuba, dad?" Rusty asked.

"You know I can't talk about that," his father said.

"I'm sorry, dad. It was on the front page of the *New York Times*."

"Well, they can talk about it, but I can't," he said.

Fortunately, the crisis ended and everyone returned home—and the missiles never made it to Cuba.

In contrast to my friendship with Rusty, I was just getting to know Lonesome George Fitzhugh, one of the more unusual characters I've ever come across.

Since there was no interstate highway yet, the three of us headed south on Route 17 through the great oaks, pine forests, small towns hugging the often visible railroad, and small clearings along the roadway. Since I had never been east of the Great Smokies and Appalachians or south of Virginia, this was an enchanting journey as we flew across the southern landscape, occasionally catching whiffs of pine in the air.

I snapped out of my reverie as we approached the two-lane suspension bridge on the South Carolina–Georgia border at Savannah. Another Beta car was closing on us rapidly, and we raced to see who would be first to get to the West Palm Beach airport, 423 miles away.

At the apex of the bridge the other car crossed the double yellow line to pass us, and George Gordon "Jerry" Guthrie leaned out to glare at us in triumph. When we exited the bridge in downtown Savannah, we cat and moused each other until we separated. I don't remember who was in the lead, but we didn't see Jerry again until we were at the airport.

The next eye-opener occurred at about dawn, in southern Georgia, as we approached a fork in the highway at about 80 mph. Lonesome was driving, and without slowing down, he asked Rusty, "Do you think we should go right or left?"

"Left, partner," Rusty calmly replied while we hurdled toward certain death in the middle of the road.

We barely made the left turn, and Rusty calmly commented, "Close call!"

Almost immediately George pulled over and said, "Take over. When my friends begin to worry, it's time to let them drive."

It was then I began to take more seriously that George had suffered a frontal lobotomy in a serious auto accident, which had altered his ability to evaluate driving situations.

When we passed east of Jacksonville early that morning, the smell of smoke reminded us of reports there was civil unrest in some cities, inspired by outside agitators. A few miles later both the smells and the thoughts were gone, and we continued southward along Florida's east coast.

Hours later we reached Fort Pierce, where Bill Tylander's parents gave us lunch. Bill had been my roommate the year before, but now he was on a two-year stint in the Navy.

From Fort Pierce we completed the final hour of the trip, arriving at the West Palm airport with about an hour to spare before our flight—plenty of time in the pre–security check era.

Since the Bahamas were a British Crown colony, as a foreign country, they could refuse entry to anyone they chose, and because the student infestation was beginning to inundate Fort Lauderdale, they might well close the country. Which was why we chose to fly out from the smaller airport in South Florida. To avoid detention, we changed into coats and ties in order to pass muster. While an enormous percentage of air travelers today are dressed to blend in with the homeless, such was not the case in 1964. We'd also rehearsed our answers to the questions that would be asked of us by Her Majesty's customs agents. Thus prepared, we were approved for admittance, boarded the airplane for the thirty-minute flight, and disembarked in Nassau.

Once we arrived downtown on Bay Street, Rutledge showed, once again, why he was a leader. While the others were packed like sardines into motel and hotel rooms, Rutledge had reserved an apartment off the main drag with three bedrooms, a living room, and a refrigerator for us (Rusty, George, me, and himself). While renting them for a week was undoubtedly a good deal for the landlord, for us it was a fraction of what the others were paying for far less. After we deposited our stuff, we headed out to explore the many nightspots on Bay Street.

While there weren't as many students in Nassau as Fort Lauderdale, there were plenty. We wore what we always did to parties: coats and ties and, as a concession to Nassau, shorts (no socks of course). This apparel had many distinct advantages. Primarily it set us apart from the others, not just for the bar owners and bouncers, but also for the girls, especially the State U-ers. Most important, we kept several cases of beer on ice at all times, and since the establishments were always crowded and the waitresses were greatly overworked, we entered each tavern with a bottle in each back pocket, which gave us two to start while we waited for our orders.

On our first night we worked our way from place to place, relishing the overwhelming number of coeds who were always ready to dance while looking for a longer relationship (like a real date).

Directly across the street from our apartment, in an old three-story, one-apartment-per-floor-wide building was a movie theater, and next door, at the corner of Bay Street, was the Tropicana Diner. To economize, I started each morning with a bowl of conch chowder and conch fritters at the diner. Then, before we went out at night, whenever I began to feel my sunburn, I would have a bag of popcorn from the theater, an Excedrin compound (which I had saved from my knee operation recovery), and a few beers.

Since there was no bridge across the narrow bay to Paradise Island at the time, and no hotels or restaurants on it, access was by a launch for a dollar a head. Once deposited on the island, we followed a sandy route several hundred yards to the beach, which offered spectacular azure waters sprinkled with flecks of sunshine. There were several well-populated counters selling beer and lethal rum-based drinks.

The island was perfectly named: Paradise. For someone who'd spent much of his summer life on beaches but never farther south than Virginia, the Bahamian beaches were beyond anything my imagination could conjure. Here we found absolute freedom in absolute charm amid absolute beauty with limitless girls and bottomless adult beverages!

In the midafternoon we returned to Nassau and explored the waterfront's shops, galleries, and fascinating straw market. The Bahamian vendors spoke in a lovely dialect of British English tempered with African roots. I especially noticed the exceedingly polite colonial policemen, clad in white pith helmets, red-trimmed tunics, and shorts. Some were ensconced on platforms in the middle of intersections and directed traffic.

When we reached the hallowed British Colonial Hotel, we toured the lobby and pool areas, and then retraced our steps to our lodgings in time for happy hour. We noticed a public beach next to the hotel that, while it was on the bay and not the ocean, was easier to access—and free. We spent about an hour back at our digs before repeating the explorations of the previous night.

Each morning we asked Lonesome George to join us at the beach, but he always replied, "Old Redeye will get me."

The only time George went out was after "old Redeye" (the sun) had gone down, and he was home by the time it came up again!

On our second night we added a new spot to our agenda, the Yellow Bird, which was over the hill and in the Bahamian section of the city. Although none of us ever thought of it, in hindsight it was another sad irony of the era. We could go to predominantly nonwhite nightspots, but the residents were never allowed to set foot in ours, other than as servants. That said, the Bahamian sector was a great place. We felt welcomed and added it to our evenings thereafter.

The next day we went back to Paradise Island, but instead of the dollar-a-head launch, the resourceful Rutledge led us to the marina, where we found a Bahamian who gladly rowed all three of us to the island (and back) for a dollar. We scheduled our return early for the afternoon. After all, sunning on the beach wasn't why we were there.

Later that afternoon, while I was walking through a restaurant, a very attractive coed said, "I'm glad you found me! What time do you want to go?"

Immediately I understood she was trying to ditch the lecher who'd intruded on the girl and her two friends, who were trying to eat.

"I'm sorry I'm late," I said. "Let's go now!"

I chatted with the girls for a while, but there was no attraction. They were attended a large state university, and we had nothing in common. So we parted ways.

In our building, the other apartment had been rented by three personable and attractive coeds. Late one morning, before heading out, all of us were having beers together.

One of the girls said, "I really would like to go on the glass bottom boat. Anyone want to go with me?"

After an awkward silence, I said I'd go. And off we went.

It turned out to be a memorable experience, and both of us enjoyed the gorgeous coral reefs and the abundance of multicolored fish and plants. By the late afternoon what had begun as an act of chivalry was a highlight of the trip and more meaningful than all the days on Bay Street.

The next afternoon we took rum and juice to the public beach. We were soon joined by a group of girls, some of whom were from Staunton's Mary Baldwin College.

Almost immediately a Bahamian joined our little get-together. And after a few minutes he turned to Courtney, one of the girls (I think she was from Greenwood, Mississippi) and asked her if she wanted him to show her what Nassau was really like.

Suddenly there was absolute silence. He had crossed the race line. Courtney was as still as if a cobra had suddenly loomed up in our midst.

"Hey, man!" I said as good naturedly as I could. "She's already taken. She's *my* girl."

Since that was a language he could understand, he smiled and said, "Sorry, mon!"

From that point on, Courtney and I were a twosome.

Having a regular date made a big difference on the last few days of our time in the Bahamas. After my usual dinner of popcorn, Excedrin, and beer, I'd pick up Courtney and head for our favorite bar on the beach. From ten o'clock until around five, we alternated between dancing, drinking, smoking, and making out (mostly on the beach).

At one point a flashlight beamed down on us on the beach. A polite policeman asked a few questions, and then said, "Have a pleasant evening." Since there appeared to be as many or more couples on the beach at night as there were during the day, the officer picked his way through the crowd, apparently keeping everyone safe.

On Easter Sunday morning, as I headed back to our apartment at sunrise, a remarkable sight unfolded at the water's edge. Amid a crowd of believers celebrating the resurrection was a black-gowned preacher baptizing a number of white-garbed new believers in the shallow waters. I thought it was a perfect ending to an eventful week and the beginning of what would be a memorable Sabbath.

Courtney and I were both Episcopalians, and we had agreed to meet at the Anglican cathedral for the eleven o'clock service. I arrived a little late because, after a panicked search for my wallet, I remembered I had hidden it under the mattress. Courtney was already seated and looked absolutely angelic, with her raven-colored hair cascading over a perfect white outfit.

The liturgy, with the exception of singing "God Save the Queen," was the same we had experienced all our lives. But it seemed more exotic here—until the spell was broken.

As we were leaving, the droll man in front of us remarked to his companion, "Well, then, that's it for another year. Now off for a martini."

That sounded like a good idea to us, so we strolled around the British Colonial in our Easter finery as if we were guests. We even encountered some friends of my parents who seemed a little surprised to see me there with a date. Afterward I escorted Courtney back to her place to gear up for a grand finale afternoon and evening, before we departed the next day.

Upon our return stateside the next afternoon, we each carried four fifths of duty-free liquor and piled into our car. We headed south to see what the Fort Lauderdale scene looked like. As we meandered through throngs of out-of-control college students (mingled with police, auxiliary police, and firemen pressed into duty), we were immediately impressed with how wonderful it had been in quaint colonial Nassau.

Rusty knew where some Sweetbriar girls were staying, and as soon as they opened the door, someone shouted, "The Virginia boys are here!"

We entered a living room populated with sunbaked revelers, including a group of Yalies, who, after a few moments of sniffing us out, determined we were some good guys with a few amazing stories.

One of the Elis was wearing the pajamas he'd been bagged in during a recent police roundup. On his way to the lockup, the paddy wagon had passed a fire that was becoming more than the fire brigade could handle, since their numbers had been thinned by the impressment of many of their brothers as auxiliary gendarmes. So the wagon was stopped and everyone was unloaded and directed to help with the big hoses.

When the conflagration was almost subdued, the pajama boy, perceptive scholar that he was, realized there were more attractive options open to him than winding up back in the paddy wagon. So he deserted his post and disappeared into the confusion.

After hearing his story, I was thankful we'd opted for Nassau, with its charming colonial mystique, and not the sprawling Florida coastal community, which was under a heavy-handed brand of martial law.

A little later Rusty and I and two girls went to a bedroom, far from the madding crowd. But don't get the wrong idea. While such liaisons became strenuously passionate, there were basic rules of decorum, including boundaries that would not be violated. When I think about it, I can still hear the words "Be sweet, Rusty!" being murmured repetitiously in the dark room.

After about an hour, my companion, apparently thinking her boundaries were in danger of being breached, said, "I think you'd better go now."

The Virginia boys started the eighteen-hour trip to Charlottesville around one o'clock that morning. I volunteered to drive, but after an hour or so my eyes were drooping so badly that I woke up George. He grumpily took the wheel, and Rusty took over when George tired.

Several hours into the trip, while speeding past a small town in Georgia (or maybe it was South Carolina), we noticed a police car parked perpendicular to the highway. We hoped we'd not been noticed, but there was no escape. Minutes later George and I were sitting quietly in the car while Rusty conferenced with the sheriff in the squad car.

I pondered our immediate future, which I understood as either spending time in the jailhouse until the Betas raised enough cash to get us out or winding up on a chain gang.

Suddenly Rusty and the lawman emerged from the cruiser, and the latter said in a deep drawl, "Y'all couldn't raise enough money to pay all the fines for all the charges I could throw at you. Boys, would it be too much to ask for a *licensed* driver *with* shoes on to drive until y'all are out of my county?"

We all readily agreed to the plea bargain, and George got behind the wheel. As we were preparing to get back on the highway, a black Cadillac with New York plates sped by. Almost immediately our benefactor, red light flashing and siren wailing, took off in hot pursuit. None of us doubted that the sheriff's kindness to us would be offset by the fate of that hapless soul.

Rusty told us he had assured his newest friend that we were nice southern boys who had been furthering our education in Nassau. And in no way had we been part of the riffraff that had taken over Fort Lauderdale.

The rest of the trip proceeded without incident. We dropped Lonesome George and his car off in Greenville, at ECTC. Rutledge picked us up, and we arrived back at 180 Rugby Road sometime after dark.

Shortly after we unloaded, a carload of girls pulled up—Courtney and her friends were on their way back to MBC in Staunton. While Courtney and I had a friendly chat, it was apparent that our odyssey in paradise was over. She transferred to Ole Miss at semester's end. And my attention and zeal turned to the upcoming Student Council nominations and elections—and the pursuit of Margaret Ann Craven.

# Chapter 16

# Politicking

After getting back from spring break in early April, I entered an action-packed extracurricular period with Easters Weekend, which began on Thursday, April 9, and ended on Sunday, April 12, and was followed by the requirement published in *The Cavalier Daily* that all Student Council candidates had to submit their qualifications to the *CD* office by 2 p.m. on the Monday after Easters and meet with the president of their political party (in my case, Bill Schenck of Scepter Society) by 7:30 that same evening. After that, at 9 p.m. the following Wednesday, the two parties (the other being Skull and Keys, with Jim Hargroves, a Zete, as president) would caucus to pick four candidates each. The election was scheduled for April 29.

Since this was my second time around, I was more savvy than the first time and had a little more name recognition. Nonetheless, with thirty-one fraternities and countless individual relationships, politicking is a form of chaos theory, with so many variables to predict the outcome.

The April 9 edition of the newspaper had several articles that presaged changes in the University that were not particularly noted as such at the time. For example, "Before revising the [Rush] Rules, Bob Harris,

President of the IFC, emphasized that Easters parties would be closed." The writer reported that fraternity presidents would be responsible for controlling their parties and for keeping out unwanted guests. It also reported the IFC had sent letters to neighboring schools to notify them of this, and the dean of students (Mr. Runk) had similarly informed deans of those schools. Notice that the student organization made the decision, not the administration, but the two worked hand in hand.

While some people were unfortunately turned away, as someone who'd stood in his own house in a packed room, hoping to see one of my own brothers, it was a necessary act of self-preservation. The alteration in the Rush rules rescheduled the formal Rush Week as November 30 through Bid Sunday, December 6, with October 14 as the first day invitations could be given for parties after the October 17 Army game.

The article also mentioned that most fraternity presidents and Rush chairmen attended the meeting with the house IFC representatives, because nothing was more essential to the University community than the well-being of the Greek community.

Another *CD* article announced "Withholding Grades No Longer Allowed: Student Council Comments on University Policy Change." The meeting was highlighted by a long and concerned discussion on the ramifications of the University's decision that the Registrar's Office would no longer withhold certification of grades of students who had not paid their private debts.

While the practice may seem archaic compared to current practices, at the time it was self-evident that a gentleman who didn't pay his debts was not a gentleman, and the University was acting in the common good. Any merchant or fraternity who believed a debt was due or overdue simply had to notify the registrar, and the individual's grades would be withheld until the matter was settled. The overall message to Charlottesville merchants was that anyone with a student ID was acceptable as a customer. When I posted overdue kitchen bills, in addition to brotherly love, I knew all accounts would be paid in full.

But many feared this new University policy would have ruinous effects. In hindsight, it was an early tear in the fabric of trust that covered commercial dealings at the Old U.

Almost a month later, a *CD* article on May 7 reported that an alternative had been worked out by the Student Council, the IFC, and Dean Runk to resume the practice of withholding grades with other creditor protections added. As I came to see later, although Dean Runk was often maligned as an autocrat, he was a firewall that kept student traditions safe.

Although there were slight portents of future changes, student independence remained fairly inviolate. For example, a much-heralded meeting to review a plan for a fraternity complex of spacious new houses in Lambeth Field and adjacent properties was held in early April in Newcomb Hall. The architectural design was to be submitted as a fourth-year project for teams of students, with a prize going the one chosen to be followed.

The plan, however, was almost universally rejected, but not for architectural reasons. The reasoning was that, no matter how fine the new houses and terms of occupancy might be, the end result was ensnarement by the administration. A classmate opined, "Better an old house with maintenance issues than a new one in a prison compound." As of this writing, almost all the houses of the 1960s—with some renovations—are still where they were.

The next Big Weekend after our return from spring break was the spring football game—and Margaret Ann was going with *me*. We ate our meals together at the Beta house and studied and spent time together, which went a long way in convincing me that ours was a mutual emotional relationship. Friday night of the weekend was incredible for me as the date of this Georgia Peach, who was devoting her full attention to me. At the game on Saturday we went through half a fifth of 151-proof Bacardi rum, went to dinner with friends, and partied at the house. We visited the DU house, which amused her. She thought we were there for political purposes, since I'd never been inside before, and we were warmly received.

Near midnight we had a serious conversation on the stairs of the house, and Margaret Ann announced she could never be serious with someone who didn't have a plan for his life. Of course, I assured her I did, and the music kept playing.

Margaret Ann was an incredible dancer, with indefatigable energy, and she was still going strong when the party ended and I was spent. I escorted her to her dorm, Mary Mumford, and when we were challenged by the security guard, she dismissed him with an almost imperious attitude by pointing out it was cold outside and telling him we were going into the parlor. There, I realized Margaret Ann thought of me as the only man who existed.

The next day, after church, lunch, and time together, Margaret Ann told me we couldn't have dinner that night because she had promised to attend a women's group thing that would tie her up all evening. So I went back to my room, still on cloud nine, while visions of my heart-throb danced in my head.

All of this was dashed to pieces around eight o'clock that night when the brother least suited to deliver this message gently—George Gordon "Jerry" Guthrie—bounded up the stairs and burst into my room.

"Boy, your date sure thought a lot of you!" he said. "She's down at The Cavalier with Beetle Bailey!"

Inwardly roiling in disbelief, I responded, "Yeah, I had a lot of work to do."

But as soon as he was gone, I hastened to the establishment to assure myself he'd invented the story. Instead, I saw Margaret Ann there, sitting in a booth with Beetle, a pitcher of beer between them. The scene is still etched in my memory.

In some kind of shock, I declined the proprietor's happy greeting with a full mug extended from his beefy arm and entered the darkness, a kaleidoscope of emotions whirling within me: fury, despair, desire, betrayal, and an urge to strike a blow. Most infuriating was that Margaret Ann was impervious to anything I said, because it had become increasingly apparent that the most important man in her life was the one she was sitting opposite from.

The striking irony that didn't occur to me at the time was that I'd been beaten in the game I'd often played against others by someone with such spectacular skill that I was but a rank amateur in comparison. Rather than try to make my case again, my ego decided I'd never call or speak to Margaret Ann Craven again.

The episode's sole redeeming grace was that it removed an enormous preoccupation from my life and permitted me to devote all my energies to school and the upcoming campaign. At the Beta house, Margaret Ann ceased to exist, as was the case when a brother had been the victim of a severe dumping. Even Jerry Guthrie left it alone.

Easters Weekend was suddenly upon us in all its glory: the Ribbon Society marches on Thursday night, with my pledge brother John Verity being one of the TILKA inductees, as well as Polk Kellam (soon to be elected fall president of the Student Council), Dave Call, Hunter Hughes, and Mac Lafferty. Also chosen was an old Blair schoolmate, Bill Mahood, who had yet to speak to me since I arrived in Charlottesville the year after he did. Two Eli Bananas were tapped who would become close friends the next year: Alex Wells and Joe Brown. But other than Verity, I didn't pay much attention other than when the march appeared at our house to tap him.

A lead *CD* article announced each new member, accompanied by a three-column picture with the caption: "Eli Tap, of the drum led, colorfully robed group on their way to becoming totally wasted." Eli Bananas were mainly known for their antics, while TILKAs were chosen for their contributions to the University as well as their ability to march.

Saturday's *CD* banner headline announced "University Staggers Under Mass Feminine Invasion: Easters Ribaldry Begins with Exuberant

Bang: Dance, Fraternity Combo Parties: Commence Weekend Merry-making." The article noted that Easters Weekend, founded in 1830, kicked off with a dance, the Thornton Sisters, and numerous fraternity parties.

On Saturday the weekend gala gained momentum with a concert featuring Josh White and the Phoenix Singers, several sporting events, and more fraternity parties. Johns Hopkins and Virginia, both undefeated and ranked fourth and fifth nationally (respectively) the year before would play each other, while Princeton, Notre Dame, Virginia, and Duke competed in the Commonwealth Cup Rugby Tournament. That spring Virginia had beaten the Blue Devils by an astounding margin to win the ACC lacrosse championship. The *CD* article noted gleefully that the score had started 1-1 and the Dukies should've stopped there. The Cavaliers went on to score 20 points and finished the competition 21-1. Since then, while most things have changed exponentially, the joy in trouncing the arrogant forces from Durham remains as pleasurable and satisfying as ever!

Also on page one was an article about the University magazine, noting "a wide range of literary genre and subject matters are in store for the reader of the Easters issue." Of particular interest was an article about economics professor G. Warren Nutter's recent article in *US News and World Report* and his debunking of the myth perpetuated by a Princeton study that Russian industrial strength was on a par with the United States. While this and several other stories were of great interest, nothing was more newsworthy than Easters Weekend.

While the weekend was magnificent as always, the following Monday's start of the official campaign season (and the deflation of my experience with Margaret Ann) made it less significant to me than others, except for visiting as many houses as possible to increase my name recognition.

The closed parties had two unexpected consequences. The first was that I had several friends from home who I didn't think knew I existed, that is, until someone said, "John Doe at the door says he's a good friend of yours. Can we let him in?"

I always said yes.

One person I was very glad to see was my old friend and Hot Springs neighbor Jackie Snead, a student at Bridgewater.

The other was when several Quantico Marine candidate officers were asked to leave the house, and one of them decided to take a girl from our party with him. He had one arm pulling her out the front door while I pulled on her other arm. It was very comforting to have University Police officer (and friend) Junior Gardner there to tell the Marine to leave without the girl.

In addition to being certain I wouldn't have to tangle with a Marine, I wasn't too sure she wouldn't have gone with him if Officer Gardner had not prevented it.

While I was concentrating on the Student Council race, it was by no means the only thing happening. April was the month in which classmates and some rising third years were chosen for every leadership position at the University for the coming year, and all but a couple would come from ten to twelve of the thirty-one fraternities.

The University Union was to be headed by Will Montague (president) and Pat Claggett (both KAs), Mike Collora, and my pledge brother Bob Greenwood.

The Raven Society was a group of outstanding scholars with broad interests, and they named Lucien Bass as president and elected forty-six new members from every school in the University, with nine from the undergraduate college, including Ted Hogshire.

The yearbook *Corks and Curls* named Bill Shenck (who also became a Raven) editor in chief, with third-year men Charlie Dunlop (a Phi Gam) and Strother Randolph (Deke).

Also active and in the news was the Virginia Players' spring production and participants, the symphony orchestra, the Glee Club, and many other vital parties of the great University. All of these, to a large extent, were removed from the world in which I lived.

On Wednesday, April 15, each of the two political societies caucused with an unusually high total of twenty-one candidates, seven each for Student Council, and the balance for the Judiciary Committee. At the conclusion of the meeting, I was one of the four nominated by Scepter, while dear friends and pledge brothers, Rutledge Young and John Verity, were picked by the other group to run for the Student Council and the Judiciary Committee. The eight Student Council candidates were joined by a ninth, Daryl Crown, who was an independent, a nonfraternity man, who had completed the arduous task of collecting enough signatures (I believe 20 percent of all eligible voters in his school).

The *CD* reported the GOP Club picked its officers for 1965 ("Redfield Elected in Clean Sweep"). At the Scepter meeting, the Young Republicans delegation made several proposals relating to procedures governing student life. I knew nothing about the group or their proposals, but that was soon to change.

The next day came the announcement that twenty-one had been tapped by Omicron Kappa Delta (ODK, a national honor society), with twelve from the undergraduate ranks, including Ben Ackerly (president of the college and Honor Committee chair), Bill Shenck, and four-years Sherrell Aston, Bill Hobbs (president of the Beta house), and Terry Sieg. From the Commerce School were Pat Vaughn and Vic Bell, and the Engineering School added Mac Lafferty and John Sakallaris. These were all people I knew or would get to know who, along with the Ravens, had achieved an amazing collection of academic distinctions, including Phi Beta Kappa.

It is fascinating to realize that all of the people I've mentioned—political candidates, academic society participants, student organization leaders, and many athletes—were members of fraternities, so that almost everything was controlled by a very small group. Since Beta was represented in that group, in spite of having a 2.20 GPA the prior semester and a 1.82 cumulative, I was a Student Council candidate along with a few others whose GPA's were much better.

In fact, someone said to me, "I'm voting for you because you're the only one running who's not on the dean's list."

Immediately after I was nominated, Robert Redfield introduced himself. He was a diminutive but purposeful man in a white shirt, conservative tie, and blue suit, and he'd recently been elected president of the Young Republicans. This was a fairly large group that existed within the University community, but since they operated in their own world of political intrigue, they viewed the election as a project. Redfield was a clever and astute behind-the-scenes operative, and he proposed sponsoring local radio spots for me and the Scepter Student Council candidates, since all the Charlottesville DJs, he claimed, were under GOP Club control. He added that his legal group had thoroughly explored the campaign finance rules, and since no funds were to be expended, this was legitimate and well within the rules.

In return, Redfield asked me to be their co-membership chairman, whose only job was to man their booth on Activities Day at orientation, which was also perfectly okay since it was a recognized student organization. Redfield had other practical advice to offer, the most valuable being to urge the Scepter nominates to run together with a platform, which we did.

After Redfield said I needed to raise the Republican banner in Senator Robert Byrd's Democrat Commonwealth, I accepted the position and the counseling.

Several nights later I received an unexpected invitation to dinner from the linchpins of Beta's small contingent of intellectuals, Tucker and Malcolm Scully, who lived with several other students in a cottage on a farm.

As we drove out Route 250 past Crozet, the beauty of the rolling hills was striking, especially to someone who almost never left Charlottesville except after dark, for road trips. We turned off the highway and traveled the dirt road to their lodging, where I enjoyed some lively banter and dinner with the occupants.

Then they came to the point of the visit, which was to prevent me from throwing my life away by pursuing the meaningless course of student government instead of the significant talents they believed were mine as a writer and academic. They offered to let me move in with them in order to redirect my path.

The expression of deep concern and conviction, coupled with their recognition of capabilities no one else had mentioned, moved me deeply and I agreed to consider it. Nonetheless, probably out of a need to prove I could achieve success as a long shot, as we returned to Charlottesville, I asked to be dropped off at the Emmet Street Dorms. By choosing to spend the rest of the evening canvassing first-year men for votes, I crossed my Rubicon.

The thirteen days between the caucuses and elections produced almost daily lead articles in the *CD*, now headed by recently elevated editor in chief Dick Carlton, who injected a sense of urgency into not only the elections but other Grounds activities. It was his start to an outstanding tenure.

Each day the paper published the views of three Student Council candidates (presenting the aspirants in alphabetical order) as well as reported the results of a candidate forum devised and moderated by the editor in chief. To summarize it all, there was only one thing on which there was unanimity: maintaining the all-male nature of the University. When the Student Council was first formed in 1930 (some said reestablished) as the Student Senate and Assembly, "Its immediate purpose was to oppose the Virginia Senate's move to establish a women's college at the University." To even think of opposing this basic maxim (no one did) was unimaginable.

In both the individual presentations and in the *CD* Forum, which also was broadcast on the University radio station, each member of the Scepter group stressed he stood firmly behind a seven-point platform. In contrast, each of the Skull and Keys contestants proclaimed the Scepter platform to be a political ploy. One opponent went so far as to exaggerate the Scepter platform promised everything but beer in the Coke machines.

In fact, the platform was a well-devised package that included (after no women) an advisory group comprised of Alderman Road Dormitory residents, more monitoring of student activities funds, cancelling the penalty for class absence preceding and following vacations, more transparency in communication between the Student Council and the student body, and the exploration of allowing female visitors and dates into the living room areas of first-year dormitories for several hours after home football games.

*The Cavalier Daily* observed the biggest difference between the two groups was whether or not the Scepter platform was valid.

On Election Day, April 29, I woke up with a stomachache and headed over to student health, where a doctor asked, "Aren't you a candidate for Student Council today?"

His diagnosis was that I had a nervous stomach.

After that I went alone to a movie to distract me from thinking about the election. Later than evening I heard the news that Scepter had taken three of the four seats on the council, with the independent (Daryl Crown) winning the other.

Out of 1183 votes cast in the College of Arts and Sciences, I had come in first with 512, followed by Daryl Crown at 511, Jim Gilwey at 511, and Tim West at 497. Pledge brother Jon Verity, in addition to being the incoming chairman of the Alderman Road Dorms, had won a seat on the Judiciary Committee. The only disparate note was that Rutledge, with 496 votes, had led Skull and Keys but missed by one vote being with me on the council.

The person who most disparaged the Scepter platform came in last, with 288 votes, which shows that people are much more apt to vote for stated objectives than for those who mock them and have no alternatives.

It also occurred to me that Robert Redfield had known what he was talking about!

# Chapter 17

# The Misstep

For me, the period after the elections was anticlimactic. After a day or two of notoriety, with the spotlight on me, life continued on the Grounds, with the final leadership positions to be decided for the following year and other important decisions pending before the Student Council, such as creating the first student medical insurance plan, inviting prominent speakers (such as Averill Harriman) to address international events, and a host of other issues. Since I had ignored all other activities for the sake of my campaign, I was now without daily extracurriculars until the fall.

In addition to the Student Council election, I had been elected vice president of Beta. The other offices went to Rutledge (president), Ted Hogshire (secretary), and Rusty (treasurer). And the time-consuming job of kitchen manager passed to Bill Abbuehl.

I resolved to concentrate on my studies, which had been in abeyance for a while. And because I needed to restore some of my depleted spending money (and I enjoyed the work), I increased my hours as an orderly at the hospital to three days a week, on the 3:00–11:30 p.m. shift.

For the rest of the semester I saw Margaret Ann only once, and that was when we passed each other in a Newcomb Hall corridor. My heart leaped at the sight of her, but I resolved to remain dispassionate and aloof.

She said, "Hey, Frank!" in a friendly tone, possibly with a questioning air.

I replied, "Hey," in what I hoped was a nonchalant manner. Better a damaged heart than a subdued ego. I also had a mouthful of tobacco juice (chewing tobacco was a fad at the time), and I was needing to expectorate, which would have made extended conversation difficult.

At the hospital, after having started in urology and proctology, where I did twelve to fifteen enemas a night, I decided there might be more varied work in some other department. Since the orderly turnover was high, my seniority was enough to transfer more than once. After trying a few areas, I settled quite happily on the third floor in thoracic surgery under the supervision of Nurse Jane Triplett.

The medical divisions at UVA formed a small homogeneous community quite different from today. For one thing, white males were doctors, residents, interns, or student orderlies, while their female and racial counterparts served as RN's, LPN's, student nurses, technicians, and secretaries. African Americans were orderlies, aides, and janitors. The thought that it might be any different never seemed to occur to anyone, and relations between the sexes and races were not antagonistic in any way.

I found there was always plenty to eat, since not all the patients could have their plates, and the pantries were stocked with snacks, juices, and Cokes. The late afternoon was usually busy, but there was always time to study in the evening.

The going pay rate was $1 an hour for the harder tasks, but not many students liked the tasks of an orderly. Overall, things appeared they would remain static until June, when I'd take the semester exams and go home for a summer of construction work and pastimes.

Everything, however, changed abruptly one Saturday afternoon in late May, shortly before exams.

The last social event for the year at the Beta house was the annual hayride, which was scheduled for the second Saturday before final exams. I had previously invited Margaret Ann to the weekend, but since that had fallen through, I couldn't think of anyone I wanted to go with. So, I decided to go stag and study later.

The last thing I remember was talking to Dean, a potential rushee, before I fell back, with nothing to hold on to. I landed on a ledge, apparently bounced off it, and found myself looking up ten or twelve feet to where I'd been. I was in a strange, dreamlike state, where I had the additional vantage point of watching myself from the outside, aware that people were around me but not knowing who they were.

Since my chest felt crushed and my mouth was full of blood, I assumed I'd punctured something serious and might die. I asked for an Episcopal clergyman to say last rites. After a while the Albemarle County rescue squad appeared, and I was taken away by stretcher. The only thing I clearly remember was the look of disappointment on Rusty's face when they relieved him as a stretcher bearer.

I later learned Caroline Edwards, a nursing student and Ted Hogshire's date, probably saved me from being paralyzed by taking charge and requiring that I not be moved. The ride to the hospital is a dim recollection, but lying on the x-ray table for what seemed like forever in severe discomfort remains a vivid memory. The next few days were something of a blur, with lots of unpleasant medical procedures.

The initial findings were a broken sternum, a dislocated clavicle, badly damaged or cracked ribs, the loss of three front teeth, seventy-six stitches running up from my forehead through my scalp, and numerous purple bruises.

Near the end of the evening shift, I was wheeled to a room, and my first happy experience since the accident occurred. Since my injuries all seemed to be torso related, the doctors decided I should be placed in thoracic surgery. There I entered the caring ministrations of my hospital family and Nurse Triplett. While there would be some harrowing, unpleasant, and demeaning procedures over the first days and weeks, at least they were done at the hands of my friends on Three East or they were with me whenever I was transported to another treatment location.

The Monday after the accident, visitors began to arrive, mostly Betas, which raised my spirits considerably. While there were early attempts at visitation rules and crowd control, they were generally overlooked, probably because the staff enjoyed being part of an ongoing fraternity party.

It was, however, disheartening for my mom to arrive at my bedside after a seven-hour trip to be with her battered eldest son and be welcomed by a group laughing at the humorous aspects of the incident. The first person to greet her was Leonard Cox.

He said, "Hi, Mrs. Briggs. Sorry about Frank. Sure, did put a damper on the hayride."

Mom said something like, "Thank you, Leonard. I'm sorry it disturbed your party."

I don't blame her for her sarcasm, but I think what most disturbed her was that I didn't seem to be particularly distressed about my predicament. She left the next day, assured that I was well taken care of.

As the week progressed, however, after short times of standing, I mentioned that my legs had a tingly sensation. The resident disregarded this as whining, but Nurse Triplett told a resident in radiology about the tingling in my legs. He took a look and found a hairline fracture of two thoracic vertebrae. I was placed on total bed rest and hyperextended (my body was placed in an arched position) so the injured vertebrae would fuse correctly. The alternative would have been traction, but it was feared that procedure would pull apart the broken bones in my chest. I suspect today the injury could be repaired with simple surgery.

The first resident, an SAE, and I formed a mutual distaste for each other.

I asked him, "I thought you said I had to get up more often."

When he ignored me, I asked, "How am I supposed eat and swallow up?"

"You'll learn," he said and left the room.

Since I faced the prospect of learning how to eat that way and realized my hospital stay might last several months, I resolved to make the most of it.

After it had been determined I had vertebral fractures, there was a move to transfer me to the fifth-floor, neurosurgery and orthopedics. Since I didn't want to leave the familiarity of thoracic surgery and people I knew and had worked with (and they wanted to keep me), the transfer was nixed, and life settled into a routine after one last necessary event.

Since I had not taken my semester exams, I was offered the choice to take them in the hospital or later, in the fall, before the next semester began. While the option to defer seemed to be a no-brainer on most of them, the thought of trying to remember Spanish vocabulary all summer seemed unimaginable.

As a result, Señora Blankenship appeared in my room one afternoon to sit by my bed and administer the exam. She was a wonderfully empathetic woman. Whenever I came across a difficult part, I would grimace, and she would say sympathetically, "Just go on, Mr. Briggs." At the end of the bedside exam, because of my knowledge, Señora Blakenship's mercy, or a combination of both, I survived another semester of Spanish with a C.

After the semester ended and my school friends departed, the number of my visitors reduced dramatically. I looked for other ways to spend my days, such as reading all the James Bond novels and going through the many cards and letters I had received but been too groggy or busy with visitors to acknowledge. Another happy preoccupation was getting reacquainted with a number of nursing students who came by regularly to check in. With them came a new crop of nursing students who didn't know anything yet about nursing and were getting acquainted with the hospital.

Since the University and the Nursing School were independent of each other—each had separate student governing bodies, eating facilities, classrooms, and living quarters—opportunities to mingle were infrequent. I proved to be of interest to the nursing students and relished the attention.

After about three weeks, my resident told me I would have to start feeding myself. He said it was not healthy or good therapy to have student nurses feed me three meals a day. Nurse Triplett also checked me out from the hospital to visit her apartment, making sure her housemate, another nurse, would be there. All in all, my physical discomfort decreased, and my interactions with the nursing students became a very pleasant existence.

One day someone entered the room, took a look at the shaved place on my head and my unrepaired front teeth, and saw me wearing glasses instead of contact lenses.

"Ugh!" she said and grimaced.

Margaret Ann was never one to conceal her thoughts.

After that empathetic visit broke the ice, she began coming by my room on her breaks to join the others who enjoyed eating my brownies in an always active atmosphere.

Soon my teeth were repaired, I resumed wearing my contacts, and I started wearing a lovely hips-to-chin back brace, which made me ambulatory.

As my appearance gradually improved so did Margaret Ann's interest, which I now attribute to several things. This occurred between semesters, and the pool of eligible men was low. And Margaret Ann was a Medical School student and took courses there, as opposed to being part of the

Nursing School. So she was something of an outsider in the day-to-day activities on the hospital floors. And she was not a Charlottesville girl, such as Allison Dwyer, who would take me to the pool at her place. I also think being on my familiar turf bolstered my case.

For whatever reason, the dead embers of our relationship began to reignite. Before Father's Day, Margaret Ann brought me a card to send my father, but she found the aforementioned Allison Dwyer presenting an array from which I could choose the card to send dad. But Margaret Ann didn't know that Allison was Shep Craige's friend from the New York City visit—and I certainly didn't explain that to her.

My first regular outing from the hospital occurred one night when Margaret Ann, now a highly trained and responsible medical technologist, used her credentials to check me out until 10:00 p.m. It was good to be outside, and we walked across the Grounds to The Cavalier, where I received a hero's welcome and a smiling Frank Kessler served us a pitcher on the house.

After a while my caregiver opined wistfully, "I guess you probably shouldn't dance."

"Of course I can!" I said.

And we did.

Hours later University officer Jim Gardner found me and said, "Frank, you're AWOL from the hospital!"

"Can you give us a ride back, Jim?" I asked.

Sometime around eleven o'clock my friend and apprehending lawman dropped us off at the hospital, and an absolutely unconcerned Margaret Ann relinquished me to the accusatory scowls of some nurses and the amused smiles of others.

The next week I was scheduled to go home to Pittsburgh, and Mom picked me up. She and Margaret Ann met for the first time over dinner. The petite southerner who came to UVA as a Chi O from the University of Chattanooga sought common ground with the tall, reserved Northeasterner from Smith College. While they had no shared experiences, there were no awkward moments, and both my relationship with the Georgia belle and my third year remained in abeyance until my return in mid-August, after an abbreviated summer.

Ted Hogshire and Rutledge Young came by Pittsburgh for a few days on their way west to visit Jon Verity in Middletown, Ohio. Since I couldn't drive, my date from the previous year's hayride often picked me up for dates. But it wasn't my best summer, and I was ready to get back.

The first thing I did as soon as I was back in Charlottesville was to find Margaret Ann, who was moving home to Atlanta. She wanted to stay until the last moment before she started a new job. Margaret Ann had completed her degree during the summer and was living in a duplex that adjoined a former residence. The space was leased to a Turkish student and his roommate from Hampton, but he allowed Margaret Ann to stay there until they arrived for the fall semester. To further complicate the arrangement, Margaret Ann had no key to the unit she was living in. However, she had access to her old place, which was empty, so she would enter that apartment and cross over by way of a shared balcony, and then enter through the kitchen door.

On my second night back, Margaret Ann prepared a dinner of pork chops and rice. After a while I asked her how long she planned to fry the pork chops.

"You're supposed to cook pork for an hour so we don't get trichinosis." she replied and then started pouring rice into a pot of boiling water.

"Isn't that going to expand some?" I asked, knowing exactly what was going to happen but not willing to intrude on the enchantment of the moment.

Moments later I was holding out various receptacles while she shoveled the excess rice out of the pan. It was actually a good thing we had so much rice, because the lima beans burned while we were preoccupied with the rice, and the pork crisps were inedible.

The next week I took exams in the morning, adding a B in American poetry and prose, a B+ in contemporary British and American literature, and C's in the course on novels and history of art. This 2.20 GPA raised my cumulative to 1.87 (which I hadn't known until doing some research for this writing). After each morning's exam, I spent the rest of the day until the wee hours with my Georgia Tinker Bell.

On Friday we got a ride to The Beach and spent a glorious Labor Day weekend with Beta friends while Margaret Ann was a guest at another house. As a sign of how times have changed, not only did we room separately, but Kelly Wood was dressed down by his stepfather for permitting Margaret Ann to change into a bathing suit in his room.

On Monday my enchantress declared she'd been stuck in labs all spring and summer and was not leaving The Beach until sundown. It was not the first time I encountered the intractability of this tiny ball of fire. As the afternoon progressed, we turned down ride after ride until Mrs. Hogshire fed us dinner, after which Teddy took us to the bus depot after dark. It turned out the bus to Charlottesville went through Richmond via Portsmouth, Suffolk, Franklin, and Petersburg.

By the time we left Norfolk, Margaret Ann was fast asleep, her head nestled on my shoulder. While it was wonderful to have my fair damsel nuzzled next to me, a three-hour trip on a bus in a full body brace can be a challenging proposition, especially since I couldn't move for fear of waking the sleeping beauty. When we arrived in Richmond, Margaret Ann awoke long enough to visit the restroom.

While our bus was segregated, the white and colored signs had been taken down in the depot, but tradition had not changed. The clueless sleepwalker tottered through the section reserved for her to reach the other area and drew quite a lot of attention. Nothing came of it and my de facto freedom rider returned to her seat with me protectively by her side there. Once she was back on the bus, she slept until we reached Charlottesville.

We intended to take a cab to Margaret Ann's digs, but a stroke of good fortune came our way and a beaming Robert Redfield appeared at just the right time. He dismissed the idea of our taking a taxi and escorted us to a waiting Lincoln Town Car and drove us home.

After we arrived, he waited for me in the car while I walked my lady to the door, engaged her in a lengthy embrace, and she began the process of entering one apartment to get to the other. Of course she opened the door to the second apartment and we engaged in the great difficulty of parting.

When I returned to the car, I was greeted by a look of incredulity and admiration.

"That was amazing!" he announced. "You kissed one girl and then, when she went inside, you went next door and kissed another."

"Yeah," I said, figuring it would take too long to explain Margaret Ann's living situation.

Tuesday, September 8, 1964, was the beginning of a momentous week in which the Beta house opened, the Turk and his roommate arrived, Margaret Ann packed to go home, and Beta John Sallee purchased a hearse. These unforgettable few days began when Margaret Ann realized she had to move everything and assumed I could arrange it.

The Betas were all at the house. Rusty had worked all summer on a Gulf oil rig. Margaret Ann considered him the ultimate gentleman because he always said, "Excuse me, Margaret Ann," whenever he uttered an inappropriate word. When the moving task was discussed, this paragon of virtue suggested we use Sallee's hearse.

John jumped at the opportunity to use his new toy but offered one codicil. Since the vehicle had no inspection sticker or license plate, he'd need to use back streets and exert caution during the operation.

The next morning Margaret Ann and I were there when the Turk's roommate and his father, a pharmacist, arrived to move in his stuff, expecting the apartment to be vacant. The little lady from Georgia assured them there was nothing to worry about. She was a little behind schedule, but her movers would be there shortly.

Almost immediately the ancient black death wagon arrived with Sallee and a press gang of goats. The Hampton pair had a front-row seat to see a slice of the old U they'd never seen before. The move was executed by a well-lubricated Beta crew, beneficiaries of a seemingly endless supply of Budweiser. As suddenly as the movers arrived, they departed quickly via a circuitous route and unloaded the stuff at the apartment of Margaret Ann's former roommate, from where it would be picked up later.

Meanwhile, the two of us remained in the grip of total infatuation and set out to experience our last few days together before the metaphorical clock struck twelve.

Late that night or early morning, after many mugs of beer, Margaret Ann realized she had forgotten her alarm clock, which she absolutely had to have for a final meeting at the Medical School. Quickly she devised a plan to get it, which was quite complicated now that the Hampton pair was in residence, but in her mind, she saw no problem for her—with me there.

She couldn't go into a bedroom where the men were sleeping, but I could. It sounded challenging to me, but Margaret Ann made it sound so reasonable. She was so convinced that I went along without question.

When we arrived, there were lights visible in the apartment Margaret Ann usually went through to get to her apartment, and this caused her to come up with a plan B. She reasoned since she weighed only a hundred pounds and I had a back brace for support, we could do it.

A short time later she ascended my shoulders and climbed onto the balcony. Then she unlocked the door, admitting me, and I was to creep up the stairs, crawl between the two sleeping men, secure the clock from the bedside table, and escape through the front door.

There's no way I could make this up!

The next day I said to her, "I bet they were surprised to see the clock gone this morning. I wonder if they woke up in time since you said the alarm was set."

"Oh, I called them," she said.

"What did you say?"

"Good morning! It's time to get up!" she gleefully replied.

Margaret Ann departed for Atlanta the next day, with plans to return the week of October 10, which made her leaving bearable for us. Her going also allowed me to turn my attention to the upcoming year.

# Chapter 18

# Final Lap Begins

During the spring of 1964 I was accepted to live on the Lawn. Since the vice president of the Beta house was also the house manager and was expected to live on premises, I'd deferred the decision but actually fell off a cliff before deciding. (By the fall, the plunge had taken on a life of its own, with a ledge becoming a cliff and then a waterfall, upon which I'd been performing daring feats.) The recovery period made it obvious to my parents and medical providers that 44 East Lawn was the better choice for me, and this proved to be another of the many blessings that grew out of the mishap.

When I told Margaret Ann I'd been selected for the Lawn, her disconcertingly predictable response was, "I didn't know you could live on the Lawn for just extracurriculars!" (which was exactly what had happened).

At the time, the committee that selected who lived there, as in all other things, was composed of fraternity men—and so were a disproportionate number of my neighbors. Many years later I attended a party at Stepping-stones in Hot Springs, where a tedious guest, referred to as the "ambassador," was told I had lived on the Lawn. Around the third time he imperiously intoned that he had endowed a room to be inhabited only by recognized scholars, I'd had enough.

"When I endow a room," I responded, "it will be for someone who's excelled only in student activities."

In fact, while the University was not as diverse in the 1960s as it should have been, most Lawn residents there were both academically and otherwise acclaimed. Neither were the citizens only from the geographically segmented Rugby Road–Mad Lane or dormitory confines. The Lawn experience was not only an ability to live at the epicenter of a renown architectural wonder of incredible beauty, but it also placed me in a vastly expanded cross section of students that were an invaluable enrichment to my life.

My room at 44 East Lawn was off-white with a pine-plank floor, a fireplace and hearth, a Jeffersonian secretary desk, a reading rocker, and a chair. On the other wall was a single bedstead nestled between two wooden closets, one for clothing and the other containing a sink and shelves. A large broad-silled window and radiator overlooked the East Gardens that gently sloped down to the Ranges, which faced Hospital Road. Opening onto the Lawn side was a stout door, while outside were a pair of louvered shutters. A covered brick walkway fronted the rooms. Across the grassy area lay the West Lawn rooms yards beyond. The identical sets of rooms, each geometrically punctuated with the two-story Pavilions, were fronted by a broad brick walkway under a metal roof that was supported every six feet by white columns.

All of this provided a magnificent setting for Mr. Jefferson's crown jewel, the Rotunda, sitting in majesty at the head, with the Lawn rolling down before it. From the crisp autumn days, with brightly colored leaves and the tang of woodsmoke in the air, through the snow-draped winter, past bursting spring blooms, to the sultry Virginia summer laden with the rich scent of magnolia, the panorama was magical. Whether entering its presence at sunup or staring up on a moonlight night, it's a scene that has never ceased to elicit a sense of wonder and awe for me.

Some aspects of Lawn living were a little less idealistic. In order to shower or use a toilet, it was necessary to go down the walkway to one of the stairways that led down to a graveled driveway and passed through the serpentine walls and gardens to a small communal bathroom. On some cold, rainy, or snowy days, it was possible to forget, momentarily, that one was in the midst of a romantic experience. It was said there were two groups of residents on the Lawn: those who used their sinks (water running) as urinals and those who lied.

Since appliances and air conditioners were forbidden, residents usually left the window and door open, relying on the louvered shutters for privacy. Because of the Honor System, if I even had a key, it was never used. Between rooms 44 and 46 was a historical marker announcing the founding of the Kappa Sigma fraternity "one chilly evening in the fall of 1869, as five students attending the University of Virginia in Charlottesville gathered in the room of William Grigsby, at 46 East Lawn, and planted the seeds of brotherhood." On muggy Saturdays, for someone who'd only recently gone to bed, it was annoying when tourists regularly read the inscription—every word—out loud to each other.

In very cold weather, I'd go to the bathroom in undershorts and my father's leather navy bridge coat, Dopp kit in hand. In favorable weather, I needed only a light bathrobe. This prompted humorous comments from visitors who were unaware of the basics.

One other thing I learned too late for that year (but of great future value) was always to make sure the firewood was seasoned and not green. My plan had been to heat only by the fireplace.

Many of my neighbors that year have been mentioned as class leaders in various spheres of University life, some of which are concentric. Others rose to new levels of recognition that could be termed notoriety. The epitome of the latter was Woolly Neck, who lived a little farther east from me.

My immediate neighbors were Doug Jordan (in the Kappa Sig room, where a member always lived) and Dick Carlton, the talented editor in chief of the *CD*. Over the coming year we three became good friends, bound together by a great many shared projects.

Three other undergraduate councilmen—Gene Angle, Woolly, and Pat McFalls—also lived on the Lawn. McFalls was an interior lineman from Pittsburgh, and he became a close friend and political ally. Will Montague, Carrington Harrison, Joe "Jose" Brown, and Rooster Singleton were others with whom I spent the most time, although there were another dozen I had more than a passing relationship with.

Although I lived on the Lawn, I was still, first and foremost, a Beta. I still took my meals and participated in all the house functions at Rugby Road. But being part of a different residential community introduced a new dynamic into my University experience. I found that living day by day with individuals is to see strengths and idiosyncrasies not visible to most outside viewers.

Shortly after I moved into 44 East, during first-year orientation, I headed to Newcomb Hall to fulfill my campaign-season obligation to the Young Republicans and Robert Redfield. It caused great consternation when I arrived wearing a Republican for Goldwater and Byrd campaign button.

"You can't wear that they explained. Senator Byrd is a Democrat! And you're our membership co-chairman."

The realization I was talking to ideologues and the pragmatic reality that I wasn't going to provide support for whoever was masochistic enough to take on the senator was immediately understood by the politically astute Redfield.

Several weeks after the semester started, Chris "Rooster," who'd heard I was dating Margaret Ann again, showed up on my doorstep. He mumbled, eyes downcast, "I'm sorry about that thing with Margaret Ann, Beta." By then I'd heard the story several times from various amused sources.

During summer school Margaret Ann and her roommates had thrown a small birthday party for Joe "Jose" Brown and told him he could ask a few friends. Instead, he invited dozens.

The birthday boy recruited Rooster to be Margaret Ann's date, but she was busy as a hostess, so Rooster was left with his friends and a bottle. By midnight he was incapacitated and then taken upstairs and dumped on a bed.

Several hours later, when an exhausted Margaret Ann finally was rid of all the guests (she thought) and had cleaned up the apartment, she found Rooster spread-eagled across her bed.

Joe responded quickly when she called, telling him to "come and get him out of here right now!"

The next morning Rooster knocked on the door. He was downcast and humiliated, so he avoided eye contact and asked if he could retrieve his wallet. It was thrown at him just before the door was slammed in his face.

I assured Chris I had pretty much forgotten about it, but I suggested, for our future friendship, that he not mention it again. Over time, Margaret Ann decided to enjoy the remembrance. But Rooster has never been able to look her in the eye. As for our exchange, it was one of the first examples of how Lawn residents grew to be a fellowship that enlarged our experience.

Since Margaret Ann had majored in premed, her transcript consisted almost entirely of science and math courses. Mine was pretty much the opposite. In my first year I had taken the two required basic-level math classes and what was considered the least difficult natural science course (geology, aka rocks for jocks). For my effort, I earned three D's and one C.

My English SAT achievement scores were in the mid-700s, but I scored a 466 in chemistry. Nonetheless, since Margaret Ann and I had decided to find out more about each other's field of study, I added basic chemistry to my course load of fourth-year Shakespeare and British literature, along with modern rational empiricism and (obviously required for me) Spanish literature.

Since I also worked at the hospital, I even thought about becoming a doctor. But things got off to a rocky start and proceeded to go downhill from there. For one thing, everyone else in the class, all first-year men, were proficient with slide rules, while I often wound up doing calculations manually.

When we had our first quiz, Mr. Glover returned to pick up the bluebooks deposited on his desk. When he saw I was still working on the quiz, he said, "Turn off the lights when you're through." And then he left. Out of ten questions I still had three to go.

But in the lab, I made a wise choice of partners and teamed up with a brilliant student from Seattle. Amid a group of tweed-and-blazer-clad preppies, he was the only one with a burr haircut and a brown suit, tie, and shoes and a leather briefcase.

My first Student Council meeting as a member was on September 29, convened by E. Polk Kellam Jr., a member of St. Anthony's Hall. He welcomed the new members and then awarded committee assignments. I was to be on organizations and publications as well as chairman of orientation and calendars, all of which was very pleasing to me.

One of the major functions of the council was to approve the organizations to operate on the Grounds as well as decide whether they would receive student funds and how much. That committee was chaired by Tom Player (one of the two Law School reps) and Ed Harper (from graduate Arts and Sciences). Tom and Ed played a significant role in my growth on the council as the year progressed.

SAE and Lawn resident Gene Angle, whom I liked very much, was in his second semester as a councilman, and he was on each of these two committees as well.

Since the bimonthly meetings involved a great deal of housekeeping (such as acting on recognition and funds requests from some sixty organizations) and lasted three to four hours, I can only highlight some major themes of the council's work. If anyone wants to know more, the minutes are available in the Special Collections Library, as are other governance groups to be mentioned in the following narrative.

After the first meetings of the council, it became clear what topics would define the year ahead. The original reason cited for the reestablishment of the body—no women at the University—never came up, since no entity or individual wanted to open that can of worms. At the time it never occurred to anyone that there was a relationship between civil rights and coeducation. The picture on the paper's front page of the nursing council titled "Pretty Politicos" was considered flattering. In the 1960s the definitions of male and female were limited to biology, and the respective roles of each was unchallenged.

Another perennial duty was to prevent any encroachment on student governance by any person or group in the administration. Early in my term, a letter was sent to the manager of Newcomb Hall food services to remind him that only the Student Council could approve a group to use any University facilities. (He had provided space and food to an unsanctioned organization.)

There was never a meeting at which the IFC report failed to produce an interesting insight into the often-dysfunctional condition of at least some and sometime all of the thirty-one houses. It often sounded like a bunch of boys saying, "Everything's fine in here. You don't need to bother yourself by coming up to our room."

The parental response—in this case from Dean Runk—was usually, "If I hear that noise one more time, there's going to be trouble!"

An area of continuous conflict, especially during football season, was between the Athletic Department and the student body. Students considered athletics to be part of the University, but Steve Sebo, the athletic director, considered it a business to be run by professionals. At the first meeting, and regularly thereafter, it was reported that ticket takers refused to take a student's word (thus disregarding the Honor System), students were permitted access only at certain gates, and students were subjected to other ungentlemanly behavior.

These allegations were all contested, and the athletic director was asked to appear before the council. Particularly irritating was the Athletic Department's decision to "appease the army" by splitting the student section, so the cadets could sit in the center as a corps. The council could not understand why the Army needed to be appeased, and therefore the student section should not be split.

At the first meeting, issues presented in the platform of the Scepter Society were introduced. Several of these passed with only a little discussion at later meetings. Under councilman Jim Gilwee's sponsorship, honor roll students were exempted from the "no cut" period two days before and after semester breaks. And regular communication was enlarged with the first-year committee, with me as their liaison.

While it was obvious to all that no one was experienced enough to govern or lead until his last third-year semester, the opportunity to have a channel for input seemed acceptable. The issue of permitting female guests in certain dorms for well-defined weekend hours sparked great opposition from the start. No women in any dorms under any circumstances was so ingrained in the University's identity that it was not to be questioned. (The only exceptions I knew of involved mothers and sisters helping move students in and out of the dorms and maids having access in order to make up the rooms.) In light of the astounding change over the decade to come, the no-women-ever rule is history worth remembering, so here are a few comments and excerpts from council minutes:

October 6, 1964: Old Business
Steve Mitchell and Lars Anderson introduced a petition with 551 signatures requesting that female guests be allowed in the Alderman Road Dorms lounges. Councilman Crown then introduced a proposal … sim-

ilar to the ... Petition except in the hours recommended....

After much discussion the motion passed.

Councilman Player then introduced a proposal ...
Monroe Hill Dorms ... Passed.

October 20, 1964:

Councilmen Player and Kellam reported on their
meeting with Dean of the University, B. F. D. Runk...
. Mr. Runk felt that control of such a proposal must be
examined very carefully to keep from overburdening
the Honor System or the Counsellor System.

A series of studies, proposal amendments, polls, and negotiations followed that lasted until the spring.

The final issue did not arise until late November, when an extremely
small organization, Students for Democratic Action (SDA), applied for
recognition. Once it did, however, it became a contentious issue.

The Commonwealth of Virginia had been content to leave things
the way they had been for generations, and this was certainly true regarding race relations. As noted earlier, the University was the first
southern state university to voluntarily integrate, but it was on a token
basis. The thinking was that progress had been made with President
Harry S. Truman's integration of the armed forces in 1950 and the Supreme Court's unanimous 1954 decision to strike down the "separate
but equal" policy regarding the public schools.

The conventional wisdom, or the lack thereof, was that full integration
would arrive in time. The SDA, however, believed the time to act was now.

My view, embraced or accepted by almost all those involved, was
that Mr. Jefferson's Academical Village should live in splendid isolation
from the outside world.

Over the course of the school year these subplots continued to play
out. However, in our community, as elsewhere, these matters were

largely peripheral, even for those chosen to deal with them. Academic activities, financial crises, dating questions, athletics, and countless other moving parts, both trivial and major, of daily living consumed our time.

For me that included spending more time on academics than before. It helped that I was living by myself on the Lawn, with the Alderman Library and Newcomb Hall being closer than the Beta house, but I also was under a lot more scrutiny than I had ever been. I still took all my meals at the house, dutifully attended to my roles as vice president and house manager, and attended all council and Beta meetings.

When the house opened and Rush was scheduled to start the following week, the following minutes reveal my state of mind. These minutes are also available in the Special Collections Library, as are the minutes of the other fraternities:

October 7, 1964

President Young called the meeting to order @ 6:45.

B. Peter reported $315.93 in the treasury.

B. Abbuehl gave kitchen report. B. Guthrie registered a complaint concerning the shitty hamburgers on Saturday. Lunch for the Army game was set for 11:30 to 12:30.

B. Hooker announced that he had signed the Checkmates for Army weekend. He was given a stomp for the Jolly Jakes. (VPI game weekend)

B. Greenwood gave touchdown club report.

B. Mather gave the IFC report and suggested that a new IFC representative be chosen.

B. Warner gave report on Rush.

President Young announced dorm visits (Rush in first-year dorms to selected rushees) Wed. Night, Oct 14

B. Warmer cautioned against rashly labeling first-year men as geeks.

B. Briggs gave house managers report. B. Mather suggested that B. Briggs come on over now and then to check on the condition of things. B. Briggs urged brothers not to tell him of maintenance problems too soon after they occur. B. Briggs also asked for help in putting in windows. Pres. Young suggested that repair sheet be used to wipe oneself if toilet paper isn't available.

Pres. Young announced a cocktail party for alumni on Homecoming weekend.

The new brothers were reminded that they must pay the $60 initiation fee.

B. Guthrie warned against offering beer to ABC agents disguised as old alumni.

Pres. Young announced plans for a Woodbury dove shoot on Friday.

B. Ellis suggested that we donate the piano to the pep rally bonfire, but B. Mather insisted that if we had a hair on our asses, we'd push it off the bridge.

After three IFC meetings B. Mather turned in his resignation as IFC representative.

B. Warner was chosen new IFC representative by acclimation.

Talk around

Doxology

Respectfully submitted

E. L. Hogshire

These are fairly representative of the Omicron chapter minutes in that the brothers weren't reticent about expressing their thoughts. During

Rush, and especially during ball sessions, they were long and could be acrimonious. The references to me as house manager were well deserved. Had I not been so self-centered, I would have decided between living on the Lawn and being house manager and living there. It was a pointed reminder from my best friends, who could have forced a choice, that I needed to attend to my business. A stomp indicated approval in lieu of clapping hands for the VPI weekend combo choice by B. Hooker.

Hokey, Hokey High! We're the boys from VPI!

Today, there is a heated rivalry between Virginia Tech and the University, but in 1964 the former was just beginning to come on everyone's radar. When I searched VPI online, the letters as a school didn't even come up, because the official name of the university is Virginia Polytechnic Institute.

In the early 1960s, the most sacrosanct rivalry for Wahoos was with UNC, and it was the oldest rivalry in the South. But there are several reasons for the long-standing history of UVA's and VPI's mutual dislike, and the first involves growth statistics and geography.

Most of the students at Hokie High in the 1960s were in the corps, and the Wahoos considered VPI to be a sleepy little agricultural school that was far down The Valley, in Blacksburg, with a 1961/62 enrollment of 5,747. And by 1964/65 enrollment had grown to 7,305, while the University remained around 6,000, with greatly criticized plans to eventually reach 10,000. Three years later, in 1967/68, the Hokies topped that with 10,254. And now, forty years after that, the Hokies numbered 34,850 while Wahoos totaled 24,639.

Culturally, what is now called Virginia Tech comes from the proud rural roots of southwest Virginia, while the school in Charlottesville has the Tidewater stock of the eastern and northern Commonwealth.

It's easy to see why those referred to as "Virginia's Public Idiots" by those they consider Tidewater and FFV (First Families of Virginia) snobs have a history of mutual contempt. These days each school has experienced vast changes, some of them good, which lessen their differences, but long-standing feuds live on. The *US News and World Report*'s rankings of colleges and universities shows the prominence of each in spite of the things they say about each other.

While Margaret Ann had chosen to return to Atlanta for a job with significantly more income—a decision she was beginning to regret— two of her five classmates, Sue Hall and Sherry Stone, had stayed in Charlottesville and shared an apartment. Sue dated and later married Tom Dugan, a UVA undergrad and law student, and Sherry was always accompanied by Igor, another med student.

Sue and Sherry knew me, and on Thursday, October 8, the morning after the chapter meeting, Sherry let me use her VW Bug to pick up Margaret Ann in Lexington. She was there because, providentially, the next-door neighbors from home, the Simmons, had driven up for Parents Weekend at Washington and Lee. Margaret Ann introduced me to them, and we indulged in some polite chit chat, but neither Margaret Ann nor I could tear our eyes from each other. We escaped as soon as we could.

In hindsight, the Simmonses—especially Mr. Simmons—seemed amused, doubtlessly because they were among the Cravens' closest friends and had been meeting the coquettish only daughter's latest one-and-onlys since she was fifteen. But for me ignorance was bliss, and my heartthrob was in the area until the following Sunday.

We drove back to Charlottesville in time for dinner at the house where Margaret Ann had become a familiar face. With the goats now having been brothers for five days and Rush to start that Saturday evening, it was the one week a year when everyone was equal, with no rushees around.

After dinner, arms entwined, Margaret Ann and I walked the Grounds together, stopping frequently to blissful enjoy each other's company. Around one o'clock, I took her to Sue and Sherry's apartment.

On Friday morning, after attending classes, I eschewed the usual Beta dove shoot, and picked up the sleeping beauty. After lunch at The Virginian, we spent the afternoon on the Lawn, and I showed her 44 East and introduced her to my neighbors, some of whom she already knew better than I. We headed for supper and spent the evening with The Checkmates, allowing their all-encompassing music to pervade the depths of our being. The group was always in high gear, and their combination of rock and roll and soul tones supercharged my date, and we danced endlessly, pausing only for occasional refueling with Rebel Yell bourbon.

Even in the midst of a gyrating crowd, as far as we knew, we were the only ones there. Around two o'clock my strength began to falter, despite how much distilled spirits I imbibed. But my partner never did.

Periodically one day transcends all others, and the Saturday of the Army game was such a day for me. After the traditional brunch at the Beta house, we walked as a group to the stadium and sat together like all the other fraternities. Because of recent concealment requirements, we carried blankets and the women were allowed to carry purses, partly for their use at the game as seat covers and necessity holders, but mostly to carry in fifths of bourbon.

Army started the game by running the kickoff back ninety-nine yards for a touchdown, which prompted my Deep South date to say, "Well, it's nice to get away from big-time football."

While we knew that was true, it was irritating to hear someone say it out loud, no matter how guilelessly. But there was more, and the *CD* headline said it all:

Cavaliers Stomp Black Knights, 35-14

The lead article was titled "Dug Out," and the writer, Alan Rosenthal, astutely noted, "If Virginia ever plays a game well both offensively and defensively, if the Cavaliers ever jell into a team, then the Wahoos might get somewhere."

While many things change, and the Hoos have had some exceptional years in the almost sixty years since that afternoon, this sentiment has recurred repeatedly over the decades.

Nonetheless it set the stage for a night of jubilant frivolity. In 1990, I was in Charlottesville when Georgia Tech defeated number-one-ranked Virginia by a field goal (after quarterback Sean Moore injured the thumb on his throwing hand and could no longer connect with receiver Herman Moore). As we were entering Alumni Hall, I remarked to a friend that I had come to join the others in drowning their sorrows.

He said, "Well, I've seen a lot of drowning, but not much sorrow."

In Hooville, we never let a loss ruin a party!

On page two of the same edition of the *CD* was the following headline: "Admissions Policies Bar Discrimination." The piece noted the University had enrolled the first African American student in the Law School three years before the historic 1953 Supreme Court decision and repeated the basic statement we all know now by heart: "accepts all qualified applicants without regard to race, creed, or color." It went on to note:

> Statistics concerning the number of students of any race now attending the University are not available because they are not compiled. This fact is itself indicative of the fact that there is no discrimination on the Grounds. Bevin Alexander, Director of Information Services, has said, "We don't know how many Negros are enrolled in the University because we don't keep records on the basis of race." There are no figures available from either the Registrar's Office or the Office of the President.
>
> The Admissions Office keeps only limited figures on Negro enrollment. Dean of Admissions Marvin B.

Perry said, "While the number of Negro students applying continues to be small, there has been an increase in the last two years. Of the nine Negro students offered admission to the University this year, five actually accepted and enrolled. The University welcomes all qualified applicants."

The article described how fully the University met the necessary criterion and concluded:

> It can be truly said that there is no racial discrimination in the admitting of students to the University.... Once admitted, no one is subject to the degradation of having their forms separated from others due to race, and no meaningless statistics are compiled.

While the University didn't know how many black students there were, my tutoring from Bebe's friends indicated they knew. There were seventeen African Americans at the University: two in each large school and one in each smaller.

A friend once said, "The University never lets progress stand in the way of tradition." Life moved on unfazed.

After the Army game we went over to Jon Verity's for a cocktail party. He lived in a substantial suite in the Alderman Road Dorms as befitted the senior counselor. Margaret Ann chatted with his date, Vicki Chainski, a Sweetbriar girl, and then we headed back to the house.

But this night was different from the prior. While The Checkmates sounded as good as ever, it was a work night, since a new round of Rush had commenced.

As the current crop of first-year men filed through, it was our job to welcome those already known, look for potential Betas, and process the rest as politely as possible. Of special value were those dates who were seasoned veterans of the Rush wars.

Since my girl had an interest in almost all males and had arrived as a sorority member from a coed school where it was a daily process, she was irritatingly good at it.

After the party I'd agreed to meet Woolly and his date, Karen. She had been at Chattanooga with Margaret Ann, but she was a member of a different sorority, and she hailed from Lookout Mountain, like Alex. It was the first of many experiences we shared and showed the potential physical and disciplinary dangers of doing things with him.

Everything went well until Alex decided we should go to Brenwanna, a black night club way out in the county. Although I had friends from the hospital who might be there, I did not feel comfortable with the idea. But what others thought never mattered to Alex. I was relieved to find the place closed when we got there.

On the way back, Woolly suddenly yelled "Depth charge!" He veered toward the right shoulder and knocked an orange-and-white construction barrel into the air with his bumper.

He laughed maniacally and swerved into the left lane of the two-lane highway and repeated the maneuver with his left bumper.

Margaret Ann grabbed my hand and then slid onto the floor.

Wooly ignored entreaties from Karen and me as well as the blaring horns of oncoming traffic. He continued to shoot depth charges left and right for several more minutes, until Karen threatened him with bodily harm. But he continued to laugh uproariously about how much fun it had been.

Margaret Ann and I were relieved when we finally reached Sue and Sherry's.

I returned to the Lawn in time to see Karen give the Mid-South wrestling champ a black eye with a skillfully delivered left hook.

Alex was an example of the separate poles that existed as a Virginia dichotomy. He was admired as a gifted athlete and student leader; he was tapped to both the Ribbon Society, Eli Banana, the coveted Ring Society, IMP; he was elected to the Student Council; and he was chosen to be dormitory counselor and mentor to first-year men. At the other pole, however, while some of his feats went beyond the pale, he was recognized for some amazing stunts.

The following week was quite probably the most fun I've ever had at the University or Blair. Since I had not been in a coeducational school since I was fourteen years old, I realized there were some advantages to having my girlfriend around all the time.

After my classes—which Margaret Ann insisted I attend and even attended a few with me—we were together constantly until I left Sue and Sherry's apartment in the evening. We shared afternoons and visited a medley of exhibits, athletic events, and other pursuits, sought out because she wanted to squeeze in as many cultural offerings as possible during the short time she had remaining in Charlottesville. Entranced as I was, I followed her around wherever she wanted to go just so I could be close to her.

One afternoon we were near Mem Gym, and a handsome self-assured athlete approached us. Margaret Ann exclaimed, "Hey, Bob!" and she disappeared from sight in an affectionate bear hug from the athlete, whose enthusiasm matched hers.

I introduced myself, and he said, "Bob Kowalkowski."

I'd now met UVA's famous interior lineman who later played for twelve years in the NFL. To my Chattanooga Moccasin varsity cheerleader, it was unfathomable we wouldn't have known each other before this.

After supper, we were together while I studied and she quizzed me on my Spanish vocabulary. Chemistry was originally in the study mix until Margaret Ann said, "I can't believe anyone would have trouble with these equations."

I said I'd get it myself, and we dropped the subject by mutual consent.

The week flew by, and on Margaret Ann's last night, Sue and Sherry had a going-away dinner for her. They had learned the lessons from Joe's birthday party, so the dinner was limited to around nine people.

Since I had missed the Beta dove shoot the Friday before, I joined the dove shoot this week, but I cautioned my love not to expect much. Yet this eternally optimistic beauty didn't believe her hunter could fail, and so she bought enough bacon wrap and fixin's for countless birds. Bear in mind that a dove is roughly the size of a tennis ball. And by mid-October Woodbury's had been well harvested. So, when the moment of truth arrived, I pulled only one cleaned creature from my game bag to present before all those who had gathered to celebrate this time together. I, however, anticipated their likely disappointment, and produced two fifths of Rebel Yell. And a good time was had by all.

The honoree's friends were well aware of Margaret Ann's culinary skills, and they generously let her entertain the guests away from the kitchen. That was fine with me, since domestic talents were the furthest thing from my mind when it came to a choice of a wife.

In fact, during the week we'd talked about marriage and talking to our parents. But we both knew it was a nonstarter, and so I never did and she didn't, either.

The funniest moment of Saturday, our last day together for a while, occurred on the Lawn, when we were talking with Jack McGauley, one of the finest people in our class.

After a while, he said, "Aren't you going to introduce us?"

It hadn't occurred to me there was anyone in Charlottesville whom Margaret Ann didn't know. I stuttered an embarrassed introduction, and since he, too, was from Chattanooga, the two of them chitchatted as she could do with anyone.

The day seemed to pass in a flash, and suddenly I was dropping her off for the last time that week. I went back to the Lawn, but around 4:00 a.m. I bolted upright, wide awake, dressed, and walked down Jefferson Park Avenue to Sue and Sherry's place. I knocked on the door, and Margaret Ann opened it. We embraced until it was time to take a cab to the depot for the 6:30 train to Atlanta.

I was in a morose mood afterward. So, I joined the Betas and their dates for an afternoon of trap shooting, which was something I usually took great delight in. This time, however, my heart was heavy, and I couldn't wait for Thanksgiving, when I would head south to be with her again.

# Chapter 19

## Institutional Isolation

The day of decision was rapidly approaching in chemistry with less than twenty-four hours before the final drop date. After that, the grade would remain indelibly on my transcript, as had happened in Latin III. I understood the lectures about as much as I did the rapid-fire Spanish dialogue in the language lab. My plan in labs was to let my brilliant partner do the experiments while and I recorded the results. But as soon as he reviewed my notes, he decided to take care of both tasks.

Since I was facing the inevitable, I went to the Registrar's office. As soon as I reached the counter and before I could say a word, the clerk asked, "Which one?"

"Chemistry," I answered.

She handed me the form and I began the search for Mr. Glover to get his signature.

When I handed him the form, he said, "I thought you were going to be a doctor."

"I've changed my mind," was all I could say.

I took the form and headed to Anderson's Bookstore. As soon as I pocketed the proceeds of selling back my books, I went to Mr.

Van's Pool Hall, where I met Rusty and enjoyed a satisfying afternoon.

My fourth-year Spanish class was carefully chosen for two reasons. First, Señor Oswaldo Chinchon was considered to be the most understanding of the instructors. Second, even though it had the negative of being a Tuesday-Thursday-Saturday class, it was the section of preference for football players and other athletes.

Señor Chinchon turned out to be an engaging man who was still acclimating to the South. On the second Saturday of the semester, he arrived to find eleven empty seats out of sixteen and asked in a bemused, wonderfully accented manner, "Where is everyone?"

"It's an away weekend," someone explained.

And then someone else clarified for him that football players were automatically excused from class for away games.

My Spanish class had a strong Deep South flavor, which included Tommy Krebs from Birmingham, Alabama, a well-liked SAE and football player. When Señor Chinchon asked him "whether Birmingham was the place where negros were mistreated," Tommy thought it was an innocent request and affably responded that it was a nice place that had a bad rap. While the use of fire hoses and attack dogs against civil rights marchers by the commissioner of public safety, Theophilus Eugene "Bull" Conner, was condemned by many as excessive and heavy-handed, in the context of UVA, it was an inappropriate question. What happened in Alabama had nothing to do with Charlottesville.

About a decade later, an attractive woman approached me at a neighborhood party and asked, "Are you Frank Briggs?"

I was impressed that she knew me, and then she explained, "I was your language lab monitor. The thing I most clearly remember is the Saturday morning you came to the lab fully dressed in coat and jacket, but your shirt had no front, just a collar and tie."

I, too, remembered the moment. I had spent the night before at the Beta house, and somehow, I was involved in a scuffle, during which my shirt was torn off. The next morning, I didn't think there was a need to get a fresh shirt just to spend a few hours in a cubicle with some headphones. I confessed to her that I never understood a word during those two-hour labs.

For me the University experience was like a smorgasbord of wonderful choices. Some offerings included dishes I had to take, but as time went on, the selection became more varied and delectable.

One genre I especially enjoyed was southern novels, including George Washington Cable's *The Grandissimes: A Story of Creole Life*, John William De Forest's *Miss Ravenel's Conversion from Secession to Loyalty*, several of William Faulkner's novels, and other compelling works. From Great Britain came semesters with more than eighty books (Yay, Master Plots!), including the works of Shakespeare, Daniel Defoe's *Moll Flanders*, and Evelyn Waugh's *A Handful of Dust*. The poetry of Rudyard Kipling, T. S. Eliot, John Greenleaf Whittier, and a dozen others inspired me to try my own hand.

One semester I audited an art course because I wanted to learn to draw and not have a grade to deal with.

Knowledge gained from philosophy, public speaking, and twenty-one hours of religion remain with me forever.

Geology and art history enriched hikes, trips, and daily life.

Economics and military science enlarged my understanding of world events.

Even my tenuous grasp of Latin and Spanish helped with word derivations in the former and ordering at Taco Bell in the latter.

But the greatest gift for me from the University was the image of a Virginia gentleman, a Renaissance man, and a liberal arts degree. I was there to get an education; learning a profession or a trade would come next.

In hindsight, while I was an English major, my real field of study was interpersonal relationships. My wife once observed that if I had spent as much time on school as I later did on my business, I could've been a Phi Bete.

"A moot point," I told her. "I did spend an average of five to six hours a day on schoolwork, with about an hour or so on academics and the rest on extracurriculars and getting to know people."

If the Bath County School System had tested me in the early 1950s with the tools now available, I would have been diagnosed as ADHD. What a blessing that gift has been to me over the years! I can and must focus intensely on a project, but only for so long, before moving to another. That ability, combined with a visual recall memory, makes it possible for me to accomplish many projects simultaneously. I'm not good at seeing the trees, but I can always see the forest. And that's what helped me so much at the U.

Rush was moving along at its usual time-consuming and expensive pace, but it was worth the effort expended for teaching so many men how to run thirty-one separate businesses and compete in the marketplace for new members, who consequently fund the enterprises going forward. Several snippets from the Beta house minutes help to illustrate the process.

> October 28
>
> B. Warner commended the house for Rush on Saturday night. [A major task of the Rush chairman and sales manager was to keep the group interested in the sometimes-laborious task of Rush and marketing.]
>
> Mrs. Elizabeth Hoskins was announced by B. Hooker as the new chaperone. [He asked the house to be courteous to her, because it was difficult to find and retain good people.]
>
> It was decided that girls would be imported from [Randolph] Macon for Friday night. [These were supplemental mercenaries for Rush. It was one of the few times when coeducation at UVA could have been worthwhile.]

B. Abbuehl reported he still had $1,500 in outstanding bills. [Contrary to what I'd told Billy Abbuehl about the necessity for the kitchen manager to be an aggressively unpleasant bill collector, he'd chosen to be a nice guy. I reminded him it was difficult to meet accounts payable with accounts receivable, and soon he'd learn what the term COD meant if he didn't get nasty quickly.]

November

[Rush chairman] B. Warner ... if any dirty Rush was planned, he didn't want to know about it (and then he got caught). [This was not elaborated on in the minutes.]

B. Guthrie asked there be no more quacking at the ducks next door. [Ducks was the nickname for Delta Upsilon, which they seemed not to like.]

Bid Sunday came the Sunday before Thanksgiving, and as always it was great fun to bump other houses by pledging people they really wanted. It was not much fun in reverse. As always there were trash cans filled to the brim with artillery punch to be poured down the gullets of brothers and pledges alike. Of the new pledges, the ones I knew best were Philip "Flip" Viles of Norman, Oklahoma; Hugh Ilgenfritz of Shreveport, Louisiana; Jeff Schmidt; Bob Strang; Joe Weller; and David "Davey" Jones.

I posted a card on the Newcomb Hall bulletin board that I needed a ride to Atlanta for Thanksgiving. A graduate student responded and agreed to take me for the price I offered.

Well before sunup on the Wednesday before the holiday, four of us—the driver and three riders—crowded into a Volkswagen for the ten-hour drive to Atlanta. The two other passengers were Laurie Croft and Ty Prince, two Zete second years from Atlanta and Savannah, respectfully. Since Savannah was two hundred miles east southeast of Atlanta, I don't remember what Ty's plans were to get there, but they were fun company. And the Crofts and the Cravens (Margaret Ann's family) were friends from church.

Most of the trip from Charlottesville to Atlanta was on two-lane highways, and it was an indisputably picturesque route. While my first trip to Georgia had been through the coastal Low Country, our present route went through the Piedmont and coastal plain, as tobacco country gave way to peach orchards and then cotton fields. Nestled within were innumerable farmhouses and sharecropper hovels. Small towns like Anderson, Livonia, and Brazelton cropped up every so often.

As the landscape changed to deeply southern, so did the drawls of the residents we encountered at filling stations, country stores, and eateries. Around five o'clock we stopped at Laurie's house, and I met his sister, Irene, an extremely direct woman. She immediately asked who I was coming to visit.

When I told her, the accusatory response was, "She's older than you!"

Although that hadn't come up at school, somehow, in real life, it seemed relevant. At any rate, the graduate student dropped me off at the Cravens'. For a moment we just stared at each other, transfixed. Then we threw each other into the other's arms.

On Thanksgiving morning, I began to realize what my Georgia girl had meant when she talked about getting away from big-time football. Not only did we attend the Georgia Tech–Georgia freshman game, but we sat with the legendary receiver John Staton, who had played for Tech and was now a senior executive at Coca-Cola, which was an unmatchable combination in the mid-1960s in Atlanta.

Staton's daughter Mary was a modern dancer in New York, and she and Margaret Ann were like sisters, although they were opposites in most ways.

As his guests, we were on the fifty-yard line in the West Stands, a mecca for the Yellow Jacket Nation. It was enough to make one consider being a Bulldog fan. Not only was the stadium full for the freshman game, but the same group would fill Sanford Stadium in Athens on Saturday for the varsity game.

My Wahoo eyes were amazed that everyone was taking the game so seriously, knew every player, and rehashed every play. Neither was it a reasonably good-natured rivalry. The two fan bases genuinely disliked each other. Most astoundingly, I didn't see one drop of alcohol in the stands. It was my introduction to Southeastern Conference (SEC) football. Georgia Tech had recently left the conference to become an independent, but they clearly retained the attitude.

Thanksgiving dinner was another learning experience for me. I had met Margaret Ann's mother and brother (Gray) before—Ruth Craven had grown up in Berryville, Virginia, and Baltimore (a southern city, she assured me)—but this was my first meeting with her father, Robert Lamar Craven, a South Carolina Gamecock from Bennettsville. He was a diminutive but energetic athlete, and he courteously and disarmingly quizzed me about my background.

I suspected he was thinking, *She's brought home a lot of them, but a Yankee?!*

Later I asked Margaret Ann, "Your dad says you went to school up north. When was that?"

With a puzzled look, she replied, "Why, when I met you!"

I now understood that I was among people for whom "up north" meant anyplace north of North Carolina (if that far).

In addition to regional differences, there were family distinctions as well. My mother was tall, reserved, and had never used prepared foods, while Ruth was more her daughter's size, didn't like kitchen duty, and used store-bought if that was good enough.

Most striking was the overwhelming difference in family governance. Hers was matriarchal while mine was paternal.

When Ruth said, "Bob, get some more rolls. These are cold," he good-naturedly fetched them.

I tried to envision what my father would have done, and I decided he would have sought psychiatric help, since Mom had definitely lost her mind.

At the time, Atlanta was just beginning to shake off its small southern town identity, but the city's tallest building was the ten-story Bank of Georgia, much of what is now called Midtown was residential, and Five Points was the epicenter of commercial activity and everything else. Over the next five and a half decades the city has remained at just under a half million residents, but the metro area has grown from just under one and half million to six million. Towns and counties that were decidedly rural are now part of the urban sprawl of the state capital. Recently Atlanta ranked as the ninth largest city in the country and third in the South, behind Washington DC and Miami. But from a southern point of view, neither Washington nor Miami is or ever was a part of Dixie.

On Saturday, Mr. Craven, Gray, Margaret Ann, and I visited their lake cabin, situated on a pristine cove on Lake Allatoona, adjacent to the Atlanta Yacht Club. To get there we went several miles north on Interstate 75 (which was under construction) and stopped at West Paces Ferry Road. From there we went northwest on US 41 toward Chattanooga. Crossing what they said was a river, the Chattahoochee, we left the suburbs behind, traveled past Marietta, and turned onto recently paved Cobb County Road, Bell's Ferry. From there we were in the countryside, with only the occasional farm, mobile home, country store, or Baptist church in view. After twenty minutes we turned onto Highway 92 and entered Cherokee County. We stopped at the ten-year-old hydroelectric and flood control lake. While Mr. Craven busied himself around the cabin, Gray and Margaret Ann took me sailing.

As we returned through the loblolly pines and harvested fields of the Piedmont, the blue-and-orange Georgia sunset spread out before us. Suddenly memories from ten years earlier, when I'd been standing on a ridge near the Alabama-Tennessee line southwest of Chattanooga, flooded back to me. When I had taken in the sunset from a point overlooking a small TVA lake, I'd vowed to be back someday.

Early the next morning, when I was picked up by the graduate student driver for the ride back to Virginia, I had a sense that I had found home, which was a powerful emotion and quite separate and distinct from having found the right girl.

Our parting was not as wrenching as her leaving Charlottesville just a couple of months ago. I knew I'd be back in a few weeks, and then my Sweet Pea would be coming to Pittsburgh the week after Christmas.

The weeks between Thanksgiving and Christmas breaks were always more relaxed and filled with a sense of winding down. The Christmas party weekend, with the new pledges in attendance, marked the end of Rush. While exams were upcoming, they were scheduled for after the new year, and professors seemed to be in the spirit of the season. Thoughts of fraternity finances and Rush violations were stuffed away, to be dealt with in January and after exams. But one item rose up at the final two meetings of the year and persisted into the spring.

The question of what to do with groups whose views appeared to be contrary to those of the University first appeared at the December 8, 1964, meeting of the Student Council. Earlier in the year the council had renewed the approval of the Virginia Council on Human Relations. One project they administered was recruitment of African American students that, while certainly not mainstream, was definitely acceptable. The council also approved placement of a U-Haul trailer in front of Alderman Library to collect needed items for Mississippi. The following excerpts from the minutes show what was considered inappropriate:

> December 8, 1964
> Organizations and Publications

The University of Virginia Outing Club requested $698.00 ... for canoes. The committee felt the request ought to be trimmed to $118.00. This amount was moved and passed.

The Graduate Education Association requested $154.50. [Requests then went to the committee before being acted upon at a subsequent meeting.]

The Univ ... Magazine requested $1,537.00, 25 percent less than last year ... committee reported the publication is moving toward solvency ... Motion [to grant] passed....

Handball Club's constitution was accepted ... Club recognized.

Then the subject matter became less routine.

The Students for Social Action presented a quickly drawn, poorly worded constitution and requested recognition the week of December 15th. The Council will consider the constitution next week and the inclusion of a "non-violent" statement of intent was strongly recommended.

Other committee reports and business followed as usual:

December 15, 1964
Organizations and Publications
The Virginia Council on Human Relations requested $316.00 ... Several speakers ... $250.00 ... Moved and passed.

Fencing Club ... equipment ... passed.

Cave Club ... $130.00 ... passed

The Students for Social Action requested recognition of their organization and distributed a revised and re-written constitution. Councilman Harper came out in favor of recognition of the group on the basis that (1) the group was non-violent and orderly, and (2) that we would be limiting their right to freedom of speech by not recognizing them. Councilman Briggs submitted an editorial from the *Richmond Times Dispatch*, December 9 issue, and a letter from students against recognition. Councilman Briggs asked their representative to answer whether or not they were aided by an outside source or would be aligned with an outside source in the future. The councilman also requested a more thorough explanation of purpose. Mr. Romain, the representative, answered these to some extent.

The constitution, with the amendment that in line 11 the phrase "open to anyone in the University community" be changed to read "limited to students, faculty, administrators and their families" was brought up for approval. A roll call vote was requested and the vote was 10 aye and 4 nay with Councilmen ... seven names ... absent.

Councilman Briggs introduced a change in the by-laws for consideration at the next meeting. His motion is as follows: "I move that the Student Council adopt a policy whereby all University organizations, sanctioned by the Student Council, be required to list any affiliations or connections with any organizations existing outside the University Community or unsanctioned by the Student Council."

Since that was the last meeting of the year, I headed back to 44 East and packed for my upcoming trip to Atlanta. I was scheduled to arrive late Thursday, with a plane ticket home on Monday. The plan was that my Georgia Peach would arrive in Pittsburgh the Monday after Christmas, December 28, and drive back to Charlottesville with Ted Hogshire and me in his car.

As I exited my Piedmont Airlines three-stop flight, Margaret Ann greeted me. She wore a matching lavender sweater and pants outfit, with a tan leather jacket and shoes. Someone had said, "You can tell the girls from Georgia and Alabama. They still wear bobby socks." To me she was perfect.

She introduced me to her amused driver, Louise Staton, who was several years older and in a big sister mode. Louise was rapidly rising in an advertising firm, and she, too, was accustomed to meeting Margaret Ann's many "forever this time" crushes. It was difficult for us to walk through the airport throng since our eyes were fixed on each other, but our caregiver kept us out of trouble.

That night we went out to introduce me to some longtime friends of hers, and Irene Croft's "she's older than you" came back to me. Libba Wight Floyd had married Billy, who was three years older than she. He was an executive with the Ivan Allen Company, and they lived in a town house and owned a dog. Her friend Lana Ball Moye's husband, Mike, was a banker, and he, too, was older than she. Even the unmarried friends were in a different universe.

I was very relieved that she and I weren't yet that institutionalized, and we retreated to the normal world of dating. Her father and I also began to relax around each other and find common ground. He was a man's man when he was free of his wife's instructions and had many experiences prior to marriage that were worthy of a Wahoo's respect.

On Saturday night we went to the wedding of Nancy Werner and Bill Gaston, followed by something I excelled at: attending a lavish reception with endless drinks and champagne. Today, I stick with bourbon, but that night it was the bubbly.

One thing I loved about Margaret Ann was she wasn't clingy, which meant that five minutes after we had gone down the reception line, she was off to check on old friends. Her brother, Gray, was a freshman at Valdosta State and a sort of pledge to me.

Periodically he'd ask, "How many glasses have you had?"

Since I had no clue, I'd say five or eight, whatever seemed like a substantial number.

When it was getting time to leave, I said to Gray, "The host would be flattered if you told him you enjoyed the champagne so much that you were going to take a bottle."

Gray was feeling no pain by then and did exactly as I suggested.

I should add that the bride's father was certainly no innocent, could well afford it, and took it in stride.

From there, Margaret Ann, feeling quite fine but totally under control, took us to an after party at a nearby apartment complex just off Peachtree (in Atlanta, everything seems to be just off Peachtree). The tenants were some guys a few years older than my girl and about a dozen of her friends.

I was enjoying the get-together, and then Margaret Ann asked if I knew where Gray was. So, I started to look for him. When I entered a bedroom, there he was, asleep on his back, mouth agape, in the center of a king-sized bed and surrounded by his champagne and dinner contents. Since I was certain that the scene might not receive a sympathetic response from the hosts, I returned to the party and found Margaret Ann.

"I found Gray," I told her. "In a couple of minutes, I'm going to head toward the door with him over my shoulder. Follow me and act like nothing has happened. Then we'll get out of here."

Thus, we made a clean getaway. We put Gray to bed and avoided detection by his parents.

On Sunday afternoon, after church and lunch, two friends of Gray's from Valdosta, Wayne Pearson and Brian McIntosh arrived. It was then Margaret Ann and I had our first less-then-positive experience.

Since I was leaving the next day, I assumed she and I would spend the afternoon together, but she planned to spend the time wrapping presents for the boys. When I complained, it only stiffened her resolve. I retaliated by refusing to help decorate the tree, which drew curious looks from the others. Margaret Ann ignored me, refusing to capitulate to my self-centered wishes, as others had done. This only served to place me further under her spell, and the trip wound up on a positive note.

I left for Pittsburgh the next day, eager for Margaret Ann to follow. And before her arrival, I enjoyed some relaxed time with my family, including my maternal grandparents and Mount Lebanon friends.

On Wednesday we went Christmas tree shopping, which was a time-consuming affair since the choice had to be unanimous. The family traditionally decorated the tree (once Santa Claus no longer brought it) when Advent ended on Christmas Eve, and we left it up until Twelfth Night, January 6, when the glow of municipal bonfires lighted the skies as the trees were burned. To me, the Deep South practice of putting up trees just after Thanksgiving and taking them down before New Year's seemed strange, even blasphemous. It would be many years before I learned the Holy Spirit's presence rendered religious traditions permittable but inconsequential.

After the midnight service on Christmas Eve, in the absence of small children, the time to open presents started later and was followed by an afternoon of visiting nearby open houses. It was always then that my dad would say he wasn't going anywhere they didn't have the television turned on to watch the games. I thought that was odd, but after meeting the Cravens, I wondered what would happen if Bob had told Ruth that he'd watch TV while she visited the hosts.

Pat McFalls called me the morning after Christmas to say he was coming by to pick me up and then we were going downtown to spend the money he'd received. After about ten minutes at Kaufmann's Department Store and then Gimbel Brothers, the city's two premiere stores, we decided the crowds were too big and went to a movie and then another, after which we decided it was too late to shop and stopped on the way home for a few pitchers. Then Pat noticed that *Father Goose* with Cary Grant was playing across the street, so we caught a third movie.

While Pat lived near me on the Lawn—he was also on the Student Council and known as an offensive line mainstay who'd played all fall with a Novocain-numbed shoulder—this was our closest encounter. Around eleven we headed off to the city's playground for twenty- and thirtysomethings, Walnut Street. After we chose which of the numerous establishments to visit, we discussed a variety of subjects, including my desire to be elected president of the Student Council and Pat's ability to help make that happen.

In the November elections four third-year men had been elected to serve two semesters at the beginning of the spring semester. Pat had completed two semesters on the council and would roll off with Eugene "Gene" Angle, Alex Wells, and Polk Kellam. Once my de facto campaign manager outlined a strategy, the place was closing and we departed.

While the temperature had warmed up considerably and the snow had receded, there was still some along the roadways and at the back of our driveway.

Pat turned in, and I wasn't paying much attention until he said, "I didn't know you had a circular driveway!"

"We don't," I said.

"Well, you do now," he smiled as he circled again.

At the time it seemed humorous to me too. After all, it was an honest mistake.

The next morning, I was awakened in my third-floor room when I heard my dad exclaim, "Who drove over our backyard!"

I knew two things for certain. One, he was not as amused as Pat and I had been. And two, I wasn't coming downstairs until I was sure dad had left.

Bright and early I called the airline and was told the flight from Atlanta was delayed because of weather. Puzzled, I pointed out that I was looking at a perfect sky and there was no snow.

"Fog in Atlanta," the airline representative answered.

But I was still perplexed, and the voice on the other end of the connection said, "Son, if you want to complain about the weather, talk to God, not me."

If only I had heeded advice like that more frequently over the years about everything.

The plane arrived in the early afternoon with me at the gate as my angel descended the stairs and entered my outstretched arms.

Dinner the first night was a discovery event for both the southern girl and my family. While we had lived in Virginia and Texas, my grandparents had not. The only family member from Dixie was feisty Aunt Samantha (Sam), who'd met Uncle Charlie while he was in OSS training in her native Louisiana and was aggressively southern. But our visitor and my nineteen-year-old sister Kingsley ("Lee"), fourteen-year-old brother Doug, and the other four meshed wonderfully. Lee happily gave up her room—which was as far removed as possible from the stairs to my room—to Margaret Ann.

While both families had Judeo-Christian values, Ruth Craven was not excessively modest, but my mother was. She made Victorian standards seem loose. At one point I put off Margaret Ann's request to see my room, knowing my mom would be aghast. It was another way in which each of us considered the other's family odd. I've since concluded that all families are odd in their own way.

The next days were a whirlwind of activity. We toured the neighborhoods from Mount Lebanon and the South Hills to an afternoon at Dick Tucker's home in Squirrel Hill. We visited Fox Chapel, the Pitt campus, and other sites. The most astounding things to the Georgian were the ethnic variety of names, the number of southerners she met, and the accents at stores, restaurants, and especially the hockey game.

Since she'd clearly not had an epiphany about moving north, it never occurred to her that others had.

In fact, because of Birmingham's steel industry, oil companies from Texas and Oklahoma and many other companies were represented in the area, and thus the southern population was extensive. There was even a Southern Club for debutantes since many from Dixie viewed themselves as a separate ethnic group and were treated as such in certain quarters. Also, Pittsburgh's determination to be a renaissance city was still something of a national secret.

After several days Margaret Ann commented to my mom in a tone that suggested surprise, "Gosh, Mrs. Briggs, I'm having a very good time. There are some nice people in Pittsburgh!"

"Why thank you very much, Margaret Ann," Mom responded. "That's awfully nice of you to say."

Since Margaret Ann was not accustomed to Northeastern irony and knowing something was happening but she wasn't sure what it was, she added, "I guess the worst place I've ever been is Newark, New Jersey!"

"Oh, really?" Mom said. "I was born there."

When I saw the look of dismay on Margaret Ann's face, I quickly said we needed to meet some people. It took a lot of convincing from me to assure her that Mom was in no way upset or offended by her comments. I told her that Mom obviously enjoyed their banter.

Early the next afternoon some friends came by to take us to lunch at Pizzeria Delphina, one of my favorite places. By then it had snowed again, about three-quarters of an inch, and Margaret Ann was prepared to trek across the Arctic. She came out in boots, rose-colored ski pants, gloves, and a white parka with a rose pattern that matched everything else.

Slightly bemused, a friend asked, "Where does she think she's going? The North Pole or what?"

But in no time this cheerful Dixie Pixie enchanted the males and won over the females.

In western Pennsylvania, after Thanksgiving, the townships flooded the asphalt tennis courts at schools and parks in preparation for winter's freeze. While often mushy or bumpy, the intermittent melting and freezing provided natural maintenance.

After my little alien marveled at the Stephen C. Foster Elementary School makeshift rink, full of skaters and hockey players, I took her to a Penguins hockey game and exposed her to a congregation of die-hard fans.

As with most things, Margaret Ann was rapturously excited, clinging to my arm and asking, "Can he hit him like that?" "Is that little box for time outs," and often "What are they saying now?"

When I answered one of her questions with "Hit the puck," she asked what that was.

"It's that little black thing they're hitting with their sticks."

Then we took the incline up Mount Washington to have drinks at Le Mont, and see the view of Gateway Center and the Golden Triangle.

On New Year's Eve day, Ted Hogshire arrived to pick up Melissa, a Wilson College student he would be driving six hours each way to take to a party. All afternoon he kept telling us, "She's so deep," "She's just deep, that's it!" It was so amusing, we started repeating it to ourselves.

Soon after he arrived, Hoggy was standing in front of the toilet, which faced the door, when my grandmother entered the bathroom. Flustered, he said, "Hey, come on in!"

Grandma took it in stride and wordlessly withdrew.

All of my Virginia houseguests tended to leave an imprint on the family. That summer Joe Brown, a former Marine, had introduced himself to my young brother, using one of his many nicknames. "Hi! I'm the Fox. I'm a trained killer." Doug still quotes that to this day.

Early in the evening a few friends came by for a drink before the New Year's Eve soiree. By then I'd begun to realize that my girl was on her own timetable, especially when preparing for a public appearance. I asked my grandmother to check on her.

When Grandma returned, she told me, "Well, that's a purposeful young lady with a mind of her own. When I told her the other girls were wearing skirts and sweaters, she said, 'This is what I brought to wear, and this is what I'm wearing.'"

Shortly thereafter the young starlet made a studied entrance down the hall stairway clad in a stunning pale blue satin cocktail dress, white gloves, and perfect accessories.

Overwhelming though her outfit was, what most astounded me was Tinker Bell's tiny waist. Though she was obviously aware of the others, her eyes were fixed on me as she came across the room. As for the others, no one would have been surprised if she'd worn a hoop skirt out of *Gone with the Wind*. In their minds, Georgia was the land of Margaret Mitchell's novel, which personified the culture.

The rest of the evening was like a dream I never wanted to wake up from. Margaret Ann's knack for making any man she talked to seem to be the only person in the room endeared her to everyone. Because of her outgoing way, she accomplished this while making female contacts as well, although that was of secondary importance to her.

Saturday, January 1, 1965, was the beginning of an eventful year. For us, like most people, it was a day of sleeping in, Bloody Marys, food, friends, and bowl games.

The next day Margaret Ann and I left for Charlottesville with Teddy. It was then we learned about the real Melissa. It turned out she'd wanted to tell him personally, not by phone or mail, that she had met someone else. Periodically throughout the trip, he'd say, "She is so shallow. She's just shallow. That's it."

Although we were empathetic, it was remarkable how Melissa could have undergone such a monumental transformation over such a short time. Thankfully, by the time we reached Harrisonburg, talk of Melissa was history.

We reached Charlottesville around eleven. After many impassioned embraces, my fair lady boarded the Atlanta-bound train at 6:30 the next morning, and another chapter ended. I was off to 44 East Lawn to catch some shuteye, mourn the absence of my beloved, and get ready for my grand-finale semester.

# Chapter 20

# Student Council President

On Monday, January 4, 1965, after hearing about each other's vacations on the Lawn, at the Beta house, and in Cabell Hall, classes resumed in earnest, with semester exams slated to begin in a few weeks. Since I had dropped chemistry, I had only four courses to focus on, and I felt comfortable about three of them. The fourth was Spanish civilization and literature, which produced in me a sense of dread. While there are better known phobias, I was the first victim of what I called Español-phobia.

The penultimate meeting of the Student Council's fall semester was the next night. Most of the issues of the term had been successfully dealt with before the Christmas break. A major item had been getting Mr. Titus of the Housing Office to permit private telephones in the Alderman Road Dorms.

Jon Verity, a Beta brother, was the chairman of the Alderman Road counselors, and he had submitted reports at almost every council meeting of the semester before reporting a successful conclusion. I marveled at Verity's ability to remain calm in all circumstances, because he never raised his voice or became emotional, and eventually the other side almost always came around and agreed with him.

By now, too, the Athletic Department seemed to be content, although someone was always ready to air some new grievance against it.

Two significant matters, however, remained unsolved in January. The first involved visiting hours for women in the public spaces of certain dorms at specific times. The dean continued to keep it under review, presumably forever, but the matter remained a major student desire and campaign plank issue and wasn't going away. The other problem concerned what steps were needed to deny potentially disruptive outside social action groups access to University resources and facilities. The next step in that process started as soon as the council was called to order.

> January 5, 1965
> Regular committee reports.
> Old Business:
> Councilman Crown saw Dean Runk and related Council's query concerning the limits of the automobile regulations. Mr. Crown was for the city limits. Mr. Runk was for the county. And that was that. [Student automobiles were subject to the University's ranking requirements anywhere in Albemarle County. Daryl Crown, on behalf of the council, asked Dean Runk if these could be changed to cover only the city of Charlottesville. Since it was not approved, unstickered vehicles, which included the vehicles belonging to first-year men, were required to remain out of the whole county. A change would have been very significant. Crown's comment showed to what extent the dean decided what happened at the U.]
> The motion by Councilman Briggs was brought up for consideration. The motion is as follows: [Motion

read as quoted earlier]. After much discussion the motion passed with two opposed.

New Business:

Committee reports are to be in by the next meeting. The election of officers will be next week.

After the council approved the recognition of organizations and the funds to be allocated to them, they went to the Student Activities Committee, which consisted of students, faculty, and administration, for consent. Although it almost never happened because of the tradition of student self-government, vetoes occurred occasionally. Because he was both the cornerstone and linchpin of everything, Dean Runk was more than just a vote, so his opinion carried significantly more weight than others.

Since a new semester was about to commence, there were many items on the agenda for the January 7 and 14 meetings dealing with the end of the fall semester and included a flurry of final approvals. The minutes reported, "Copies of a listing of monies distributed thus far during the first semester were supplied committee members. Allocations to date total $33,429.37."

After a short discussion, two final requests were presented:

> Mr. Player presented his first item of business, a request of $318.00 from the Virginia Council on Human Relations. Student Council had recommended this be cut to $250.00 by eliminating money for high school recruiting.
>
> Mr. William Leary, president of the organization, was on hand and reviewed the request.
>
> Mr. Scott asked about the high school recruiting program, and Mr. Leary stated Human Relations Council members have been visiting negro high schools

[and] advising students of opportunities open to them at the University of Virginia.

Mr. Runk asked about the relationship of the Virginia Council of Human Relations to the newly organized Students for Social Action.

Mr. Leary stated there was no connection. He also stated that the Council's speakers' programs are open to the public.

After Mr. Leary withdrew, Mr. Runk clarified this statement, saying that he felt Mr. Lowry was mistaken about the public being allowed to attend such speeches in Cabell Hall; he believed that attendance was by invitation only and that this was the basis on which the Virginia Council on Human Relations was permitted to use University facilities.

Dean Runk's understanding was in keeping with University policy, that is, meetings were for students. Such scrutiny, however, was not generally manifest. The funds request was approved, as was a request from the Fencing Club for $86.00.

While there was an understanding that things concerning racial matters needed to change, there was also a belief that the University should not permit the school to host disruptive demonstrations similar to those that were occurring on other campuses across the country.

I believe most of the community believed the owner of a place of business had the right to decide who they wanted to invite into their establishment. As an example, Buddy's Restaurant ("Where the neat meet to eat!") on Route 29, across from The Cavalier, was picketed by a history professor and a few students in the only protest incident I can recall during my time in Charlottesville. An equally small group of counterprotesters (rednecks) abused the picketers while the student patrons of the restaurant watched the entertainment from their window-side tables. It was not an indication of partisanship; it was a belief that such matters were not part of the University experience, but academics, athletics, and party weekends were.

These sentiments were part of the larger desire for isolation from the winds of change blowing across the country. Several items in the *CD* of February 9, 1965, serve to illustrate the attitudes of the time. An article concerned the Student Council motion to participate in a newly established Student Governments of the United States of America (ASG). Councilmen Pat McFalls and Phil Stone had been instrumental in its creation at a meeting at the University of Oklahoma, which was also attended by *CD* editor Dick Carlton.

In a lead editorial titled "A. S. G. Constitution: The Need for Ratification," the writer noted: "Established by a number of schools disenchanted by the National Student Association, the new group [ASG] seeks to provide a common meeting ground on which problems of student government can be discussed. This will be done without the political overtones which have come to plague the NSA."

Equally telling was another editorial titled "Change of Sets in Vietnam?"

> With the announcement that their next Asian target for concentrated political action would be Thailand, the Chinese Communists have notified the world of their intentions to increase subversive maneuvers throughout the area. The first indication that such a policy was definitely being put into effect came just a few days ago, when the Viet Cong, continuing its struggle to overthrow the vestiges of democracy in South Vietnam, carried out a military operation directed against the forces of the United States ... Secretary of State Dean Rusk stated bluntly, "It is they [the Communists] who set the scenario." Every action which the United States takes,

then, is a reaction to Communist policy. We have allowed them to make a move, and then have attempted to counteract their infiltration with a token show of strength ... .

The United States has allowed the Communists to set the scene in Vietnam, and other Asian nations, for too long a time. If Vietnam does fall, then there can be little doubt that the Communists will direct their subversive lines in a concentrated effort against Thailand. And if the United States does not change its policy, if the policy makers do not decide to take more positive action, if the democratic armies serving in Vietnam do not attempt to grab the initiative, then assuredly the Communists will not have only set the stage, they will also have acted the play.

As the fall semester came to a close, two impactful things happened, the most important of which to me was my election as Student Council president. While it was not a forgone conclusion, it meant that my final semester experience would be exponentially expanded.

The other was my academic result, for had it not been for a C- in Spanish, I would have achieved a 3.0.

Although less important to me at the time, my career choices expanded quite a bit. As at Blair, starting at the bottom made it easier to show continued improvement. From a 1.37 GPA at the end of my first year, I'd now rocketed to 1.97. At the University, while a B+ was nicer than a B or a B-, numerically it meant nothing. A student with all A-grades had a 4.0 GPA while one with all B+ grades had a 3.0.

The first of my regular meetings with Dean Runk occurred a few days after my election. We had a pleasant conversation, and he outlined the several University committee meetings I would now attend and their purposes. Then he told me I could represent the University in early February at the thirteenth annual Presidential Prayer Breakfast and the first annual Seminar of Student Leaders in Washington. I was very excited, told him so, and accepted right away. It proved to be an incredible experience.

As Dean Runk instructed, the following week, I went by the bursar's office to pick up an advance on my expenses. As I was leaving the office, Señor Chinchon was entering.

He asked, "Ah, Señor Briggs, what are you doing here?"

After I told him about the prayer breakfast, the seminar, and the expense money, he said, "You're graduating this year, right?"

I seized the moment and said, "That depends a lot on you, Señor Chinchon!"

When I arrived at my hotel in Washington, I met my roommate, a nice enough person who attended a school I'd never heard of. In the lobby I met the student government presidents of Yale and Columbia. We decided to talk over some beers, and I returned to my room to get my jacket.

I was surprised to see my roommate and a friend kneeling by the side of his bed. He smiled up at me and said, "Frank, we're talking to Jesus. Would you like to join us?"

I stammered my thanks and explained I was meeting some people and escaped, wondering what those two were thinking. Ten years passed before I knew the answer. They were committed to the Lord while I had yet to be.

The next several hours were an education for me as the two Ivies discussed things I'd never thought or cared about. For me and almost all my constituents, the boundaries of our world did not extend beyond our self-contained community. Virginia decided each year not to participate in *Who's Who in American Colleges and Universities*. If people at the University knew, what difference did it make who else did?

At least the Yale guy was a Beta with whom I had some commonality. At one point the Columbia Lion asked me, "What are you people doing about curriculum control?"

Clueless as to what he meant, I said, "The deans do that."

After a while we discontinued that kind of talk and indulged in what we all had in common: beer.

The next morning, I rose early and headed over to the breakfast. As I was about to enter the building, a limousine pulled up and Vice President Hubert Humphrey emerged and walked only ten feet away from me.

After the prayer breakfast I went to the student leaders' meeting, which had several speakers followed by a Q&A. One of the speakers was a man I'd heard make a successful campaign speech for senior class office at Mount Lebanon High School eight years earlier, when I was a brand-new freshman. I introduced myself and we had a nice talk, which ended with our setting a time to meet up again for him to tell me more about his group, Moral Re-Armament, after I returned to Charlottesville. That chance encounter went much further than I anticipated.

While I waited for the Capitol subway, I recognized a slender well-dressed man standing next to me and said, "Hello, Congressman Kennedy. I'm Frank Briggs, representing the University of Virginia at the Prayer Breakfast. People tell me I was trying to emulate you when I had my back accident. I tell them I had mine first, so you must be the one following my example."

He looked at me with a friendly smile, patted my stomach, and asked, "Still wearing a brace?"

"No sir," I said.

"Looks like it," he grinned.

I'd met Ted Kennedy, the youngest of the three famed brothers.

After chatting with an aide to my senator, Hugh Scott of Pennsylvania, I headed back to Virginia to reenter the happy life of academics, road trips, and party weekends.

Ash Wednesday was on February 12, which marked the annual trek to Mardi Gras in New Orleans by a number of dedicated road trippers. Stories abounded. One concerned itself with how well the city's cops could wield billy clubs. And an attempt to place a beer bottle into the hindquarters of a mounted police officer's steed was dealt with swiftly and efficiently.

One group of returning road warriors continued their shenanigans along the road back to Virginia and decided to moon a Greyhound bus. Afterward they roared off toward Charlottesville, happy as larks. But several days later they received a summons to report to a variety of authorities. The bus driver and passengers had noted the car's license plate. At that point the boyish prank became a serious offense, and as a result, one of our most distinguished classmates was not permitted to graduate with the rest of us in June. While the sentence was severe. It was generally thought to have been the best of many options. The event also established the perpetrator even more firmly in Cavalier lore.

About the same time a young SAE pledge fell under the spell of Wooly Neck and rolled with him to Mary Baldwin. They had a wonderful time. As they were leaving, Wooly spotted a large road scraper parked by a landscaping project in the middle of the campus and induced the pledge to climb aboard. Once he was in the saddle, after maneuvering a few levers, the behemoth began to rumble forward. When the panicked pledge tried to ask Alex how to stop it, he turned and saw his hero standing on the ground, doubled up in laughter.

The vehicle came to a stop seventy-five yards later against a large tree, surrounded by an increasing number of official vehicles, all with sirens and flashing lights.

When the pledge later appeared in court, he was accompanied only by his father, a small business owner in Roanoke, and legal counsel. His mentor, as Wooly was adept at doing, had convinced the pledge to not identify him. The case was settled, but only after the dad produced more than $15,000.

As agreed, the Moral Re-Armament leader contacted me shortly after I returned to school and impressed upon me the importance to the nation of having a program at the University. While I knew nothing about the organization, the idea that our country was in a spiritual crisis and the desire to please this defender of morality led me to present the idea to Dean Runk at our second meeting.

Mr. Runk explained to me that this group had been around before in different wrappings, and he implied that he gave the venture little chance for success. Nonetheless, since I was enthused, he did not contest it.

The presentation was to be made by a panel of ten, led by two U.S. Olympic gold-medal holders. Next, my friend Will Montague, a KA and president of the University Union, presented the proposal to the Student Council. They approved it unanimously, as did the Committee on Student Activities. And Dick Carlton dutifully supported it in the *CD*.

On March 25 Newcomb Hall's ballroom was emblazoned with Moral Re-Armament banners and materials. From the University community were maybe a hundred students, Dean Runk, and me. The University was no less apathetic to the Religious Right than any other movement.

While the event was not a success, the matter built a bridge between Dean Runk and me. He never referred to the Moral Re-Armament event, but he showed me he was willing to work with me. And it made me eager to work with him. As the semester progressed, he became a sort of father figure to me, often stern but always courteous, taking advantage of opportunities to instruct me in a reasonable manner. He often said to me, "There is more to being a leader than simply being elected to a position." That phrase still resonates with me. While we would often disagree over student activities, there was always a sameness of mind on our overriding objective: preservation of the University way of life.

When the spring semester began, it looked as if I was not going to win my appeal with the Army concerning ROTC, and I began to think about what I was going to do after graduation. It seemed that law school was the most acceptable option. And in the fall, like 68 percent of my class, I'd taken the LSAT and done very well.

We could all have done a little better had the test not been administered on the day of the UNC football game. It was a very high scoring affair, with lots of lead changes. The first time there was a roar from Scott Stadium, Bud Simpson, the law student monitoring the test, left the room. When he returned, he wrote the score on the blackboard. Each time he updated the score, many in the room were distracted.

Of course, my dad suggested an alternative, namely, I should get a job. While I thought this was the most distasteful option, a friend suggested I sign up for some job interviews at the placement office. Naturally I protested, vowing I didn't want a job yet, but my friend said that was a perfect reason to do the interviewing, because there would be no pressure.

The next Monday I signed up for the first four on the bulletin board. They were listed in alphabetical order: American Cyanamid, American Tobacco, AT&T, and Atlanta First National Bank.

American Cyanamid wasn't a fit.

I liked the tobacco company because the first year was spent in the tobacco fields and at auctions, learning to grade tobacco. When I mentioned the soon-to-be-released Surgeon General's report, they assured me that would pose no problem to them.

AT&T was the hardest interview. First, the evaluator asked me what made me most proud of my years at Virginia. I started with being Student Council president, and he asked, "What else?" After I rolled out at least six extracurriculars, he said, "Son, has anything academic ever excited you?"

I had no good answer.

So, he asked, "Why do you want to work for the telephone company?"

That was a tough question since I really didn't want to work for the telephone company. All I said was, "Because it's a big company."

He struggled not to roll his eyes. "Why is that important?"

"Because there's plenty of room to go to the top," I said. It was all I could think of.

The interviewer ended the interview. "You have a great future," he said, "but it's not with the telephone company."

In the fourth interview, I struck pay dirt. After about five minutes, the interviewer said, "We want to fly you to Atlanta. When can you come?"

I could scarcely believe my good fortune! I'd been trying to think of how to get to Margret Ann's the next weekend for spring break. He said the timing was fine and they would reimburse me. When I told him I didn't have the money to start with, he said they'd work out transportation and lodging. I told him I wanted to stay with friends, and he was okay with that.

When I arrived at the Atlanta airport in the evening, I was told to catch the airport shuttle to the Biltmore Hotel on West Peachtree. Since my family usually picked me up whenever I arrived in town, I interpreted this as a cool reception by the Cravens.

The shuttle had to drop off passengers at five other hotels before I eventually arrived at mine. But I was enthusiastically embraced there by Margaret Ann and realized this was not a mark of disaffection but the pragmatic decision of a different mindset. The Cravens simply didn't do things that were less convenient.

I spent the next day at First National Bank of Atlanta, escorted from one interview to the next. And lunch was included, with all the interviewees, at the restaurant on the top floor of the Bank of Georgia Building, the city's tallest structure. We were reminded more than once that First National's new building was under construction and would be the tallest building in town at forty-four stories.

While I probably did all right at lunch, I didn't think I had. In the company of eight other prospects I didn't know, I felt aloof and out of character. It didn't seem to matter, though, and I received a warm send-off, with a lot of materials to complete and return.

Bob Craven's office was a few blocks from the bank, so I rode home with him and two women who carpooled with him. At that time the downtown connector was two lanes each way, and we sat in traffic for ages.

That night, Margaret Ann and I had a lover's quarrel. While I was used to the partygoer who stayed up until all hours, she was now a Grady Hospital lab technologist who went to bed by 9:30. I had never let sleep deprivation get in the way of having a good time, but Margaret Ann never passed up eight hours of sleep. It was another reminder to me that if we had separate opinions, hers would prevail.

The next morning a well-rested me was dropped off at the Greyhound station for a ride to Athens and an interview with Lindsey Cowan, dean of the University of Georgia Law School. It was well known at Virginia that Georgia was on its way to being a splendid law school, because Mr. Cowan had come from the UVA Law School. After a very pleasant meeting with him, I headed back to the bus depot in that delightfully sleepy southern town, and the bus meandered through a series of even smaller towns on the way to Atlanta.

The next day was Friday, and I headed to the Emory Law School for a meeting with Col. Jacob Shacter, the head of admissions, for an agreeable meeting. The bus ride, though circuitous, afforded me a view of a different side of Atlanta, between Five Points and Decatur, the suburban city where the campus was located. As an urban school, at least relative to Charlottesville or Athens, Emory stood out in distinct contrast to the other two law schools.

That night, with no one scheduled to work on Saturday, my beloved transformed back into the girl I knew, and we went with a group of friends to the Whiskey A Go-Go, a new spot several blocks from the famous Fox Theatre. It was there, in between dancing the twist and embracing on the dance floor that I was introduced to Mary Staton, Margaret Ann's best friend since grade school.

After Northside High School their paths diverged significantly. Mary had gone to the University of Colorado in Boulder to become a modern dancer. After that she was a member of the famed Martha Graham School of Contemporary Dance in New York, specifically Greenwich Village.

She happened to be in town for a visit, and she and I spent the evening battling over our mutual loved one. Mary was a devout feminist and saw her task to be saving Margaret Ann from the life of a southern matron. She should quit her humdrum job, cast off the shackles of conventionality, and move to a liberal land.

But I was equally determined to keep Margaret Ann from that life. At the end of the evening, although the romantic idea of becoming a medical missionary was enticing, Margaret Ann did not cast her lot with the anarchists.

The next day the status quo was back and Margaret Ann returned to being as conventional as she was capable of. But I'd glimpsed the seed of exploration buried just below her surface and feared it.

On Sunday morning another of her many facets emerged: the need to take whatever amount of time she deemed necessary to complete dressing (an all-inclusive term for all the things she did before leaving her room to dazzle whoever might see her). Her family, especially her father, alluded to it, but this was the first time I would be significantly inconvenienced.

When the belle announced we'd walk the half mile to a new church, St. Anne's Episcopal, rather than ride with her parents to St. Philip's, I thought it was a great idea. Ruth Craven pointed out that we'd need to leave early if we wanted a seat, since the sanctuary was being remodeled. As they left for St. Philip's, she repeated her admonition.

Finally, we left the house all of six minutes before the service was scheduled to start. Nevertheless, my escort was very happy and totally unconcerned about the time. When we entered, all the seats had been taken, and while folding chairs had been brought in for the overflow crowd, there were no two seats open together. So, I glowered from a chair five rows behind Margaret Ann.

An hour later, not knowing how to ask the Holy Spirit for guidance, I complained on the way home. Margaret Ann peevishly pointed out that we'd left home as soon as she was ready. After we'd walked some distance in silence, I capitulated, knowing if a mistake had been made, it wasn't going to be hers.

After that we were at one again and snuggled happily, until she and her father dropped me off at the Biltmore to catch the airport shuttle.

# Chapter 21

## Road to Easters

After exams and spring break were over, Student Council business resumed, and I began to understand the presidency was going to consume at
least four or five hours a day. This was the first time in my life when something extremely demanding charged me with excitement and anticipation.

To start, I reviewed my predecessor's correspondence and learned
the presidential officeholder was the chief negotiator for the student body
and was responsible for presenting all student demands to the administration and for making sure the council clearly understood the administration's positions. Next, I realized I would be attending some alumni
and other schools' meetings as a representative of the Virginia student,
which would require an exemplary demeanor. Finally, the previous president had two responses to requests: since we've participated in the past,
we will continue to do so, or since we did not participate in the past, we
will not participate now. It struck me as a sound path to follow.

I decided to move the Student Council meetings from the Newcomb
Hall boardroom to the Rotunda. The meeting was pictured on the *CD's*
front page and captioned "Mr. Jefferson's Rotunda again quakes at sounds
of Student Government."

In response to significant student criticism about a rise in dairy product prices, I met with Bernard C. Fontana, the food service director, and invited him to defend the action. After significant discussion, some middle ground was achieved.

Also, the council had received no answer from Mr. Herring, director of Newcomb Hall, agreeing that he could not approve groups to use the facilities without the council's written consent. I investigated.

A motion was passed reiterating the long-standing Jeffersonian position that religious groups must coordinate any activities through the University YMCA. A request from the Christian Fellowship Association, which had been advanced in error, was withdrawn.

A motion to inform the Students for Social Action that the sale of SNIC (Student Nonviolent Coordinating Committee) buttons was regarded as an affiliation with that group was passed.

After this meeting, I met with Dean Runk and began to understand more fully how his significant presence kept the University's often disparate parts balanced and running smoothly.

President Edgar F. Shannon was a greatly respected academic and received well-deserved credit for the increasing prominence of the University, but he left the day-to-day operations to Dean Runk. The dean made no comment about the council's actions regarding the food services, because they were on course. But when I mentioned our problem with Mr. Herring, he explained there were no written guidelines and pointed out the advantages of that. He then offered to take care of the matter if the council wanted him to. I reported this at the next meeting, and there was no further discussion, because everyone knew this was a done deal that required no paperwork.

While I missed Margaret Ann tremendously, things were going very well with us. She would be coming to Easters Weekend in a little over a month. Meanwhile, we corresponded several times a week or I called her.

In 1965, long distance was a big deal, expensive, and operator assisted. For an extra charge, a call could be made collect, which meant the receiving party had to agree to pay. Another option was station to station, which meant the caller had to deposit the money when the right person picked up.

Since I never wanted to waste money paying to talk to her parents, I used the latter. And I especially didn't want to pay to hear Bob Craven grumble, "Can't that boy ever call you at a decent hour?"

Both letters and calls were filled with love and affection. One day I was treated to a second letter in two days. When I opened it, my happiness turned to shock and dismay!

"After giving it a lot of thought," she wrote, "I've decided that you and I are not meant for each other." It was signed "Sincerely," presumably to make sure I didn't misinterpret the message.

I absolutely couldn't believe what I was reading. How could this have happened in a single day? How could it be happening at all? For several hours a barrage of emotions flooded through me, especially anguish, rage, betrayal, and nausea.

Midafternoon, before heading to the shelter of my always loyal support group at 180 Rugby, I set out to find Margaret Ann's friend and former roommate Sue Hall. I poured out my tale of woe to this no-nonsense New Englander.

When I was through, she said, "You're better off! It's the best thing that's ever happened to you. She is fickle, fickle, fickle!"

It was exactly what I needed to hear.

Sue added, "I know exactly who you should go out with. Ann Marie. I'll fix it for this Friday."

At the Beta house, the gathering of brothers wounded in the feminine wars reinforced Sue's opinion. It was widely known at the house that if someone dumped a Beta, there was something the matter with the dumper and not the dumpee.

While Ann Marie wasn't my soul mate, we had a good time, and I reminded myself how messed up Margaret Ann was. At least I was trying to convince myself that she was.

When the Virginia spring began to burst forth, the backdrop of the Lawn changed from winter's steel gray to early fruit blossoms. The piles of firewood next to every door disappeared. Late at night or at sunrise, whenever I was alone, the beauty of my home was overpowering. In those times I could almost feel the presence of those who'd preceded me in this spot over a century and a half. Occasionally an unwelcome awareness crept around me that this time was going to end quickly, that I couldn't stay here forever. This was such an unwanted thought that I rushed into some activity to push it away from me. I wished that time could warp and we'd all remain here forever, as in Brigadoon.

The fraternities resumed their road trips, and women's schools all around the Commonwealth placed their security on high alert. Typically, this type of road trip was a bus roll and the destination rested heavily on how many brothers had potential dates at a particular school.

In the case of Beta, Rutledge (aka President Young) was very involved with a Hollins girl, Mary. So, one afternoon a bus pulled up out front of BOII and we piled aboard. As the de facto first lady, Mary had arranged dates for all who needed one—including me. The 120-mile trip required many cases of beer, so the trip was much easier as an upperclassman, because pledges could be bumped from the line to the restroom at any time.

Upon our arrival it was crucial that everyone remain on the bus and keep his mouth shut while Rutledge and some others escorted the ladies through the campus checkout and onto the bus. An unruly group could be summarily dismissed and their conveyance banished.

My date was a tall Louisiana blonde who announced to me that she did not go to bed with people. I didn't know how this act might be accomplished on a bus trip to the Sportsman Club dance floor and back.

So, I assured her that I certainly wouldn't try to take advantage of anyone. She and I had a lovely time together, and the roll was a great success. One way I knew this was that it took several washings to get her lipstick out of my collar.

Another roll to Hollins was not so successful. One morning I went down to Alex's room to retrieve my favorite madras shirt. He handed it to me with the pocket torn off and said, "It's your fault. You knew what I was like when you lent it to me." He was right, but I had to ask where he'd been. He told me a sad tale.

The previous afternoon his uncle, a Hoo alumnus, showed up and announced he was tired of Lookout Mountain and had come to visit. A large group of SAE brothers and pledges had rented a truck and moved the E's living room into it for a truck roll to Hollins. Wooly invited his uncle along, and they all had a great trip over. But when the living-room-carrying truck full of boisterous Cavaliers rolled up to the gate, they were told to vacate the premises. The uncle did not take this well and told the administrators what they could do with their demand. Wooly opined he might be the only Wahoo whose uncle had been banned from Hollins.

As council president, I began to meet various members of Virginia's minis-cule dissident community as it pertained to off-grounds causes. The pressing concerns of almost all of us were centered around issues such as food and maid services, fraternity regulations, academic calendars, and student freedom, individually and communally. The University was ded-icated to Mr. Jefferson's concept of being an "academical village" in which all points of view could be explored.

During this semester the Students for Democratic Action requested funds for three speakers, among them James Farmer, director of the Congress of Racial Equality (CORE). This was readily granted. The majority of the council, however, believed it was in the best interests of our social order to prevent anything from disrupting that social order.

Disturbances that occurred within our confines, although sometimes challenging, were not visible to public scrutiny. Infringement from outside causes posed a very real threat to this comfort zone.

The SDA was represented by Howard Romaine and his attractive and omnipresent girlfriend, who was rumored to be the daughter of a very conservative state legislator. We all got along, and in different circumstances, we could have had a beer together. But our meetings followed a predictable course. Howard would ask me to present something to the council, and I would explain why I wasn't. Then he would threaten to petition the council, and I would tell him to go ahead, knowing that the possibility of obtaining signatures of 20 percent or more students was impossible.

Once Howard said they wanted to have a meeting the second weekend in April to which they would invite delegates from the other chapters. Other groups, such as the Young Republicans, did that. I told him I didn't need to consult with the dean or the council to tell him that this was impossible.

"Howard, it hasn't got anything to do with First Amendment rights. It has to do with security. That's Easters Weekend, and there's no way the University could keep your group from being annihilated! Pick another weekend and we'll talk about it."

A few law students with Ivy League and other northern undergraduate backgrounds sought to enlighten me.

The Garden Clubs of Virginia had scheduled a large event to dedicate the renovation of the East Gardens. The keynote speaker was to be the first lady of the United States, Lady Bird Johnson. And she would be accompanied by Margaret McNamara, wife of the secretary of defense. As Student Council president, I was invited to the dedication and reception on the Lawn that followed the event.

Several days before the dedication, I was visited by a contingent of students opposed to the Vietnam conflict (it wasn't called a war until later). When they told me it was my duty to inform Mrs. McNamara that her husband should end US involvement in Southeast Asia, I was shocked.

I tried to inject reality into their misguided thoughts and said, "There is no war in Vietnam. The president clearly says that this is a peacekeeping force necessary to protect South Vietnam from communist aggression."

I reminded them that the ladies were guests of the University, and it would be the height of rudeness to bring up a political matter at the reception.

The afternoon of the dedication was a perfect spring day, and the long, quite boring ceremony went off without a hitch.

Bill "Root" Powell, a Zete, representing the Darden Graduate School of Business, and I headed off for the best part: tables laden with tea sandwiches. After searching them for something recognizable, we each took a sandwich with something white in it. As soon as we bit into them, we looked at each other and wanted to spit out the food.

Suddenly a group of ladies arrived, and we heard Eleanor Shannon's delightful hostess voice as she introduced us to the first lady and Mrs. McNamara. Root and I engaged in very brief conversations with mouthfuls of cream cheese stuffed to the back of our jaws.

Because of my cliff accident I had no savings from the prior summer. So, my hospital job was very important, and I worked two or three shifts a week. I had enough seniority to become a floater, which meant I stayed in the auxiliary nursing office until I was needed on a floor. While the ER and ICU were the most fun, if I needed to find the time to study, the best place was the psychiatric ward—unless there was a full moon, which tended to make the patients restless.

One function of the floater was taking DOA's to the outpatient morgue and making sure they were cleaned and stuffed. One night I was accompanied by a new trainee orderly. He was squeamish, and the task made him nervous, even more so when we had to use a long, dimly lighted tunnel to get to the morgue.

While the inpatient facility had pull-out compartments for the bodies, the outpatient area had white metal tables. On the wall was a kitchen cupboard marked "For Babies Only." All of this made the trainee even less eager.

When I said, "I'll take the top and you take the legs," I did but he didn't.

This forced air out of the contracting lungs of the cadaver, which came out as a long groan. The trainee's face turned into a look of absolute horror, and he was out of the room in a blink. By the time I reached the door, he'd disappeared down the hall, never to be seen again.

That and many other experiences, some heartrending, made the job satisfying.

During my time at the hospital I befriended an intern who showed me how to do stitches. Under his supervision I practiced on some clinic patients and achieved some skill with a needle. When this became known, I became an unofficial ear piercer.

In general, pierced ears were considered foreign and unladylike, but they were coming into vogue. My procedures usually occurred very late in the evening, and there were several girls who sought my services.

First, an ice cube would be placed on the earlobe. Then a large sewing needle, the dull end stuck in a cork, would be sterilized with a cigarette lighter. Another girl would serve as my assistant and help me with the trickiest part. It was important to make sure the holes were placed uniformly. Later, my customers would proudly show me the result. I always reacted with satisfaction and relief. Since my talent was provided pro bono, there was never a refund request.

As the year progressed, I attended more meetings of the Committee on Fraternities as an ex officio member. The March 3 minutes are fairly descriptive of the typical items discussed:

Mr. Runk opened the meeting by bringing to the attention of the Committee the following matters: [Eight of the eleven concerned individual fraternity chapters: disciplinary actions, sanitation concerns (particularly in kitchens), and chapter finances. Only a few fraternities were involved. The other three concerned everyone]

8. Read present rule regarding pledges on probation having to be de-pledged.

10. Commented on disgraceful condition of Fraternity area following Mid-Winters Weekend: broken bottles, paper cups littering street and fraternity grounds long after they should have been cleaned up.

11. Reported to committee in general and students present in particular that community is fed up with ungentlemanly behavior of fraternity residents and guests and is pressing hard for University remedial action. Once again urged students to govern themselves.

IFC president Alan Goldstein then had the thankless task of representing a group of thirty-one unconcerned and unrepentant fraternities, almost none of whom cared about the academic requirements for pledges or chapters, litter, or noisy parties. Nonetheless, Goldstein and the IFC scholarship chairman, Edward "Ted" Feinour, spent the ensuing meetings discussing fixes.

It was noted that thirty pledges had GPA's less than 1.0. An IFC vote also found that only five fraternities were interested in establishing regulations relating to scholarship.

Later, during one of our meetings, Dean Runk suggested it would be nice to have a rule against carrying open containers in the streets. When I presented that at the next council meeting, it was greeted with derision and formally rejected by vote.

At another meeting, Daryl Crown suggested that Mad Lane be closed on party weekends:

> Councilman [Will] Rouse remarked that hitting one person a year was better than having police on the Lane.

One of the three faculty members of the 3-3-3 Committee on Fraternities was law professor A. J. Gustin Priest, a nationally acclaimed expert on public utilities law. He was also a devoted leader of his college (University of Idaho) fraternity, Beta Theta Pi. While he'd remained actively involved with the general fraternity since 1924 and visited many chapters over those years, he despised the Virginia Omicron chapter. Some said his first visit to 180 Rugby Road was for a faculty cocktail party and that he arrived wearing a Beta tie with the pledge manual, *Sons of the Stars*, tucked under his arm. According to legend, someone poured a beer on his head. (I referred to this story in chapter 6, but there's more to the professor's relationship to the UVA chapter.)

Whether the story above is true or not, the Law School website biography of the professor includes the following nugget: "The chapter at the University of Virginia both annoyed and worried A. J. for years because [its] organization and activities never met his own standards for fraternity life; finally in 1970 he was instrumental in having the Virginia Chapter dissolved."

Mr. Priest's disdain for the Wahoo Betas was made clear to me at every meeting of the committee. He never failed to inquire, "How are *those* Betas?!"

After a few encounters with him, I made a motion to the brothers to invite both Mr. Runk and Brother Priest to dinner at the Beta house. I consider inducing Mr. Priest to dine with the fraternity to be one of my greatest accomplishments at Virginia.

On the day of the dinner I received some pushback from Rusty, who conveniently forgot the matter had been discussed beforehand and unequivocally stated he didn't come to the house to eat with deans. It was an absurd comment, and the others told Pony as much. But he was on a roll and even forbade the goats from dining with Runk and Priest with threats of serious repercussions. My blood was up as well, and I reminded everyone that dinner with the dean and the law professor was a required pledge event. Eventually calmer minds pointed out to Pony that, right or wrong, Dean Runk and Mr. Priest would be at dinner that night.

When Mr. Runk and Brother Priest appeared, they received all the gracious hospitality the Beta brothers had to give, and a good time was had by all. There was a slight silence when Dean Runk noted Rusty's absence. He was immediately informed that Rusty was unable to attend because of an unusually heavy study load that evening.

Dean Runk never missed anything!

At the next chapter meeting, the dean's thank-you note was read aloud. Among the new business was the following recommendation: "B. Warner suggested the house adopt a policy of psychological intimidation toward the goats in the spring. He stressed the need for a concerted effort in this respect." Since the IFC had tightened the rules on physical hazing, this was a necessary precaution.

Other new business included the following report: "The annual ball grabber check was held with horrendous consequences. An unprecedented seven goats were found wearing grabbers. These same goats were cautioned on the dangers and inconveniences of such inappropriate and unfashionable underclothing."

Another task I had was meeting with Mr. Bus Male, assistant athletic director, about never increasing student athletic fees for any purpose. He had a woebegone approach and began each meeting with the same statement, "We make more money playing one game at Georgia Tech than in our entire home season."

I knew my job was not to commiserate with his woes, so I reminded him how hard pressed many students were to pay the current excessive fees, and then we'd schedule the next meeting.

Mr. Male's son, Buzzy, was a Zete pledge who was considerably more outgoing than his father. The elder, however, like many other second-level administrators, was well liked by the alumni, and his job was safe until he chose to retire in a world where nothing really changed.

Something else that looked as if it would never change was the policy against permitting female visitors visiting hours in certain dorms. After receiving no definitive response during the previous semester, Jim Gilwee requested that the question be renewed at the first council meeting of the second semester. A committee of Daryl Crown, Tim West, and Tom Ammons was appointed to pursue the matter, which they did with vigor. For more than a month they conducted an extensive poll of other schools, clergy, faculty, and administrators. And while the vote was close, the ayes outnumbered the nays, and the council triumphantly presented it to the administration.

After a suitable period in which the matter was allegedly considered, the administration sent its answer. Citing the Honor Code, compliance, and manpower concerns, the request was rejected.

The response caused an immediate fury. Dick Carlton wrote a scathing editorial titled "Dean Runk; Get Thee to a Nunnery!" On the afternoon it appeared in the *CD*, Dick visited me and asked what I thought about it and what the council was going to do next.

I told him the editorial was very good but perhaps a little too much in the attack mode, but the council intended to pursue it no further.

I can still see the look of pained betrayal in Dick's eyes. For me there were bigger issues involved. Preserving the fraternity system from attempted changes by the Committee on Fraternities and preserving our culture were by far the prime issues. I also had a comfortable relationship with Dean Runk. I knew he'd made up his mind, and further discussion of this matter would serve no purpose other than to impede our compatibility.

After Margaret Ann's "Dear John" letter, my dating activity increased significantly, but with no more than a date or two with any one individual. For a few weeks the physical education teacher at St. Anne's and I enjoyed each other's company, but it wasn't a good fit.

Pam Jones, one of the most beautiful and sought-after girls at Sweetbriar, and Jose Brown had become regulars, to the sadness of many Virginia men. Joe was a neighbor and good friend, both on the Lawn and as a Zete across the street from BQP, so their connection seemed quite natural.

One weekend Pam fixed me up with Eleanor, a junior schoolmate, and it was a great fit. El was a lovely blonde with myriad attributes. In addition to being good looking, she was smart, personable, easy-going, and an all-state field hockey player. One of the games at The Patch, a small pub near Sweetbriar, was bowling for beer. While I was a below-average bowler, El was great! As I sat with the other dates at a table, she'd win pitcher after pitcher from the other guys. After a while I asked her to come to Easters Weekend and she accepted.

The Thursday of Easters my mentor, Chuck Spence, told me to be in my room from eight o'clock on. That meant I was going to be tapped by TILKA, which was a very exciting moment for me. Several hours later I was marching through fraternity land, and the ceremony was described in the *CD*: "A pounding drum and loud chanting awakened early sleepers Thursday night as the two ribbon societies, Eli Banana and TILKA, performed their annual ritual of tapping new members."

In addition to me, joining fellow pledge brothers Rutledge Young and Jon Verity, who'd been tapped the year before, was Ted Hogshire from Beta as one of the eight tapped by TILKA that night. Also chosen was Ray Sutherland (Chi Phi), who I knew from my first year, and Will Montague (KA), a Lawn neighbor and friend.

The march went on until the wee hours, when the revelers began dropping out. Some left because they were dedicated students with Friday classes, and others became alcohol impaired. Two Elis fell in the line of duty. Bear fell off the back of the Zete parking lot and broke his leg, and the other required forehead stitches.

The next morning, I was awakened by Alex, an Eli, who thrust a letter at me.

"Sign this," he said.

I did, but a little later I went down to his room and asked what I had signed.

"A letter to the Zete house, apologizing for the damage we did to their kitchen," he explained.

"I wasn't at the Zete house," I objected. "I wound up at our house before coming back here."

"Well, if you'd been there, you would have," he responded. "That's not good enough."

"Give it to me," I said, and I struck out my signature and left before he had a chance to talk me out of it.

In any endeavor, continued practice improves performance, and party weekends were no exception. The April 10 issue of the *CD* proclaimed:

Mass of Pulchritude Come for Party Weekend

Fraternities Schedule Usual Revelry

Combos Produce Music as Dancers

Imbibe Copiously in Easters Spirit

Alumni Pour onto Grounds for Gridiron Contest

Pro-Studded Ex-Cavaliers to Test

Mettle of Davis-Led Varsity Squad

In Annual Scott Stadium Encounter

The alumni game article stated, "For many of the Alumni the trembling is over. After weeks of worry, the special conditioning party held last night at Alumni Hall bolstered the spirits of all and the Alumni have sworn to show up. Rock Weir is holding the final practice at eleven this morning, when he will try to sober up his team and organize them into a fighting unit."

The Wahoo party spirit didn't stop after graduation. The article noted that Coach Blackburn's varsity, coming off four weeks of spring training, wasn't taking the game lightly.

An accompanying article informed readers:

> Easters 1965, long considered the "biggest and best" of the big dance weekends, has arrived and is now underway. After an audacious start last night with the PK-German dance featuring Chuck Berry, the festival promises to reach a peak today and tonight. The Weekend, which was initiated in 1930 as a celebration of Mr. Jefferson's birthday, may be marred by disagreeable weather, as the weatherman has predicted "cloudy and cool" with possible showers for today and tomorrow. But it will take more than a few raindrops to dampen the spirits of University men and their dates this weekend.

As I recall, it never rained that day, but if it had, more spirits would have been sufficient to overcome any inclement weather.

With a new TILKA button on my lapel, the travels from house to house with El on my arm, bourbon bottle in my side coat pocket, were even more fun. No party was more enjoyable than at 180 Rugby Road, where B. Hooker had arranged for The Checkmates to deafen us with their assortment of speakers, instruments, and singers.

Sunday afternoon was a time for fraternities to have their weekend combos to finish off the weekend, so I'd always gone to ours. The most infamous of all Easters Weekend Sunday events was the SAE-ZBT Grain Party, a bacchanalia of such magnitude that it was in a class of its own.

Another afternoon highlight was the annual Ribbon Societies competition at Mad Bowl. This year it was changed to a polo game and moved to Brook Hill Bowl. Since there were four Beta participants, we staged a pregame preparation with a concoction prepared by Rutledge Young and called Liquid Courage. It consisted of a bottle of Beaujolais wine to a pint of grain alcohol and was rationed one per player plus a spare. We started drinking around one o'clock, which meant we were loaded to the gills with valor by the midafternoon game time.

Wooly Neck Wells (an Eli Banana) submitted a detailed account of the game to the *CD*. It was published the following Tuesday with the headline "Easters Tilt Sees Ribbon Jocks Deadlocked; Milk Toasts, Banana Peels Each Score -69."

I have several vivid memories of the joust. I had been riding trail animals and jumpers since I was five years old, but I had never tried polo. Most of my Beta brothers were the same. Since there weren't enough horses to mount everyone, some played on foot.

The first goal was scored by Eli Jose Brown, who ran in the soccer ball we were using on foot. But it was ruled a no score because a mounted opposing player knocked him over the goal by mistake.

Some players rode double, while others alternated by mounting and dismounting. After the second chucker, Macy Wall, a fraternity brother and nationally ranked polo player, hurried across the field to me. With a pained, accusatory look, he took the reins of the horse he had loaned me, and I played on foot thereafter. I don't blame him at all.

My last memory is of running the ball toward the goal. As I approached it, I sensed someone behind me and instinctively rolled to the right. I moved just in time to avoid being ridden over by Jose and Rooster Singleton, who grinned at me as they rode by.

The game was a perfect end to my last Easters Weekend as a student.

# Chapter 22

## Cow Day

The end of March saw the changing of the guard with third years taking over positions for the coming year. William S. "Steve" Hopson IV took over as editor in chief of the *CD*. In elections for class officers, the College of Arts and Sciences, with a 70.5 percent turnout, elected Scepter Society candidate George Morrison with 642 votes. His Skull and Keys and independent opponents secured 521 and 460 votes, respectively. Charlie Dunlop (Scepter) defeated his Skull and Keys opponent 1173 to 300 for vice president. Secretary and historian each went to the Skull and Keys candidates. David Greenburg (Theta Tau, the Engineering School's major political party) won the presidency of the Engineering School. Including Student Council, only one independent had chosen to run, and he received 28.3 percent of the vote. At the Beta house, Henry Warner was elected president, Doug "Woogie" Kincaid won vice president, Shep Craige became secretary, and John Sallee was made treasurer. Houseboy Sam Ragland was also nominated but failed to win.

With Easters over and many significant positions passed on, for fourth years especially, only final exams and the Judiciary Committee served as a governor to an otherwise unbounded enthusiasm for the hijinks our world had to offer. On the Lawn, rocking chairs were moved from the hearths to the walkways, both for studying and increasingly frequent cocktail hours. From early afternoon until dark, Frisbees, boomerangs, and a variety of balls flew across our expansive front yard.

At the Beta house and the others on Rugby Road, front porches became living rooms, with goats serving beers upon request from the concessions. Jerry Guthrie and Rutledge owned our concession, set competitive prices, collected overdue bills, and avoided ABC agents.

Enjoying the porches on late Sunday afternoons was always a bevy of women who'd not left for their respective schools. They ranged from seasoned favorites of each house to new girls who, like pledges, were being checked out.

In previous years I enjoyed wearing bib overalls with a jaw full of chewing tobacco. When chatting with new girls, I'd periodically release a stream of tobacco juice onto the grass. If she ignored or mocked me, she was a keeper. Girls like Eleanor realized this was a stupid male thing, very rarely displayed in mixed company, and ignored it.

Sometimes the camaraderie would enlarge to include the Zetes across the street and become a sort of block party. Rugby Road would become the center of Frisbee and football tossing, with pedestrians crisscrossing to the detriment of passing traffic. In addition to my Lawn friends and neighbors—Joe Brown, Mac Caldwell, Bland Hoke, Lance Schaffer, and Chris "Rooster" Singleton—there were many more cross-street relationships, including classmates Bob Barron, Jim Edmonds, Doug Pollard, George Nelson, and Jim Hargraves, not to mention other classes.

Up the street was another porch-load of Sunday afternoon comrades at the SAE house who were always up for action. Gene Angle, Carrington Harrison, and Alex "Wooly Neck" lived on the Lawn as well, so I knew them best, but Bob Blackwood, Reid Lunsford, Tom Bornhauser, and Charlie Lincoln were other sixty-fivers. Ken Reisinger and Rick Graham were from the DKE house and part of the neighborhood, as were my close KA Lawn neighbor, Will Montague and John Kettig. AEPi often joined the fun with Alan Goldstein and others.

While the ZBT house was isolated on the other side of Scott Stadium, my friend Larry Gold often dropped by with his brothers Charlie Glazer, Chuck Rotkin, Mark Levinson, and Don Zackery. Ken Adatto had left after three years to enter the LSU Medical School. It would be years before UVA would award an undergraduate degree to someone who'd left early. When they finally changed the rule, and Ken received his bachelor of arts, it was dated 1981—thirteen years after his doctor of medicine degree!

By the spring of '65 the differences and distances between Madison Lane, Rugby Road, and other locations had evaporated. Over the four years of going to classes, partying, extracurriculars, and road trips, each of us felt close enough to transcend fraternity lines. In a few months we would all scatter to varied lives and careers, but for the time being we'd grown into a homogenous group.


One day Dean Runk summoned me to explain I had an unpleasant task to perform. Under the Honor System, only a student could accuse another student. A University man had been charged by the police with theft and been convicted. I formally charged him with an honor offense, and as the accuser, I attended the honor trial. It was truly an educational experience for me, since honor trials were totally private.

As I described earlier, the Honor Code was very simple in that a person either lied, cheated, stole, or violated his word of honor. It was a yes-or-no question. It either occurred or it didn't.

The Honor Committee was comprised of the president of each school in the University, seven in all, to be judges. The president of the College of Arts and Science (Ben Ackerly in 1964/65) presided at any hearings. Legal counsel, both prosecution and defense, came from the Law School. No records were kept of any trials, and the results were never revealed or discussed. As a final safeguard, a guilty verdict had to be unanimous.

In the years since my time at Charlottesville, the Honor Code has been amended several times. The sure knowledge that I lived in a community where total trust could be placed in my fellows, although altered in execution, remains in place. The basic principle—that honor is not relative—is still the cornerstone of the Honor Code. Like pregnancy, one is either honorable or one isn't.

On May 4 the Student Council met in the Rotunda and discussed the part students might play in the Rotunda's upcoming restoration. The next day after classes, Lance Schaffer, Alex, and I were heading up the Lawn and noticed a large crowd at the south steps of that building, all looking toward the roof parapet. When we got closer, we noticed some people on the roof, and they appeared to be surrounding a large animal. We were told a cow was stuck on the roof and some groundskeepers and doctors from the hospital were trying to decide what to do next.

At that point Wooly said he might as well go back to his room and wait for the Dean's call, certain that he'd be on the list of suspects for such a prank. It was then I remembered never to let a gathering go to waste. I encouraged my two companions to join me, and we ascended to the porch. And there, facing a crowd of a few hundred people, I gave what has become known as the "Cow Day Speech." The *CD* reported it as well.

> Student Council President Frank Briggs addressed the crowd from the Rotunda steps around 12:15 commemorating the occasion. Said Briggs, who proved to be an eloquent impromptu speaker, "The Cow Day Committee, myself, Lance Schaffer, and Alex Wells, today join together on the steps of the Rotunda to pay homage to those valiant forefathers of ours who, fifty

years ago, gathered on these same hallowed steps in order to place the first symbol of bovinity in its proper place—on the Dome of the Rotunda." Briggs was referring to the first time such a stunt had been pulled, when, according to the 1963 issue of the Alumni News, "it took seven hours of engineering ingenuity to remove a cow placed on the roof of the Rotunda by students." A rumor which was circulating through the crowd put that first "Cow Day" in 1915, although the article in the Alumni news gave the date as 1887.

Since I'd given the talk on the spur of the moment and made it up as I went along, none of this information was true. It was just an opportunity to have a little fun. I left my podium to good-natured cheers and headed off with my compatriots for lunch at our respective houses.

While we were going to lunch, someone said, "Hey, Briggs, phone call." On the other end was an excited staffer from WUVA who'd reported the event and called to tell me he'd put the information, with pictures, on the AP and UPI wire services. That seemed cool and I thanked him. As we were about to hang up, he asked, "Did you know the cow died?"

The next day I opened the *CD* to see the cow story, and then I learned the cow and I were also on page one of the *Charlottesville Daily Progress*, most of page two of the *Richmond Times Dispatch*, and prominently mentioned in other East Coast newspapers. I also learned more about bovines in general and this one in particular, namely, cows have shorter front legs than rear legs, which makes it possible to lead them upstairs but impossible to do the reverse.

The animal on the Rotunda roof was a recently born Angus bull, weighing four hundred pounds. As a newborn, it was dehydrated that morning, and its system was too sensitive to withstand the tranquilizer used to prepared it for transport. So, it died. While all of this was interesting, my day in the spotlight was done.

The following Saturday was the beginning of fourth-year comprehensive exams for each course, followed by a May Day weekend at Sweetbriar with El. So, I put the whole matter behind me and began to prepare for the exams. It would be the following week before I realized Cow Day was not over.

As an English major, I'd taken a third-year comprehensive exam, which required reading the Bible and the full body of Greek mythology, because all English literature was derived from those two sources. Fourth-year's exam covered every genre each student had studied in his two years, so the exam was separated into sections. Each examinee chose the parts that tested his genres and went at it. As someone with a good memory and a general overall knowledge, it was my type of exam. In my opinion it was much harder for people who knew it all in depth, for they tended to look too deeply at the questions. At any rate, after the two or three hours given, I handed in my exam and felt quite confident.

Shortly afterward I met Jose Brown at his room, and we prepared a very large jar of rum and juice for the fifty-two-mile trip to Sweetbriar. Jar in hand, we headed down to Jefferson Park Avenue and stuck out our thumbs. A few minutes later a married instructor and doctoral student at the Engineering School picked us up. He lived in Lovingston, which was about thirty miles down Route 29 toward our destination. As we got to know each other Joe offered him some of our hooch. Several times Jose graciously refilled his cup, so by the time he dropped us off, he had a happy glow. We wondered how he was going to explain to his wife how he'd managed to get slightly looped on the way home.

Putting out our thumbs again, we could see in the distance the Lovingston constabulary approaching. But before the officer arrived, a car with several students pulled over and we hopped in. They were headed to May Day as well, so we drained the last of our jar just as we met up with Pam and El. I had a reservation with other Betas at the Holiday Inn in Lynchburg, since Sunday promised to be fun as well.

The last time Jose had gone to May Day was in 1962, shortly before he'd departed for his two years in the Marine Corps. That year he and several friends had hopped a freight train that regularly traveled the route and disembarked as it slowed down around Amherst. This method of travel, while never becoming a daily occurrence, was a tradition for some. Because of comprehensive exams, however, Joe had missed his connection. Others, such as his admiring young friend Ridgely, continued the practice and arrived before we did.

May Day was an incredible party, with Mary Wells featured as the keynote entertainer. At one point she was joined by Ridgely, Jose, and two others on the stage. I would say they leaped onto the stage, but it was a little late in the evening for that. Mary played along with them, and the crowd enjoyed it. The party was a winner and extremely spirited.

Much later I climbed into Jon Verity's convertible, planning to meet Eleanor for chapel the next morning. When I awoke from a dream, I realized the car was moving and Verity was at the wheel. Since I was supposed to be at the nearby Holiday Inn, something seemed amiss, but I dozed off.

When next I opened my eyes, I quickly shut them. I opened them slowly and realized I was in my room on the Lawn. And it was around 10:45. Clearly Jon had not been planning to stay in Lynchburg.

Quickly I rushed to Wooly's room and called Eleanor.

"Hey, El," I started. "You're not going to believe this—"

But she cut me off. "If you're going to tell me you're in Charlottesville, I already know it!"

While I was disappointed as I could be, I knew one thing for certain: El would adapt. And that made her a real keeper.

Alex, meanwhile, had an eventful Saturday afternoon of his own. An incredible salesman, he'd gathered a group for an afternoon of beer drinking and infused them with patriotic zeal by continually warning them of the dangers posed by godless communists. In short order, this pied piper led his band to the Marine recruitment office. The next morning, they all woke up as enlistees in officer's training for the Marine Corps. As usual, his presence had provided an unexpected result for his companions.

Monday and Tuesday's mail was unusually heavy and revealing to me. The farther from Charlottesville a newspaper was, the scantier the Cow Day coverage. One clipping was titled "Students Kill Cow in Virginia." Much of the correspondence, though, was from animal lovers. One poignantly noted, "The wrong SOBs are dying in Vietnam."

On a happy note, my mom read only the *CD* coverage and an editorial in a Pittsburgh paper that said it was nice to see students acting like students.

Dean Runk, however, requested my presence "at your earliest convenience." The word *earliest* expressed the gravity of the topic he had in mind. When I asked if this was about student activities funds, he said, "I want to talk about cows, a specific cow." He added that this had become a concern also of the president and the board of visitors. I now understood this was not considered a silly prank by the administration.

The Restoration Ball for the Rotunda occurred on Saturday, May 15, and it remains one of most salient memories of my years in Charlottesville. The event was sponsored by the Jefferson Society and the Student Guide Service, and the ball committee was chaired by my friend Henry Currie and included twenty other guides and faculty wives. Among them were Mrs. Mary Betts (Rotunda hostess), Mrs. Bernard Mayo (wife of my favorite teacher), Dean Perry's wife, and a first-year hallmate Calder Loth.

The event was held on the building's broad terrace, with bars and serving tables inside. The weather cooperated, producing a vintage central Virginia spring evening under an almost full moon. The air was heavy with the scent of magnolia blossoms. A string orchestra rounded out the setting. I was happy to have Eleanor with me as a perfect complement to the evening.

The most significant moment of the event (for me) occurred when El and I paid our respects to President Shannon and his wife, who were standing with a group of muckety-mucks, including Dean Runk. While not an exact quote, the University first lady said, "It was so much fun reading about your Cow Day talk. It was so clever!"

I thanked her but didn't want to come across as particularly triumphant, so I changed the topic to the event and praised the committee for its excellent execution. I rejoined my peers and realized that Cow Day was behind me. At the end of the ball, the schoolgirls were taken home to meet curfew, and an after-party commenced on the Lawn and continued long into the night.

By now Will Montague and I had started to share a nightcap or two before turning in. We were in the process of doing that when there was a pounding on the door, and Wooly Neck announced he wanted to join us. Will and Alex were both from Lookout Mountain and had gone to the McCallie School together. He knew that opening the door for Wooly would mean a noisy extension of the evening, so he told him to go away.

There was a mighty thud against the door and then another. A vertical segment of the upper door panel splintered. Wooly pulled out the rest and triumphantly entered the room. It created such a racket that Bob Hunt, a law student and Lawn counselor, dashed over to see what was going on.

All of us stared at the instigator in amazement. None of us could believe what we'd just witnessed. It was over the line, even for Wooly. Bob tried to find the appropriate words to cover the incident, but there were none. And since Alex graduated with us, he must have wiggled out of yet another scrape.

I believe the dean, who went to school with Wooly's father, felt that both the young man and Virginia would be better off with his departure. But one had to wonder just how many more scrapes with authority he could survive.

By now final exams were close enough to take seriously. The Beta hayride, the last social event of the school year, was the most uneventful one I'd ever been on. I had a date and I didn't fall off a cliff. Out of that weekend, however, a complication arose that was to become significant.

Eleanor told me she'd be with me at The Beach for the traditional blowout between final exams and graduation ceremonies, but she could not be my date for Finals Weekend because her summer job at the English-Speaking Union would start before then. This was a real downer for me, because I was looking forward to it. Moreover, since she was a native of Wilmington, Delaware, my parents would have liked her.

Several days later, I called Margaret Ann and asked her. I was surprised when she said yes. I would meet her at the Richmond airport on my way back from The Beach.

Problem solved!

But the next day an excited Eleanor called to say she'd gotten her starting date moved back and could come to Finals!

For a moment I was speechless. A pros-and-cons list flashed through my mind, revealing the right choice was El and telling me to cancel the date with Margaret Ann. Sue Hall's words flooded my mind: "She's fickle, fickle, fickle!" I reasoned that Margaret Ann wanted only a weekend in Charlottesville while El wanted to be with me. The Atlantan had no tangible advantage over the Sweetbriar beauty. After May Day and the other spring events, she'd earned her place on the Finals squad.

But in spite of all that, I said, "No, El, you made a commitment. They need you. I wouldn't want to have you renege on my account."

I realized once again what an a-hole I was. There was something about the Georgia girl that enticed me beyond common sense. Had Eleanor expressed indignation, I might have decided differently and the future would have been inexorably changed.

What followed next was crunch time. All exam periods were anxiety ridden and largely devoid of joy. This one was the last chance to finish on time and the final one for some. For many of my classmates it was the stress of knowing whether their degree would be with honor or with high honor.

For me it was a far simpler question: How would I do in Spanish?

For many years after Virginia and occasionally even now, I wake up in a cold sweat. It takes a few minutes to realize it was just a nightmare. The theme is always the same. It's the week of exams and I suddenly realize I have one more Spanish course to pass. But I've forgotten about it. The agony comes in trying to decide whether to go for the test or hope the school doesn't notice because I'd never been to class. Happily, I've never had to decide because that's the point at which I always awaken.

The other incentive for taking my degree on time was to not have to tell my parents to cancel their hotel reservations.

For someone like me who was trying to condense four months of class into several weeks, it was a time of frenzied activity. Since I had scant notes of my own, I borrowed Dick Tucker's meticulous records. As I reviewed them, I could see why Tucker was a Phi Beta Kappa who would go on to Columbia Law School and appear before the U.S. Supreme Court.

I lived on coffee and my remaining supply of Dexedrine, putting in several twenty-hour days. I saw the Lawn and Rotunda at 3:00 a.m. and again at sunup through a lens of exhaustion. Mindful of the stories about students who'd succumbed to the effects of powerful drugs to keep awake, I took great care to make sure the effects had worn off before exam time, especially before the Spanish exam.

Finally, for better or worse, the exams were over. To find out my results I'd need to wait until each teacher posted the results on the classroom door, which could take several days. To ensure privacy, most professors, but not all, used initials next to the grade. Since one generally knew who was in the class, this was not a particularly effective solution. In my case, it was only my result that mattered to me. In the left column was the exam grade, while on the right was the total result.

That day Rutledge's close friend Mimi, one of my favorite people, had lunch at Farmington with her parents and invited him, El, and me to join them. It was a wonderful time at one of the finest clubs in the country, with the conversation at our table being witty and fun. The only problem I had was, after days of sleep deprivation, I kept ordering bourbon to stay awake. Afterward I returned to my room and sank into a deep slumber.

The next morning, I was awakened by an exuberant Eleanor, who entered on her way to The Beach. After she departed, I buoyed myself to go to Cabell Hall to find out the verdicts. By early afternoon the results were all posted, and I was to receive a BA in English from the University of Virginia. There was no graduation from Mr. Jefferson's University, for learning never ended. I was to earn the honor of all honors: a degree from *the* University.

While all the grades were meaningful, I saw that I received a C+ in Spanish, the highest I'd ever received in a foreign language (not counting the bogus B in third-year Blair Latin). My other grades were all B's, with one exception, a C in group discussion. That was a clear mistake that I could have appealed, but I couldn't have cared less.

For the first year since matriculating at Charlottesville, my GPA exceeded 2.0 with a 2.07 overall and a 2.667 for the semester. More important, I was ready for The Beach!

# Chapter 23

# Finals Week

Since my ride to The Beach wasn't leaving until the next afternoon, I planned to take a day of R&R. And then I had an unexpected visitor. My former girlfriend Joan drove down from Pittsburgh with a friend. She was now a bank teller and living at home. While she didn't spell it out, she missed her school days. Since I had nothing else to do and they had wheels, we went down to The Tavern, a place with great burgers and pitchers. We left Joan's friend at their room, waiting for a call from some guys. I knew the call was never going to come, but she didn't believe me.

After a pitcher of beer, Joan and I headed out to a country fair. I'd visited the fair before, with Betas, for the express purpose of visiting the skin show. It was held in a large tent at the end of the midway, and it was definitely not family entertainment. Other than the stage lights, the place was dark, smoky, and crowded with men. Seated in the rear were always one or two deputies, presumably for security. The performers had not seen better days, and they weren't likely to. They were neither attractive nor artistic. But we were a gang of young males in a society that prohibited nudity, sexual displays, or vulgar language in any setting. For us, this was novel entertainment, base though it was. Props were thrown from the audience to be used as erotic tools. There was always one guy whose glasses were snatched for an act. It was a kind of rite of passage.

But there was no way I was going to take Joan there, so we strolled the midway, stopping occasionally to play a game of chance or buy something from a food booth. After a while we arrived at a tattoo artist's tent and saw Wooly. He said he was there to get an "IMP" on the top of his left hand. Alex was in both a ribbon society, Eli Banana, and a ring society (IMP). I pointed out that having an imp face on his hand would probably be an impediment in his later careers. He agreed and redirected it to his ankle. It seemed like such a fine idea that I joined him and got a TILKA symbol on the inner side of my left ankle. The tattoo artist casually mentioned keeping it covered for a few days.

Before midnight we headed back to check on Joan's friend, who was still waiting for her call. Then we headed to the Lawn. As we approached on a University side street, a police light turned on and I pulled over and said hello to my friend Officer Jim Batten. I explained the car belonged to my date and she was leaving with it. He opined it was symbolic he and I had met when I first arrived at school and now as I was leaving.

Joan and I hung out for a while. She left but agreed to drive me to a brunch the next morning at eleven. It had been a very satisfying day.

The next day was Sunday, and Joan and her friend chauffeured me to the brunch. Uncle Merrill and Aunt Louise Smith were guests at one of the many magnificent farmhouses to the west, along Route 250 around Farmington. They were not actually kin, but he was my dad's close childhood friend and they'd been part of my life for as long as I could remember. Since they were favorites of mine, I'd delayed The Beach trip a day to see them and have another country house experience.

We drove a brief distance through the sparkling Virginia morning and entered a short driveway bordered with a glorious display of bright pink climbing roses and honeysuckle. Circling right around the traditional brick house, we saw the Smiths with their hosts seated by the pool. As the men rose to great us, I alighted, thanked Joan, and sent her on her way.

At first there were five of us to enjoy the premeal Bloody Marys and mimosas. Their daughter, Sarah, recognized me from numerous previous encounters and joined us. It was a special time among friends. After several hours we said goodbye, and Sarah dropped me off at the Beta house.

From there, Walter Hooker and I went to Richmond in his car. A younger Beta, Walter was one of those gentlemen liked by everyone who knew him. He was a Richmond native who always knew what was happening, and so we went that night to an unforgettable graduation party at the American Legion.

A wonderful thing to me about Virginia was the Alcohol Beverage Commission (ABC), which permitted only beer and wine to be sold by the drink. The Commonwealth was a brown-bag state where if one wanted liquor, it was brought in a paper bag. Buying pitchers of beer, ice, and setups was a far more economical way to drink a lot. It also meant that an enterprising person or group could rent a place and charge admission (a cover charge) to get in. Football games at Scott Stadium were a lot like that.

Walter and I entered the crowded ballroom of mostly Richmond folk from a variety of colleges and universities. One overriding commonality pervaded the room: "School is out! It's time to party!"

Soon an irritating nasal voice drawled my name in my ear.

"Hello, Ford," I answered.

He had been my cabin mate from Camp Shaw-Mi-Del-Eca ten years ago. The memory of a long-forgotten conversation flooded back.

"You told, Ford!" I'd exclaimed.

"No, I didn't," he responded. "I just said, 'I bet you don't know where Briggs is.'"

As a result, I spent one week of the seven returning to my cabin immediately after supper. From there I could hear all the other campers going to the evening activities. My punishment was because I had left camp on my own to visit a nearby country store.

Ford was now just graduating from Princeton. As we talked, he came across as a real person and not a distant distained memory. It was nice to shed a grudge after only ten years.

The revelry in the ballroom went on unabated, as the music and spirits enveloped the blissful congregants. Eventually the place thinned out, and Walter and I left to get some rest before the next funfest.

I don't remember how I got to Virginia Beach or where I stayed. I do remember being warmly greeted by El at the place she was staying. After that, we joined some friends on a beach near her place and started a nonstop celebration that lasted until Thursday.

When we left the beach the first day, we joined a Zete named Winky and his wife for supper. I was cognizant of my dwindling cash, so I chose to save money and stopped at a convenience store. I purchased a quart of Colt 45 malt liquor and a bottle of apple wine for a total of $1.85. More bang for the buck.

Then the four of us went up Atlantic Boulevard to a field that was filled with parked vehicles. We walked toward some dunes and climbed to the top. An incredible sight greeted us. Spread out before us was a vast Army surrounding sporadic bonfires. Rugby Road and Mad Lane had moved to The Beach!

As we moved through friends, Jose and Pam appeared in the firelight. In dazed wonderment, Jose kept repeating, "I'm graduating! I'm graduating!" While he went on to the Washington and Lee Law School and achieved great prominence, he couldn't help but remember how his last year at Virginia had begun.

He had finished a stint with the Marines and stood in line for registration when Dean Runk spotted him.

"Why, hello, Mr. Brown. Welcome back to the University," he said pleasantly and added more ominously, "for the *fourth* and *last* time. Do you understand me, Mr. Brown? This is the fourth and final time."

Jose's third departure from the University was the result of a firecracker prank. Raymond Bice was a much admired and loved dean, and he had been amused by the prank, so he told Joe he would have intervened had he thought it would help.

Just a day before my encounter with him on The Beach, Joe realized he was three grade points short of graduation. Providence, however, was with Joe and Pam when they found Mr. Bice, and Joe told him he could intervene now, if he wanted to. He asked him to look over his final exam, and the professor noticed some grading errors. When he corrected them, the result was an increase from a C+ to a B-, and Jose would join us in the graduation procession down the Lawn.

Lee Winton "Rusty" Mather Jr.'s problem was more complex. For years his aim had been to take his degree with a perfect gentleman's C. His final grades were very disappointing when they showed a B- instead of a C+ or C. It turned out getting a grade reduced was as difficult as getting a grade increased. I can't remember if Rusty was successful in this quest.

In the great scheme of things, the difference between 2.0 and 2.07 doesn't really matter, but the difference between 2.0 and 1.93 has tremendous significance! Like Joe, Rusty's future career as a successful Wall Street investment banker was not evident in June 1965.

But those with high GPA's have always invoked my greatest admiration. In looking back, it appears that academic performance is just one factor in creating a satisfying legacy.

Sometime after midnight the four of us left the beach party and headed to a pancake place. As we cruised along Atlantic Boulevard, we were suddenly airborne as cars flashed past us. We'd slowed considerably, Wink took a hard left, and we merged onto Atlantic. The street had veered left, around a restaurant and parking lot, but we'd gone straight. Our driver announced he'd forgotten to turn the headlights on, and we proceeded to our destination.

I was famished, so I ordered a tall stack of buckwheat cakes with drawn butter, sorghum syrup, sausage, and coffee. Wink suggested someone who'd been drinking apple wine and malt liquor all night might not want to have such a robust meal. I assured him I had a cast-iron stomach and ate the whole meal.

They dropped El and me off where she was staying with a Sweets group. Since it was only about one, we enjoyed the beach patio together in solitude.

The next morning, I awoke a little sooner than planned, and Winky's words of caution came back to haunt me. I knew that physically fit Eleanor wouldn't be up yet, so I decided to walk the beach. But for digestive reasons, I stayed close to some plumbing facilities.

Also, I began to understand why the tattoo artist had told me to keep my ankle TILKA insignia covered. When it began to itch, I only had cortisone ointment to put on it. While it eventually healed, the red and gold disappeared, leaving only the black triangle I have today. Still, it lasted long enough to finish the beach trip.

Very close by was a house of Hollins girls. Among them was one of the all-time great people, Barbara Beamon. I spent a pleasant morning on the porch talking to her and Eden White, her knockout classmate from Atlanta.

At one point we saw a girl walking on the beach.

"Who's that?" someone asked.

Someone else answered, "It's one of the Sweetbriar girls."

"How can you possibly tell?" several asked.

"She teases her hair," came the definitive answer.

It was fun being a fly on the wall at an all-female gathering.

Toward midday my gastric distress subsided, so I headed down to Kelly Wood's house, knowing the Betas would be there. I resolved to drink only beer until happy hour.

Over the years I have become certain that heaven is a real place. Moreover, it is indescribable and beyond the finite mind's ability to grasp the perfection it embodies. In my midthirties I was led to understand the only way I would get there was by the grace of the Holy Trinity, not my own powerlessness. Since then I've had a growing sense of peace by following the Holy Spirit's guidance.

That said, being on a beach is as good an approximation of perfection as earth can offer. While my vantage point and perspectives have matured, the ability to feel the Creator's majesty in nature has not. That afternoon I was a dissolute twenty-two-year-old with a hedonistic mindset. And I loved every minute. My perspective has changed over the years, but the Creation hasn't.

The next several days were filled with all The Beach had to offer: ocean, sand, bars, beer, and music. For those of us who were graduating, it was our last call, one final chance to be together. Although very few of us, certainly not me, would get overly philosophical, a subliminal awareness existed. Twenty-four years later and twice thereafter I could empathize with each of my children as they went through the process. While tremendous changes had occurred in the school by then, leaving the University and Rugby Road had not.

Thursday was pretty much a repeat of the prior days with one notable difference. I was going back to Finals Weekend in Charlottesville and Eleanor was going home to Wilmington. It didn't really strike me until late that night, after all the hullabaloo had ended. We were alone on the porch and it was there between us. She had never mentioned or asked about it. It certainly wasn't something I was going to bring up. And so we parted.

I don't remember who took me to the Richmond airport, maybe Teddy. Margaret Ann had told me to meet her at the baggage claim and suddenly there she was. Since we were a lot alike in this respect, it was as if nothing had happened between us. She was very excited at being back in Charlottesville, and we began to visit all the places on her itinerary.

She stayed with her old apartment mates, Sue and Sherry. I got the impression Sue was thinking, *Some people never learn.*

My parents had arrived the night before graduation. Mom relished the event while Dad was probably happiest that there would be no more tuition and fees to pay. After lunch, we spent the time packing my belongings on the Lawn and enjoying the general ambiance of the day. The Beta house graduates' reception was midafternoon. It took the first thirty to forty-five minutes of ice breaking to loosen up the gathering. As parents grew more acquainted with each other and the drinks kept coming, it became a more relaxed affair, though still stilted. A collection of successful people with only their sons in common was never destined to become a typical Beta party. I recall Rutledge's mother and Ted's dad as the most outgoing of the parental group.

I had dinner with my parents along with Lee, my sister, now a college sophomore, and my ninth-grade grade brother, Doug, and Margaret Ann. We went to the elegant Silver Thatch Inn, which was far beyond an undergraduate's pocketbook or inclination. It was a perfect choice for us, because it was quiet and discrete and offered impeccable cuisine.

I realized that no one in the family was aware of Margaret Ann's perfidious letter, and I was not going to enlighten them. We dined in a carefree atmosphere, although my parents, from long experience, might have had their fingers crossed. There was still over fifteen hours to go before graduation was a done deal.

Around ten o'clock, Dad was ready to turn in, and they dropped us off at the Lawn. No more lending of autos in Charlottesville!

In 1965, every graduate walked from the Rotunda to Cabell Hall for the ceremony. There, each College of Arts and Sciences degree candidate remained seated, alphabetically, until called by name. Those from the other schools—Architecture, Commerce, Education, Engineering, Graduate Business, Law, and Medicine—went to their respective buildings.

Today, aluminum walkways and steps are installed to protect the grass. A primary ceremony is still held in the traditional place, but not the awarding of degrees. Only the English Department, about half as large as our whole class, stays on the Lawn. It now takes two days and dozens of sites to complete the graduation process.

As Margaret Ann and I approached through the West Gardens, the sounds of music and laughter grew more intense. In front of every third or fourth room was a congregation of happy souls. As on other big weekends, revelers mingled freely. This convocation was comprised principally of graduates and their dates. I sensed it might be a tad more subdued than a usual party weekend. No one wanted to test Dean Runk's conviviality on the day before graduating.

We eventually settled down by Rooster's and Jose's rooms, where Pam was the de facto hostess. I noticed Rusty had brought Shep Craige's sister, Carol, with him.

Sometime after midnight, my Georgia girl decided she wanted to see the Rotunda one more time. I pointed out that it was closed and locked, adding that my key had been returned.

With a smug look, Will Montague revealed he'd never turned in his key.

As far as Margaret Ann was concerned, that settled it. She started off with Will trailing along. While I saw potential pitfalls in the plan, I had no choice but to join the conspirators.

We went through the south entrance and entered a sanctuary dimly illuminated by the outside lights. Standing on the marble-tiled floor of the large circular room, we could see the domed ceiling three flights above. Naturally, we thought it would be fun to see the view from the top, so we went up the stairs. When we reached the upper balcony, we saw a view well worth the climb. Then we began to reminisce about Cow Day.

One of the striking features of Mr. Jefferson's Pantheon design for his masterpiece is its remarkable acoustics. To demonstrate this, Will mooed like a cow, and we all joined in. The cacophony reverberated so wonderfully that we redoubled our efforts. Suddenly our symphony was shattered when all the lights came on and two University police officers entered the center of the room.

Will immediately led us into an attic space and shut the door. I knew that being found hiding was the worst possible result. Leading my doubtful co-conspirators back to the open balcony, I yelled, "Hello, officers! I bet you're surprised to see us in here."

I instructed my companions, especially Margaret Ann, not to look guilty while I launched myriad explanations at the uniformed authorities. Since the truth was a time-honored method that often worked, I started there.

We were graduating.

Will had a key.

I had once had a key.

Our guest is from Georgia.

There was a two-word response: "Come down!"

I resumed my cheerful explanations while my escorts uttered not a word.

After a minute or so, an officer said, "Y'all leave now and don't come back."

We were only too happy to comply.

Sunday, June 6, 1965, was a bright, sunny day that dawned not long after many of us had concluded our Saturday. Since graduation at Virginia relies on the beauty of the Grounds for most of the allure, some rain is unpleasant, while an all-day downpour borders on catastrophic. Happily, monsoons seldom occur, and one didn't this year.

Academic processions are majestic and beautifully archaic. At Virginia the black-robed Grand Marshal of the University leads with an impressive mace. Then, and for many years, it was Dean Runk. The parade continues with rank upon rank of dignitaries and faculty members, each in a robe with a stole or cowl. The variety of designs and colors is dizzying, but each represents a different degree, school, and rank. In prior centuries they would have been worn to class. Today, they come out of mothballs only once a year for most. They are the officer corps of academia. Every commencement exercise is a medieval spectacle of pomp and circumstance.

For those of us in the horde of black-clad undergraduates, there was a very different thought process. Many had markings to indicate they were cum laude and a few magna cum laude graduates. The rest of us were there simply for the moment on the stage. We'd receive a handshake, a piece of sheepskin, and move our tassel from one side to the other. Those symbolic actions would complete the long, arduous path of being a college graduate.

There are three things I remember clearly. My parents standing as proud spectators. Pam standing next to the parade with a large antacid-filled pitcher, distributing the contents in paper cups. Finally, Joe Brown and I returned to our seats.

After a moment we each received a tap on the shoulder from the row behind us. Someone asked, "Are you guys sure those aren't blank?"

We laughed good naturedly, and then each surreptitiously peaked under a corner to make sure.

And then the pageantry was all over.

My parents planned a celebratory dinner. The next day the family was going to Hot Springs to visit Steppingstones, a massive estate owned by friends. While there we'd see our old friends and neighbors. The Homestead hotel, which dad had once run, would provide dinner and entertainment.

But I explained to them that my obligations weren't quite over. I'd promised to drive Margaret Ann to the Richmond airport for a midafternoon flight to Atlanta. I vowed to be back in time for dinner. Alas, that was not to be.

Always optimistic, Margaret Ann was to leave early the next morning from Atlanta with my arch nemesis, Mary Staton, for a summer at the University of Colorado to be followed by a month in Mexico. And since a leopard never changes its spots, Margaret Ann had not yet begun to pack for the three-month trip. She needed to be on time for her flight.

Unfortunately, as we approached Richmond, I became confused and went the wrong way. By the time we made it to the airport, her flight was well on its way to Atlanta. She panicked and had me wait until the airline took the necessary steps to place her on a later flight. I gallantly complied. After that, we should have made the intelligent decision for me to leave, but we didn't.

We went to Uncle Charlie's to wait for the plane. Sizing up the situation in an instant, he noted I was just as likely to get lost the second time. He announced that I should leave for Charlottesville immediately and he'd get Margaret Ann to the airport.

By the time I reached Charlottesville, dinnertime was long past. I have no doubt that Mom was thankful to her brother for his intervention. She said, "It was too bad we had to eat our dinner with all the other graduates and their families—without our graduate."

In a twisted way it seemed a fitting end to my University career. Happily, the time in Hot Springs went flawlessly as planned. And once again Margaret Ann effortlessly vacated my life.

After seventeen years of preparation, Virginia had been the grand culmination. Now I would find out what I had been preparing for.

# Chapter 24

# Beyond Finals

As I write this, it's been fifty-five years since I walked the Lawn to take my degree. We had wanted to celebrate it in Charlottesville, where it all started, but the 2019/20 coronavirus pandemic proved an obstinate obstacle. Many milestones have been toasted there over the years with our friends and classmates, and with God's almighty grace, more will be commemorated there in the future. Since the future hasn't happened yet, I'll go back to the weekend of our milestone fiftieth. From that vantage point, I'll recall key moments about the reunion and the years leading up to it.

We came down Route 29 from the airport to our lodgings at the Colonnade Club on the Lawn. Located in Pavilion VII, with a cornerstone dated 1817, it is the University's first building. I often sit in the library, with the many portraits of some mighty academics from the past sternly staring down at me. I often get the impression they're thinking, *Who let you in here?* Driving past the site of long-gone establishments, such as Carol's Tea Room, a host of memories flood through me. As has happened often before, my mind drifted back to my first year, I've been pushed out of my Charlottesville comfort zone.

Since I had no plan for my life, by default I submitted an application to the Emory University Law School in Atlanta, and I was accepted. My preference would have been an Army commission, but that seemed increasingly unrealistic. While my appeal for a new physical was in the works, there was no reason for optimism. Going to law school meant raising funds for room, board, and incidentals. Dad was right that I should have a lot of my own skin in the game. As he put it, "You seemed more excited about being a lawyer if you could have done it in Charlottesville."

Three weeks of heavy construction labor showed that my post-trauma back wasn't up to the task, and I was forced to quit. This time my dad observed, "Unless your study habits change dramatically, you're not apt to be law review. Maybe you should get a job."

When we discussed my options, he asked, "How many people in your class are going to law school."

"Sixty-eight percent took the LSAT," I told him.

Although it went over my head at the time, his answer defined the rest of my life: "If I were you, I would pick a product or service to sell to that 68 percent."

In early July I was flown to New York for a day of interviews with the Equitable Life Assurance Society. After the interviews, I went several blocks down Sixth Avenue to say hello to Mom's other brother, Doug, who was second in command at Uniroyal.

I spent a week with him and Aunt Marise at their home in Mountain Lakes, New Jersey. With the National Lawn Tennis championships at the Orange Lawn Tennis Club going on, it was a glorious time. From early afternoon until late at night, my savvy, good-looking younger cousin Dana and I enjoyed the many social activities at and around the club in South Orange. As both a Blair and recent UVA graduate, I was well positioned for the opportunity.

In the mornings I would drive my cousin Joe to a chemical plant to apply for a summer job. Then, while he applied for a job, I slept in the jeep. Joe would wake me up and we'd drive to the next place. A Mercersburg grad, as were his father and Uncle Charlie, he'd matriculated at the University of Arizona. It was a wonderful vacation, and the last one I would have without time constraints until I retired fifty-three years later.

When I returned home, a letter from Equitable was waiting. I had been accepted as a management trainee and was to report on August 16 to the Western Regional vice president of Group Insurance Operations in San Francisco. It sounded great. If I was going to work, it would provide a chance to explore some unknown territory.

With that accomplished, I spent the next month enjoying my final days of freedom. Mostly it was with my longtime friend Sally Dickson, who was moving to a job in New York. We spent a lot of time at each other's country club pools. Nights were spent at one of the many places on Walnut Street. Sometimes Pat McFalls picked me up for parties at Larry Molinari's family house in Natrona Heights. It was always fun to party with the football guys like Pat, Larry, and Charlie Hart.

There I had my first contact with the Vietnam War. My date was shipping out as a nurse the next week. It soon became clear she'd become part of a world I knew nothing about but would get to know over the ensuing decade.

My mom reminded me several times that I was now a college graduate. And then she'd ask when I was going to start to act like one. In the absence of more input, I had no clue what she had in mind. (I still don't.)

A few weeks before I was to leave for San Francisco, I received another letter from Equitable. Because of a resignation, I was no longer needed there. I was told to report to the Southern Region Group vice president in Atlanta!

Although I didn't yet understand it, the Lord had put me where he had planned to all along. Even more amazing, he did it in a manner that left no doubt about how it had happened. At the time I chalked it up to good luck and fate.

Thus, on a hot, sticky August evening, I checked into the Cox-Carlton Hotel, catty-corner to the famous Fox Theatre. My future roommate Mike McGehee, an Elmo, would not be back in town until early September. He hadn't yet learned I would not be joining him at Emory Law.

I called the Cravens and learned their daughter would be returning to Atlanta, at least temporarily, around September 10.

To describe my first year in Atlanta and Georgia would take another book. In summary, being a business trainee was an abysmal experience. Doing so as a transplant only added to the sense of loneliness. Only the constant support of my Virginia friend Bill Crawley and his parents offered any sense of family companionship. They toured me, fed me, and introduced me to the Cathedral of St. Philip. The fellows at work were friendly and helpful, but they were all married with children. And they lived in the new suburbs, like Tucker in dry DeKalb County.

After a week, I fell into a mutual attraction with a raven-haired beauty interning at Equitable. While south Fulton County is now developed, back then it was deep in rural Georgia. On weekends she stayed with a married couple. They would pick me up to sample the urban dens of iniquity. Heretofore, she'd only heard about them.

One Sunday morning, she picked me up and we went to All Saints' Episcopal, a lovely church with typical Anglican liturgy and communion. To her it was altogether new and awe-inspiring. That night when I dropped her outside the little Baptist church she attended, I knew why.

Meanwhile, Margaret Ann came home and all other thoughts departed. Once again it was only the two of us. However, she'd taken a job at the University of Colorado School of Medicine in Denver and was scheduled to start there in ten days. We spent as much time as possible together before yet another parting.

The night before she was to leave, we had dinner together. Then I left her to pack.

During the night I was awakened from a sound sleep by the ringing telephone.

"I'm not going," she said. "I don't want to go back to Colorado. I want to stay here with you."

It was Margaret Ann at her zaniest, whom I was destined to love.

A week later I made a foolish, ego-driven move. Since I'd been the jiltee of our relationship, I decided to even things up a little. I knew we were finally in the same place, and I felt I was on safe ground. Although I had no intention of following through on what I was going to say, I suggested we should date other people.

She didn't respond, and I decided things were even, and we moved on.

The next day I called to ask her out.

"I'd like to, but I can't," she said. "I'm going to Minneapolis to be a stewardess for Northwest Orient Airlines."

Reason might have dictated a number of ways to respond to this latest bizarre impulse of hers. Instead, ego spoke up and said, "Go ahead. I'm sure you'll be happy."

My brain reminded me that she had backed out of the Colorado job and she would doubtless change her mind again.

What I didn't know was that she had already applied at Eastern and Delta, but they had turned her down as too short. When she was applying at Northwest, a passing senior vice president heard her appealing southern accent and suggested she stand on her tiptoes when she applied. And two weeks later I waved goodbye as she boarded a plane.

With Margaret Ann gone, I plunged into a funk for which I had only one answer. Keep moving! One way would have been work. Unfortunately, I had no assigned functions and no one to lead me. Athletic activities never entered my mind. There was only one thing, I reasoned, I was exceedingly good at. After work hours I excelled at enjoying Atlanta's many nightlife opportunities.

In this I was helped by the only kindred soul I knew in Atlanta, my roommate, Mike McGehee. His parents had recently returned to Atlanta, and they had substantial connections. His ability to have most women seek him out was astounding. He also had a radar-like quality to find action. In a self-destructive way, Mike was a formidable ally.

That fall I dated many people. Rutledge Young's family invited me to a memorable Thanksgiving weekend in Charleston. There was a wonderful ball with a young lady from Summerville. His sister Courtney was a sister to me as well. Since I had no vacation days to use for a trip to Pittsburgh, the Youngs were my surrogate family.

Sally Dickson met me in Charlottesville for a party weekend. I also spent a weekend visiting her in New York. And by late November I had formed a relationship with an Atlanta girl, and it only strengthened in December. On a good week I tagged along with a coworker to Macon, Georgia, and then Opelika, Alabama.

Meanwhile, my alleged girlfriend, Margaret Ann, was an increasing source of exasperation. One weekend she came to Atlanta and it was awful. She'd write and call me from Winnipeg, Chicago, or New York to tell me about her experiences. I'd hear how none of the Minnesota Vikings players who lived in her apartment complex interested her. None of her Midwestern dates were as much fun as I. It was miserable.

In mid-December my Atlanta girlfriend was becoming impatient. Were we in a relationship or weren't we? I didn't know the answer and was tired of the question.

I wrote Margaret Ann and told her I was dating someone else and that we were broken up. A few days later my Atlanta girlfriend and I went to a wonderful Christmas party. I didn't get home until two in the morning. And then the telephone rang. It was Margaret Ann from Vancouver.

"I got your letter. I can't believe it."

"Read it again," I said.

"I'm coming home."

"What for?"

314

"To be with you."

"Suppose I get transferred?"

"I'll go where you go."

"If you do, we might as well be married."

"Okay."

"What did you say?"

"I said good, let's get married."

The final piece had fallen into place. I was ecstatic, but remembering who I was talking to, I knew it wouldn't be real until the rings were on our fingers. Much happened over the next few months, but on June 3, 1966, one year after my last Finals Weekend at Charlottesville, Margaret Ann and I were married.

My dad was my best man and Joe Brown, Doug Briggs, Gray Craven, Mike McGehee, Alan Rimer, and Rutledge Young were groomsmen.

As our class traveled through the fiftieth reunion weekend it was hard to believe how many things were the same and totally different at the same time. They were alike in that the Rotunda, the Lawn, and the central Grounds remain remarkably unchanged. However, if one moves outward concentrically, almost everything is new. Nationally acclaimed John Paul Jones Arena is two basketball venues removed from the pathetically inadequate Memorial Gymnasium of our day. My sport, swimming, enjoys the second new Natatorium since the murky waters of the old pool. Scott Stadium maintains its same classical demeanor, but the venue is vastly expanded in both size, facilities, and ambiance. All the other athletic facilities were remarkably enhanced as well. It was eye-opening, as always, for us old grads to see the newest advancements each time we return to C'ville.

The new law school is no longer close to being new, nor is the new home of the Darden School of Business. Buildings have sprouted since 1965. The student body has also changed dramatically. From the party school of the first half of the twentieth century it has grown into the world-renowned academic institution we came back to. For starters, many of my classmates and I couldn't qualify academically for admission today.

I've already commented on the exceeding pleasant presence of females at the University. What could we have we been thinking about in fighting their presence so strenuously? As to African American students, there is a universal regret that we were so abysmally ignorant in our youth. How could we have ignored the obvious? I simply have no answer. Fifty years has caused a sea change in our attitudes. While the percentage of white students is somewhat below both the Virginia and national averages, the African American population still lags way behind in each. The good news is that black students as a population has grown from around seventeen African American students when we took our degrees to over 2,700 now. We are reassured the University will continue to forge ahead in its quest for improvement. New, since 2019, President James Ryan leads admirably on the course set by his predecessors.

Walking back down the Lawn with my classmates, my mind wandered back to 1968, which was a significant time of challenge for all Americans, including Margaret Ann and me. For the first time in our lives, we began to interact with African Americans on a person-to-person basis. Our office moved to the eighteenth floor of the new Equitable Building on Peachtree Street downtown. Right across the hall was a consulting group composed of black men. Our first conversations were tentative because neither side was used to it. As the weeks and months passed, friendships were created. One of those for me was Rob Pitts, who is now chairman of the Fulton County Board of Commissioners. Another was Ben Brown, who moved to Washington DC. A frequent visitor was Charles Stevens, at the time fundraising director for the Butler Street YMCA. Tragically, Charles died of cancer in 2013.

On April 4, 1968, the unthinkable happened when Atlanta native son, Dr. Martin Luther King Jr. was assassinated in Memphis. Because of the many thousands of one-on-one relationships across the city, we were able to grieve together. Out of this tragedy, each of us grew significantly.

As I looked around me at Virginia that day, it was obvious. A reality of individual dialogues between those of divergent understandings is what has made the University a vibrant enterprise.

If it wasn't obvious to you from the last chapter, it should've been that Margaret Ann and I did not enter into holy matrimony with a great deal of foresight. Therefore, the last fifty-five years have been a series of adjustments, and a few were especially momentous. Since it would take another book to begin to tell it all, I will hit on a few highlights.

The first few years were an extension of our Charlottesville life. However, by year six, Margaret Ann was the mother of three, and I was fully engaged in developing my business. Being married to a partier and being one herself had begun to lose its allure for her. For my part, I was frustrated at feeling as if I were fourth in line at home. Sticky, gooey was rapidly vanishing, and we began to travel separate paths.

Two events finally brought the issue to a head. First, Margaret Ann cornered me in the den one night and asked me if I thought it was strange that the children called both of us "Mom." She also wondered if I knew what it was like to have no adult conversation for days on end. The second occurred when I woke up one Saturday morning, after a night of poker, and I went for a walk with my family. Under a glaring sun outdoors, I was afraid my head would fall off if I bent over. Right then and there, I determined that my family was more important than my night life. While I certainly did not become a teetotaler, I reduced my intake markedly. I also scheduled date nights and attended my children's ballgames, plays, concerts, and parents' nights. In hindsight, my Steel Magnolia had made her presence known.

As in all reunions, the overwhelming focus is on being together with our friends of yesteryear. After fifty years we were all the same people in terms of personality, but all of us had arrived there by significantly different routes. After leaving Virginia, many of our class entered the Vietnam War. Some never came home. Others returned with significant impairments. Coleman Goodwin still struggles with the effect of Agent Orange. The rest came back with considerably altered views of life. As one decorated Marine officer told me, "Vietnam taught me that there are no black or white Marines. There are only green Marines, and we all bleed the same red blood."

Many other classmates dropped out from our ranks for a plethora of reasons, not the least of which was death, our pledge brother, Kelly Wood, among them. Undeterred, the rest of us have marched on, typically in the same smaller groupings we had formed a half century earlier. For me it was my Beta pledge brothers.

On the Saturday morning of our fiftieth, the reunion classes walked down the Lawn, each in its own grouping. Looking around, I saw Rusty Mather, who spent four years in the Navy with Underwater Demolition Team 12 and Seal Team 1. After two tours in Vietnam, he earned an MBA at Berkeley and went on to become a prominent investment banker in New York.

Rutledge Young also served in Vietnam and learned the language, so he could interview villagers and search out Vietcong infiltrators. As a UVA law grad, he returned to Charleston and became a highly successful lawyer, civic leader, and president of the South Carolina Bar Association.

After he finished at Columbia Law, Richard Tucker became a VISTA volunteer in Kansas City and Providence. After years of providing legal services for the underrepresented he returned to Pittsburgh. Dick's the only friend I know who has tried, and won, a case before the US Supreme Court.

After serving as an Army signal officer on the infamous thirty-eighth parallel in Korea, Ted Hogshire spent a lifetime in the practice of law, dedicated to representing the underserved. He became a circuit court judge for Central Virginia, and he is nationally known for his groundbreaking efforts in the development of specialty courts. Ted is currently an adjunct professor at the Virginia Law School.

Another banker, Jon Verity retired as president and CEO of First Chicago's Trust Company and joined his brother at Verity Partners. In 2006 he moved his business to Beaufort, South Carolina, where he later became chairman of the City Redevelopment Commission.

Bob Greenwood was an officer on the USS *Enterprise* when she was in Southeast Asia, but now he is the CEO of a successful San Francisco–based fundraising company.

Bill Tylander returned from New York to his native Florida to head Chemical Bank Trust operations there. He later joined his wife, Gigi, in their thriving office supply company.

With our group for a while was Zate Joe Brown. After graduating from Washington and Lee Law School, he moved to Las Vegas, where his legend continued to magnify. Joe is currently one of the most prominent lawyers and men of influence in Nevada and the western United States. According to many articles about him, he is also beloved for his polite and gentlemanly demeanor.

Who'd have thought the immature group of eighteen- to twenty-two-year-olds I've described in this book would turn out to be mature men such as these in their later days?

After seeing old friends at a class lunch, visiting the current Beta house brothers, and various breakout sessions, we reconvened for the traditional pledge brother dinner. It's a superb blending of old stories and recent happenings for each of us. The reunions are always held on or near our wedding anniversary, and they have become a special way to celebrate our anniversaries with the people we've loved for over fifty years. Three of the wives—Pam Brown Jones, Vicki Chainsky Verity, and Carol Craige Mather—were around on graduation day. I met

Kathleen Kimmel Young at their wedding in 1968. Lynn Tucker, Gigi Tylander, Diane Hogshire, and Glee Greenwood became Beta wives shortly thereafter.

As Margaret Ann entered the terrace at Farmington with some of the other ladies, I marveled once again that this self-possessed beauty was really my wife. Suddenly my mind dredged up a period thirty-five years before, when she began to think there was more to life than what she was experiencing. My sweet pea then accepted an invitation from a group of women to join their Bible study. As the months passed, this commitment to her faith transformed the way she saw things and intensified her concern for social justice. For me this became an enormous irritant. While I didn't mind some changes here and there, a total transformation was much more than I had signed up for. On the one hand, Margaret Ann became a more complete wife and partner. On the other, her focus changed, and I was no longer the center of her life and I didn't like it.

One night I told her that she had stopped being as much fun as she had been before.

Her anguished response was, "How can I make you see that I'm not the shallow, fickle person you married?"

My retort was, "I liked you when you were shallow and fickle. That's why I married you!"

To the outside world we remained an ideal couple, and finally, after three years of growing aloofness, everything changed. Several things in my life cried out to me that it was time to listen to the Lord and make a commitment of my own. And when that was done, everything changed.

We became a partnership once again but under the Lord's leadership. We even began to sail our Snipe better as a team (although Margaret Ann still had difficulty resisting input, especially at the leeward mark).

When I snapped out of my reverie when the ladies approached the table, the men stood to seat them, and our wonderful fellowship went on. We relished more things from our days at 180 Rugby Road, and then remembered as many events of the intervening years that added richly to the tapestry of our conversations.

Sunday was a day of farewells. Final visits and brunches presented last opportunities to see many old friends. For our pledge class, it would only be an interruption between periodic visits. In fact, Rutledge announced plans for a mini-reunion in Charleston. But some of the other attendees we would never see again. However, leaving this time was far different from our parting in 1965 in that now we were all going back to established lives.

For Margaret Ann and me, the years that followed our realization of eternity was a time of incredible growth. While always placing her family first, those days of my beloved's life have been spent serving in urban communities or volunteering at the Fulton County Jail and the Georgia Women's Metro Penitentiary. And my nonfamily and business times were enriched with a multitude of youth activities. (Margaret Ann tells friends that some of my emotional maturity was arrested at the junior high level.) Together, we are part of a group that many years ago started the Atlanta Youth Academy, which provides an academically superior education in a Christian environment for children at risk from kindergarten through eighth grade.

Nowadays we play more of a sideline role, but we still provide mentoring, fundraising, and organizational experience to those who ask for it. Significant amounts of time are also spent with our children and grandchildren.

That last night we walked hand in hand on the Lawn, drinking in the magnificence of the scene, and I realized what had occurred here long ago. Although we are still far from perfect, and we still bicker at times like children, fifty years ago we began a love story with a very real but emotion-driven infatuation with each other. And now we were joined as one, as the loves of each other's lives, walking together through life and all that lies ahead.